Camino de Santiago

Andy Symington

Credits

Footprint credits
Editors: Felicity Laughton, Sophie Jones
Production and layout: Emma Bryers
Maps: Kevin Feeney
Cover: Pepi Bluck

Publisher: Patrick Dawson
Advertising: Elizabeth Taylor
Sales and marketing: Kirsty Holmes

Photography credits
Front cover: Marques/Shutterstock.com
Back cover: Poliki/Shutterstock.com

Printed in Great Britain by CPI Antony Rowe, Chippenham, Wiltshire

MIX
Paper from responsible sources
FSC® C013604
www.fsc.org

Every effort has been made to ensure that the facts in this guidebook are accurate. However, travellers should still obtain advice from consulates, airlines, etc, about travel and visa requirements before travelling. The authors and publishers cannot accept responsibility for any loss, injury or inconvenience however caused.

Publishing information
Footprint *Focus Camino de Santiago*
1st edition
© Footprint Handbooks Ltd
February 2013

ISBN: 978 1 909268 06 7
CIP DATA: A catalogue record for this book is available from the British Library

® Footprint Handbooks and the Footprint mark are a registered trademark of Footprint Handbooks Ltd

Published by Footprint
6 Riverside Court
Lower Bristol Road
Bath BA2 3DZ, UK
T +44 (0)1225 469141
F +44 (0)1225 469461
footprinttravelguides.com

Distributed in the USA by Globe Pequot Press, Guilford, Connecticut

All rights reserved. No part of this publication may be reproduced, stored in a retrieval system, or transmitted, in any form or by any means, electronic, mechanical, photocopying, recording, or otherwise without the prior permission of Footprint Handbooks Ltd.

The content of Footprint *Focus Camino de Santiago* has been taken directly from Footprint's *Northern Spain Handbook*, which was researched and written by Andy Symington.

Contents

- **5 Introduction**
  - 4 *Map: Camino de Santiago*
- **6 Planning your trip**
  - 6 Best time to travel the Camino de Santiago
  - 6 Getting to the Camino de Santiago
  - 9 Transport on the Camino de Santiago
  - 12 Where to stay on the Camino de Santiago
  - 14 Food and drink on the Camino de Santiago
  - 19 Festivals on the Camino de Santiago
  - 20 Essentials A-Z
- **25 Camino de Santiago**
  - 26 **Western Pyrenees: Camino Francés**
  - 32 *Map: Pamplona/Iruña*
  - 34 Listings
  - 40 **Western Pyrenees: Camino Aragonés**
  - 43 *Map: Jaca*
  - 47 Listings
  - 51 **Western Navarra**
  - 53 Listings
  - 56 **Route through La Rioja**
  - 58 *Map: Logroño*
  - 64 Listings
  - 68 **Burgos**
  - 70 *Map: Burgos*
  - 76 Listings
  - 80 **West from Burgos**
  - 85 Listings
  - 87 **León**
  - 88 *Map: León*
  - 93 Listings
  - 97 **West of León**
  - 102 Listings
  - 105 **Route through Galicia**
  - 108 Listings
  - 110 **Santiago de Compostela**
  - 114 *Map: Santiago de Compostela*
  - 120 Listings
- **125 Footnotes**
  - 126 Index

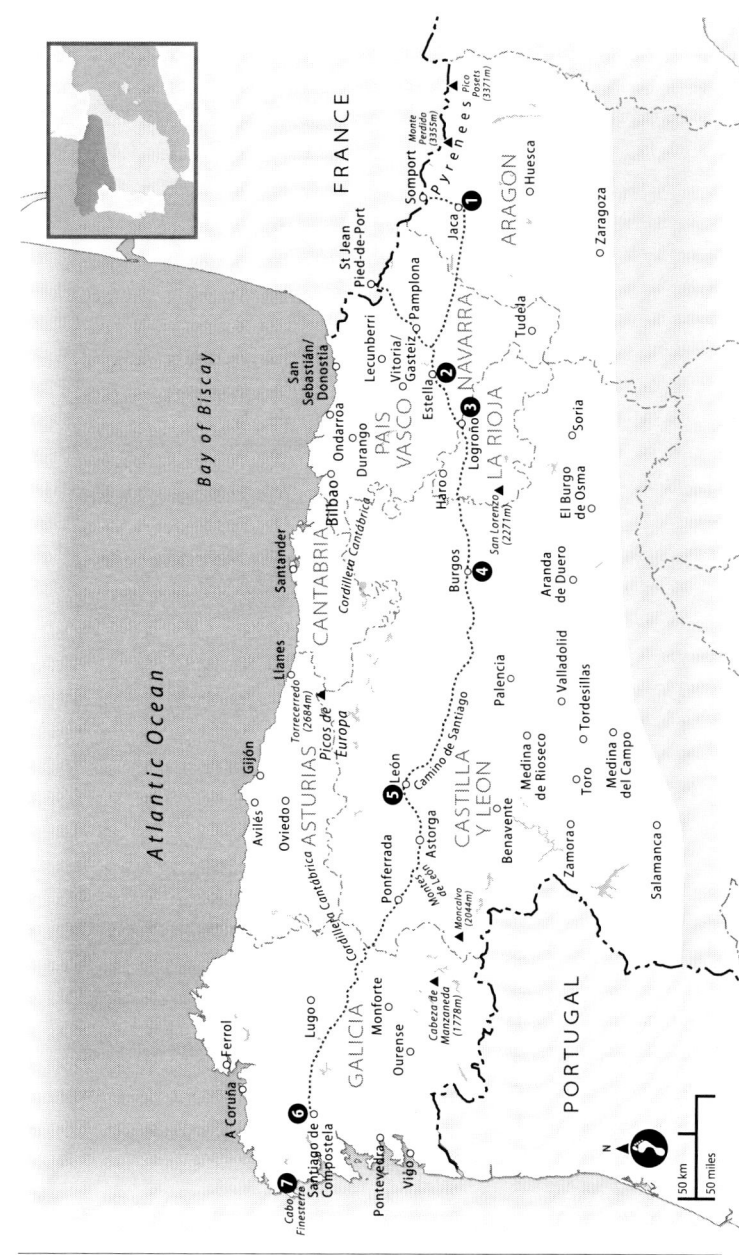

The revival in recent years of the medieval pilgrimage route across Spain to Santiago de Compostela has been a striking one. Today, over 100,000 make part of the journey on foot or bike every year. These *peregrinos* come from all nations and backgrounds, and are drawn by a range of motives. Some seek spiritual redemption, others time to think, and yet others just a good long walk.

One of the joys of the Camino is that it's very much what you make of it. If you're there to make friends around the table at sociable communal dinners, you can. If you want some time out from modern life and prefer pacing the pathway alone, you can. The network of *albergues* (pilgrim hostels) means that you can plan your route according to your abilities and whims of the day. Some do the walk from France to Santiago in one go, while others prefer just to do the final section. Some do a week a year, picking up the trail where they left off last time.

There are as many Camino routes as there are starting points, but the main one, the Camino Francés, is what we cover in this guide, along with its tributary, the Camino Aragonés. The Camino Francés, starting in the French Pyrenean town of St-Jean-Pied-de-Port, is a fantastic way to see Northern Spain. The route crosses the entire region, taking in Pyrenean passes and valleys, Navarran and Riojan wine country, the flat plateau of Castilla and Galicia's verdant hills. Many of Spain's most picturesque villages, evocative monasteries and interesting towns lie on or close to the route, and, by the time you see the granite towers of Santiago before you, you'll have taken a crash-course in Spanish culture and architecture along the way.

Planning your trip

Best time to travel the Camino de Santiago

Pilgrims walk the Camino throughout the year but you've got to be pretty hardy to do it in winter, when there's lots of rain in Galicia and the Pyrenees, and snow and freezing days and nights on the Castilian plain. May or September are the best months for walking the Camino de Santiago as you'll avoid the crowds and worst of the heat, but it will be cold at nights on the plains and wet in the mountainous parts. In summer, Galicia and Navarra are pleasant, but the haul across the plains from Logroño to León is gruelling. Summer is very hot in Castilla and La Rioja too – expect days in the mid to high 30s, if not higher. That said, it's an enjoyable time to be in the country as there are dozens of fiestas, and everything happens outdoors. Santiago de Compostela's main fiesta, the feast of Saint James, is on 25 July. Bear in mind that summer is by far the most popular time for walking the Camino, so facilities are stretched and the trail is crowded with walkers.

Getting to the Camino de Santiago

Planning your route
One of the benefits of the Camino Francés is that there's an *albergue* in nearly every village along the way, so you can be fairly flexible about how far you walk each day. Many of the towns and cities that you pass through are worth a stop of a day or three, so if you aren't pressed for time, pause to enjoy the richness of northern Spanish culture.

For this guide, we've assumed a normal walking day of 24-32 km, which means a journey of some 28 to 32 walking days to complete the 780 km from St-Jean to Santiago. Some pilgrims walk it in just a fortnight – a gruelling, fun-free march – while others dally to their hearts' content, stopping to smell the flowers along the way. The choice is yours.

Air
With budget airlines now flying to several regional airports, it's easier than ever to get to the Camino and away again. **Ryanair** fly to Santiago de Compostela, Valladolid, Santander, Madrid, Biarritz and Zaragoza from London, while **Easyjet** serve Santiago, Asturias, Bilbao and Biarritz, and **Air Berlin** go to Bilbao and Asturias (among others), with a connection, from many German and Austrian airports. These airlines also run routes to other European cities. Other international airlines serve Bilbao (which is connected with London, Paris, Frankfurt, and several other European cities), Vigo, Santiago de Compostela, Zaragoza and Asturias. If you're not on the budget carriers, however, it's often cheaper to fly to Madrid and connect via a domestic flight or by land transport. Madrid is a major world airport and prices tend to be competitive.

If you are planning to start your journey in the French Pyrenees, the easiest route is to fly to Biarritz, get the airport bus to Bayonne train station, where you then get a train to St-Jean-Pied-de-Port. Otherwise, **Iberia** serve Pamplona daily from Madrid and Barcelona.

The big advantage of using budget airlines at the start and end of your Camino is that you can fly into one airport and out from another without the financial penalty that other airlines tend to apply for this type of 'open-jaw' return.

Before booking, it's worth doing a bit of online research. Two of the best search engines for flight comparisons are **www.kelkoo.com** and **www.kayak.com**, which compare

Don't miss...

1 The extraordinary monastery of **San Juan de la Peña**, page 44.
2 The monuments of lovely **Estella and the nearby tap dispensing red wine**, page 51.
3 **Wine-tasting around Logroño** while your blisters heal, page 57.
4 Learning about Europe's oldest **hominids around Burgos**, page 68.
5 The wonderful **stained glass of León's cathedral**, page 90.
6 **Santiago de Compostela**, the end of the Camino, page 110.
7 The extra days' journey to the soul-stirring **clifftop views at Finisterre, the 'end of Europe'**, page 112.

Numbers relate to map on page 4.

---

prices from travel agencies and websites. To keep yourself up to date with the ever-changing routes of the bewildering number of budget airlines **www.whichbudget.com** is recommended. **Flightchecker** (http://flightchecker.moneysavingexpert.com) is handy for checking multiple dates for budget airline deals.

Rail

Travelling from the UK to Northern Spain by train is unlikely to save either time or money; the only advantages lie in the pleasure of the journey itself, the chance to stop along the way, and the environmental impact of flying versus rail travel. The quickest rail route from the UK is to take the **Eurostar** ① *T0870 160 6600, www.eurostar.com*, from London St Pancras to Paris Gare du Nord, then transfer to Gare Montparnasse to board a TGV to Bayonne, which is the gateway to St-Jean-Pied-de-Port and the start of the Camino Francés. The journey will take just over nine hours, if the connections are kind. Once across the Channel, the trains are reasonably priced, but factor in £100-200 return on **Eurostar** and things don't look so rosy, unless you can take advantage of a special offer. Using the train/Channel ferry combination will more or less halve the cost and double the time.

If you are planning the train journey, **Rail Europe** ① *T0844 484 064, www.raileurope.co.uk*, is a useful company. **RENFE**, Spain's rail network, has online timetables at www.renfe.es. Also see the extremely useful **www.seat61.com**.

Road

Bus Eurolines (www.eurolines.com) run several buses from major European cities to a variety of destinations in Northern Spain. There's a Eurolines service from London to San Sebastián from where there are buses to Pamplona, and from Pamplona there are buses to Roncesvalles. There's also a bus that leaves London Victoria at 0800 on Monday and Saturday, and arrives in Bilbao at 0430 the next morning. The return leaves Bilbao at 0030 on Thursday and Saturday night, getting to London at 1945 the next evening. There's an extra bus in summer. A return fare costs about £100; it's marginally cheaper for pensioners and students, but overall isn't great value unless you're not a fan of flying. Book on T01582 404 511 or www.gobycoach.com.

Car The main route into Northern Spain is the E05/E70 tolled motorway that runs down the southwest coast of France, crossing into Spain at Irún, near San Sebastián. More scenic but slower routes cross the Pyrenees at various points. Most other motorways are free and in good condition.

Packing for the Camino

The amount of baggage you carry on the Camino will greatly impact on how tired and sore you are at day's end, and how difficult it is to get going again the next morning.

Bear in mind that it's not a wilderness expedition, so there's no need to stuff your pack with trail rations, litres of water, and pharmaceuticals for any eventuality. Food, water and supplies are available at fairly regular intervals throughout the day, and you're never going to be far from help should you suffer illness or accident. All of which means travelling light is a key to enjoying the walk.

Another key is footwear. Much of the Camino is along hard paths or roads, so comfort is the most important factor. Some favour hiking boots, but if you do the route in summer, these will overheat your feet and you'd be better off in hiking shoes, trainers, or even durable walking sandals. Outside summer, waterproof footwear is essential. To avoid wet feet and blisters, carry and use extra socks and dry out your footwear as completely as possible every night. And don't start the Camino with a brand new pair of shoes, or you'll likely be in agony after the first day. Wear them in first! Gel insoles are another good idea; the cushioning effect helps avoid knee and heel pain.

A possible packing list could include: small backpack with rain cover; sleeping bag and/or sleepsheet; earplugs (for snorers in hostels); broad-brimmed hat; sunglasses (but if you walk in the mornings you won't use them much as you're heading west); suncream; walking pole; water bottle; flipflops or spare trainers (to change into on arrival); sticking plasters (for blisters); paracetamol; light waterproof poncho; minimal clothes (say walking shoes/boots, two walking shirts, one evening shirt, walking shorts, evening trousers, three pairs socks and underwear and a fleece jacket); inner socks/sock liners to prevent blisters; microfibre towel; Swiss army knife; small toiletries bag; book (you can swap for another at hostels); a diary; mobile (unlocked if you want to buy a Spanish SIM card); small camera; waterproof bag for documents.

To look like an authentic medieval pilgrim, many people don the traditional garb. A long staff is a sensible option anyway, as are a gourd for water and broad-brimmed hat to keep out sun and rain.

Cars must be insured for third party and practically any driving licence is acceptable (but if you're from a country that a Guardia Civil would struggle to locate on a map, take an International Driving Licence). Unleaded petrol costs about €1.50 per litre in Spain.

If planning to leave your car in St-Jean-Pied-de-Port or Roncesvalles, contact the pilgrim *albergues* in advance to see if someone can keep an eye on it.

Sea

For competitive fares by sea to France and Spain, check with **Ferrysavers** ⓘ *T0844 576 8835, www.ferrysavers.com* and **www.ferrycheap.com**, which list special offers from various operators. The website **www.seat61.com** is good for investigating train/ferry combinations.

The only UK–Spain ferry are services run by **Brittany Ferries** ⓘ *T0871 244 0744, www.brittany-ferries.co.uk*, from Plymouth and Portsmouth to Santander and Bilbao. There's one weekly sailing on each route, taking around 24 hours from Portsmouth and 20 hours from Plymouth. Prices are variable but can usually be found for about £70-90 each way in a reclining seat. A car adds about £150 each way, and cabins start from about £80.

Alternative routes

As well as the Camino Francés, the main route followed in this guide, the Camino Aragonés is also popular, differing only initially as it crosses into Spain in a more spectacular section of the Pyrenees, and descends the Canfranc Valley to the lively town of Jaca (see page 41). It joins the Camino Francés near the town of Puente la Reina in Navarra.

A less frequented route, the Camino del Norte, follows the north coast and is arguably the most scenic, while the Ruta de la Plata, taken by people coming from the south of Spain, passes through Salamanca and Zamora. The Camino Primitivo starts from a village near Lugo, the Camino Portugués starts from Porto and heads north, and the Camino Inglés starts at A Coruña (where English pilgrims arriving by boat traditionally disembarked) and tracks south. These alternative routes have the benefit of far fewer pilgrims in high season.

Transport on the Camino de Santiago

Public transport between the larger towns in Northern Spain is good; you can expect several buses a day between adjacent provincial capitals; these services are quick and efficient. The new network of high-speed **AVE** trains link major cities in double-quick time, but are significantly more expensive than the bus. Other train services are slow.

Rail
The Spanish national rail network **RENFE** ① *T902 240 202 (English-speaking operators), www.renfe.es*, is becoming a very useful option for getting around Northern Spain. AVE trains run from Madrid to Valladolid, Zaragoza and Huesca, with other routes under construction to nearly all of Northern Spain's major cities. These trains cover these large distances impressively quickly and reliably. It is an expensive but excellent service that refunds part or all of the ticket price if it arrives late. Elsewhere though, you'll find the bus is often quicker and cheaper than the train.

Prices vary significantly according to the type of service you are using. The standard fast-ish intercity service is called *Talgo*, while other intercity services are labelled *Altaria*, *Intercity*, *Diurno* and *Estrella* (overnight). Slower local trains are called *regionales*.

It's always worth buying a ticket in advance for long-distance travel, as trains are often full. The best option is to buy them via the website, which sometimes offers advance-purchase discounts. You can also book by phone, but they only accept Spanish cards. In either case, you get a reservation code, then print off your ticket at the terminals at the station. If buying your ticket at the station, allow plenty of time for queuing. Ticket windows are labelled *venta anticipada* (in advance) and *venta inmediata* (six hours or less before the journey).

All Spanish trains are non-smoking. The faster trains will have first-class (*preferente*) and second-class sections as well as a *cafetería*. First class costs about 30% more than standard and can be a worthwhile deal on a crowded long journey. Buying a return ticket is 10-20% cheaper than two singles, but you qualify for this discount even if you buy the return leg later (but not on every service).

An **ISIC student card** or **under-26 card** grants a discount of between 20% to 30% on train services. If you're using a European railpass, be aware that you'll still have to make a reservation on Spanish trains and pay the small reservation fee (which covers your insurance).

The credencial and the compostela

The *compostela* is a certificate issued by the Church on your arrival in Santiago stating that you have completed the pilgrimage. To qualify, you need to have completed the last 100 km on foot which means starting from Sarria (see page 107), or the last 200 km if riding a bike or horse (from Ponferrada, see page 100).

The document that proves that you have done this is called the *credencial*, popularly known in English as the 'pilgrim passport'. This document is issued by the Santiago diocese and lets you access the network of pilgrim hostels along the various Caminos. You should get it stamped once or more per day in churches and hostels along the way as proof that you have walked the route.

Once you arrive in Santiago, you present this document at the pilgrim office (see page 111) to receive your *compostela*.

Credenciales can be obtained in your home country via various associations, but are easily available on the Camino itself; nearly every church and pilgrim hostel along the way issues them, usually either free or for a small fee. Though in practice they are issued to all, in theory your journey needs to be motivated by Christian principles to be awarded the *compostela*.

For many, at the end of the journey, the dog-eared, sweat-stained, weatherbeaten *credencial*, with its stamps and memories, is a more treasured keepsake of the Camino than the *compostela* itself.

Road

Bike About one in every four or five pilgrims does the journey on a bike. The whole of the Camino Francés is rideable, although there are steep descents and bumpy sections that you may prefer to bypass by using the road, unless you've got a mountain bike with proper suspension.

It's a long ride to Santiago, and while some do it in a week or so, most take two or a little more. The most important thing is that the panniers are robust and balanced, and that the rack can take their weight without making for an uncomfortable ride.

As a cyclist, you need to complete 200 km to Santiago to be eligible for the *compostela* (which means starting at Ponferrada). Be aware that some pilgrim hostels give priority to those arriving on foot, as they figure it's easier for a cyclist to ride on to the next *albergue* if that one's full. Many *albergues* have lockable bike storage and washing facilities.

From Santiago, you can transport your bike back to other parts of Spain on some bus routes, but most trains don't offer this service. However, the train company **RENFE** has an agreement with a courier service, **Halcourier** ⓘ *www.halcourier.es*, that lets you transport your bike anywhere in Spain for €45 provided you are in possession of a long-distance train ticket. This should be booked a day or two before.

Not all riders on the Camino are on two wheels however; a handful of people each year do the route on horse-, donkey- or mule-back. It's a picturesque way to do it, but requires a fair bit of logistical planning and support. However, there are tour companies that offer this experience.

Bus Buses are the staple of Spanish public transport. Services between major cities are fast, frequent, reliable and fairly cheap; the five-hour trip from Madrid to Pamplona, for example, costs around €26. When buying a ticket, always check how long the journey will take, as the odd bus will be an 'all stations to' job, calling in at villages that seem surprised

Lightening the load

The tradition of the Camino is that pilgrims carry their own necessities on their backs, up hill and down dale. But there are various baggage transportation services available along the route, some run by private hostels, some by locals in the villages you pass through.

There are several reasons that you might want to use these services, whether to ease the physical load, to be able to take more cultural detours, or because you want to carry a decent amount of clothes to be able to look your best for the city nightlife. Some pilgrims only avail themselves of these services once in a while, others do the whole trip this way.

The most popular and reliable of these services is **Jacotrans** ⓘ *T610 983 205,* *www.jacotrans.com*. Based in Navarra, along the first portion of the route, they work with partners on each stretch so that the whole route from Roncesvalles to Santiago is covered. As well as baggage transportation, they can also help out with other logistical support and bike transport and repair.

If using a baggage transportation service, do be sensitive to the feelings of other pilgrims. Although it's only a small minority that get snooty about those who don't carry their own packs, it can be understandably annoying if you get beaten to the last berth in the *albergue* by someone who strolled past you up the last hill whistling a tune and carrying nothing heavier than a digital camera!

---

to even see it. *Directo* is the term for a bus that doesn't stop; it won't usually cost any more either. Various premium services (called *Supra, Ejecutivo* or similar) add comfort, with onboard drinks service, lounge area in the bus station and more space, but cost around 60% more.

Most cities have a single terminal, the *estación de autobuses*, which is where all short- and long-haul services leave from. Buy your tickets at the relevant window; if there isn't one, buy it from the driver. Many companies don't allow baggage in the cabin of the bus, but security is pretty good. Most tickets will have a seat number (*asiento*) on them; ask when buying the ticket if you prefer a window (*ventana*) or aisle (*pasillo*) seat. There's a huge number of intercity bus companies, some of which allow phone and online booking; the most useful in Northern Spain is **ALSA** ⓘ *T902 422 242, www.alsa.es*, which is based in Asturias and runs many routes. The website www.movelia.es is also useful. The platform that the bus leaves from is called a *dársena* or *andén*. If you're travelling at busy times (particularly a fiesta or national holiday) always book the bus ticket in advance.

Rural bus services are slower, less frequent and more difficult to coordinate. They typically run early in the morning and late in the evening; they're designed for villagers who visit the big city once a week or so to shop.

All bus services are reduced on Sundays and, to a lesser extent, on Saturdays; some services don't run at all at weekends. Local newspapers publish a comprehensive list of departures; expect few during siesta hours. While most large villages will have at least some bus service to their provincial capital, don't expect there to be buses running to tourist attractions like monasteries, beaches or castles; it's assumed that all tourists have cars.

Most Spanish cities have their sights closely packed into the centre, so you won't find local buses particularly necessary. There's a fairly comprehensive network in most towns, though; the Transport sections in this guide indicate where they come in handy. In most cities, you just board and pay the driver.

Taxis Taxis are a good option (and the only way to get to St-Jean-Pied-de-Port from Roncesvalles at the start of your route); flagfall is €2-3 in most places (it increases slightly at night and on Sundays) and it gets you a good distance. A taxi is available if its green light is lit; hail one on the street or ask for the nearest rank (*parada de taxis*). In smaller towns or at quiet times, you'll have to ring for one. All towns have their own taxi company; phone numbers are given in the text.

Where to stay on the Camino de Santiago

Albergues de Peregrinos (pilgrim hostels)
For most people travelling the Camino de Santiago, the network of pilgrim hostels is where they spend the majority of nights along the way. These have largely been set up in the last decade or two as the popularity of the route has soared, and they come in many varieties.

The standard *albergue* might be run by the local community or municipality and will offer no-frills sleeping in bunks, some kitchen facilities, and simple showers and toilets, often with little privacy. The cost of a night's sleep tends to range from €5 to €10; some are by donation. You'll need the *credencial* (pilgrim passport) to sleep in most *albergues* of this type, and many will require you to have your own sleeping bag or sleep sheet. Some offer tent pitches, and many put down mattresses or mats on the floor once the bed spaces have been taken. You'll find many that offer evening meals, often prepared communally.

These *albergues* are supplemented by a growing number of privately run hostels, which also often double as *hostales* (see below), offering private rooms as well as dormitory accommodation. These tend to be smaller places, with better facilities, and cost around €10 for the night.

As you'll discover, the *albergue* experience often has more to do with the *hospitalero* (warden) than the facilities. Good *hospitaleros* (often volunteers) make pilgrims feel at home, supply valuable local information, and foster the social side of the hostel, introducing people, organizing communal dinners, prayers or singalongs and not waking sleepers too brusquely in the morning. Pilgrims seeking the 'spirit of the Camino' will find it in the kindness of some of these *albergues* and their guardians.

There are several downsides, however, to the *albergue* network. There's usually a curfew, normally 2200 or similar, so if you fancy a meal in a restaurant that doesn't open until 2100, you risk being locked out. Most require you to pack and leave by 0800 in the morning or so, and in many you can only stay one night. Regular complaints include overcrowding, lack of heating, no privacy in the shower room, bedbugs, and occasional theft of cash or personal items by other pilgrims. The other problem is that, as the municipal ones tend to not take bookings, there's a race to bag a bed, with walkers getting up ever-earlier to ensure they get a cheap sleep in the next town. Racing anxiously to the next *albergue* is no way to enjoy the Camino.

Hoteles, hostales and pensiones
Hoteles (marked H or HR) are graded from one to five stars and usually occupy their own building. *Hostales* (marked Hs or HsR) go from one to three stars. *Pensiones* (P) are the standard budget option, and are usually family-run flats in an apartment block. Although it's worth looking at a room before taking it, the majority are very acceptable. Spanish traditions of hospitality are alive and well; even the simplest of *pensiones* will generally provide a towel and soap, and check-out time is almost uniformly a very civilized midday. Most *pensiones* will give you keys to the exterior door; if they don't, be sure to mention the fact if you plan to stay out late.

Price codes
Where to stay
€€€€ over €170 €€€ €110-170
€€ €55-110 € under €55
Price codes refer to a standard double/twin room, inclusive of the 10% IVA (value-added tax). The rates are for high season (usually June-August).

Restaurants
€€€ over €20 €€ €10-20 € under €10
Price codes refer to the cost of a main course for one person, without a drink.

There are a reasonable number of well-equipped but characterless places on the edges or in the newer parts of towns in Spain. Similarly, chains such as NH, AC, and Hesperia have stocked Northern Spain's cities with reasonably comfortable but frequently featureless four-star business hotels. This guide has expressly minimized these in the listings, preferring to concentrate on more atmospheric options, but they are easily accessible via their websites or hotel booking brokers. These things change, but at time of writing, by far the best booking website for accommodation in Spain was www.booking.com. If you are booking accommodation without this guide, always be sure to check the location – it's easy to find yourself a 15-minute cab ride from the town you want to be in. Having said this, the standard of accommodation in Northern Spain is very high; even the most modest *pensiones* are usually very clean and respectable. Places to stay (*alojamientos*) are divided into three main categories; the distinctions between them follow an arcane series of regulations devised by the government.

All registered accommodations charge an 10% value-added tax (IVA); this is often included in the price at cheaper places and may be waived if you pay cash. If you have any problems, a last resort is to ask for the *libro de reclamaciones* (complaints book), an official document that, like stepping on cracks in the pavement, means uncertain but definitely horrible consequences for the hotel if anything is written in it. If you do write something in it, you have to go to the police within 24 hours and report the fact.

Agroturismos and casas rurales
An excellent option is the network of rural homes, called a variety of things, normally *agroturismos* or *casas rurales*. Although these are under a different classification system, the standard is often as high as any country hotel. The best of them are traditional farmhouses or old village cottages. Some are available only to rent out whole, while others operate more or less as hotels. Rates tend to be excellent compared to hotels, and many offer kitchen facilities and home-cooked meals. While some are listed in the text, there are many others. Each regional government publishes its own listings booklet, which is available at any tourist office in the area; some of the regional tourism websites also list them. The website **www.toprural.com** is another good place to find them. Many *casas rurales* within a few kilometres of the Camino are happy to do pick-ups and drop-offs for pilgrims.

Campsites
Most campsites are set up as well-equipped holiday villages for families; many are open only in summer. While the facilities are good, they get extremely busy in peak season; the

social scene is good, but sleep can be tough. They've often got playground facilities and a swimming pool; an increasing number now offer cabin or bungalow accommodation, normally a good-value option for groups or families. In other areas, camping, unless specifically prohibited, is a matter of common sense.

Food and drink on the Camino de Santiago

Nothing in Spain illustrates its differences from the rest of Europe more than its eating and drinking culture. Whether you're halfway through Sunday lunch at 1800, ordering a plate of octopus some time after midnight, snacking on *pinchos* in the street, or watching a businessman down a hefty brandy with his morning coffee, it hits you at some point that the whole of Spanish society more or less revolves around food and drink.

Eating hours are the first point of difference. Spaniards eat little for breakfast, usually just a coffee and maybe a croissant or pastry. The mid-morning coffee and piece of tortilla is a ritual, especially for office workers, and then there might be a quick bite and a drink in a bar before lunch, which is usually started between 1400 and 1530. This is the main meal of the day and the cheapest time to eat, as most restaurants offer a good-value set menu. Lunch (and dinner) is extended at weekends, particularly on Sundays, when the *sobremesa* (chatting over the remains of the meal) can go on for hours. Most folk head home for the meal during the working week and get back to work about 1700; some people have a nap (the famous siesta), some don't. It's common to have an evening drink or *tapa* in a bar after a stroll, or *paseo*, if this is extended into a food crawl it's called a *tapeo*. Though pilgrims will have a different timetable (see below), dinner (*cena*) is normally eaten from about 2200 onwards; sitting down to dinner at midnight at weekends isn't unusual. In smaller towns, however, and midweek you might not get fed after 2200. After eating, *la marcha* (the nightlife) hits drinking bars (*bares de copas*) and then nightclubs (*discotecas*; a *club* is a brothel). Many of these places only open at weekends and are usually busiest from 0200 onwards.

Food
While the regional differences in the cuisine of Northern Spain are important, the basics remain the same. Spanish cooking relies on meat, fish/seafood, beans and potatoes given character by the chef's holy trinity: garlic, peppers and, of course, olive oil. The influence of the colonization of the Americas is evident, and the result is a hearty, filling style of meal ideally washed down with some of the nation's excellent red wines. The following is an overview of the most common dishes.

Even in areas far from the coast, the availability of good **fish and seafood** can be taken for granted. *Merluza* (hake) is the staple fish, but is pushed hard by *bacalao* (salt cod) on the north coast. A variety of farmed white fish are also increasingly popular. *Gambas* (prawns) are another common and excellent choice, backed up by a bewildering array of molluscs and crustaceans as well as numerous tasty fish. Calamari, squid and cuttlefish are common; if you can cope with the slightly slimy texture, *pulpo* (octopus) is particularly good, especially when simply boiled *a la gallega* (Galician style) and flavoured with paprika and olive oil. Supreme among the seafood are *rodaballo* (turbot) and *rape* (monkfish/anglerfish). Fresh trout from the mountain streams of Navarra or Asturias are hard to beat too; they are commonly cooked with bacon or ham (*trucha a la navarra*).

Wherever you go, you'll find cured ham (*jamón serrano*), which is always excellent, but particularly so if it's the pricey *ibérico*, taken from acorn-eating porkers in Salamanca, Extremadura and Huelva. Other cold **meats** to look out for are *cecina*, made from beef and, of course, *embutidos* (sausages), including the versatile *chorizo*. Pork is also popular as a cooked meat; its most common form is sliced loin (*lomo*). Beef is common throughout; cheaper cuts predominate, but the better steaks (*solomillo, entrecot, chuletón*) are usually superbly tender. Spaniards tend to eat them rare (*poco hecho*; ask for *al punto* for medium-rare or *bien hecho* for well done). The *chuletón* is worth a mention in its own right; a massive T-bone best taken from an ox (*de buey*) and sold by weight, which often approaches a kilogram. It's an imposing slab of meat, best shared between two or three unless you're especially peckish. *Pollo* (chicken) is common, but usually unremarkable (unless its free-range – *pollo de corral* – in which case it's superb); game birds such as *codorniz* (quail) and *perdiz* (partridge) as well as *pato* (duck) are also widely eaten. The innards of animals are popular; *callos* (tripe), *mollejas* (sweetbreads) and *morcilla* (black pudding in solid or semi-solid form) are all excellent, if acquired, tastes. Fans of the unusual will be keen to try *jabalí* (wild boar), *potro* (foal), *morros* (pig cheeks) and *oreja* (ear, usually from a pig or sheep).

Main dishes often come without any **accompaniments**, or chips at best. The consolation, however, is the *ensalada mixta*, whose simple name (mixed salad) often conceals a meal in itself. The ingredients vary, but it's typically a plentiful combination of lettuce, tomato, onion, olive oil, boiled eggs, asparagus, olives and tuna. The *tortilla* (a substantial potato omelette) is ever-present and often excellent. *Revueltos* (scrambled eggs), are usually tastily combined with prawns, asparagus or other goodies. Most **vegetable** dishes are based around that New World trio: the bean, the pepper and the potato. There are numerous varieties of bean in Northern Spain; they are normally served as some sort of hearty stew, often with bits of meat or seafood. *Fabada* is the Asturian classic of this variety, while *alubias con chorizo* are a standard across the region. A *cocido* is a typical mountain dish, a massive stew of chickpeas or beans with meat and vegetables; the liquid is drained off and eaten first (*sopa de cocido*). Peppers (*pimientos*), too, come in a number of forms. As well as being used to flavour dishes, they are often eaten in their own right; *pimientos rellenos* come stuffed with meat or seafood. Potatoes come as chips, *bravas* (with a garlic or spicy tomato sauce) or *a la riojana*, with chorizo and paprika. Other common vegetable dishes include *menestra* (delicious blend of cooked vegetables), which usually has some ham in it, and *ensaladilla rusa*, a tasty blend of potato, peas, peppers, carrots and mayonnaise. *Setas* (wild mushrooms) are a delight, particularly in autumn.

Desserts focus on the sweet and milky. *Flan* (a sort of crème caramel) is ubiquitous; great when *casero* (home-made), but often out of a plastic tub. *Natillas* are a similar but more liquid version, and *arroz con leche* is a cold, sweet, rice pudding typical of Northern Spain.

Though the standard Manchego-style cheese is still the staple of its kind (it comes *semi-curado*, semi-cured, or *curado* – much stronger and tastier), there are a number of interesting regional cheeses that are well worth trying. Piquant Cabrales, Galician Tetilla, Basque Idiázabal, and punchy blue spreadable Valdeón are some of the best.

Regional cuisine
Regional styles tend to use the same basic ingredients treated in slightly different ways, backed up by some local specialities.

Navarran and Aragonese cuisine owes much to the mountains, with hearty stews and game dishes featuring alongside fresh trout. Rioja and Castilla y León go for filling roast meat and bean dishes more suited to the harsh winters than the baking summers. Galicia is seafood heaven, with more varieties of finny and shelly things than you knew existed; usually prepared with confidence in the natural flavours; the rest of the area tends to overuse the garlic. Inland Galicia relies more heavily on that traditional northern staple, pork.

Food-producing regions take their responsibilities seriously, and competition is fierce. Those widely acknowledged to produce the best will often add the name of the region to the foodstuff (many foods, like wines, have denomination of origin status, DO, given by a regulatory body). Thus *pimientos de Padrón* (Padrón peppers), *cogollos de Tudela* (lettuce hearts from Tudela), *alubias de Tolosa* (Tolosa beans), *puerros de Sahagún* (Sahagún leeks) and a host of others.

Eating out
One of the great pleasures of travelling in Northern Spain is eating out, whether it's a simple pilgrim set menu in the village bar, or a splash-out in some temple of the new Spanish gastronomy in a regional capital.

The standard distinctions of bar, café and restaurant don't apply in Spain. Many places combine all three functions, and it's not always evident; the dining room (*comedor*) is often tucked away behind the bar or upstairs. *Restaurantes* are restaurants, and will usually have a dedicated dining area with set menus and à la carte options. Bars and cafés will often display food on the counter, or have a list of tapas; bars tend to be known for particular dishes they do well. Many bars, cafés and restaurants don't open on Sunday nights, and most are closed one other night a week, most commonly Monday or Tuesday.

Cafés, especially those along the pilgrim trail, will usually provide some kind of **breakfast** fare in the mornings; croissants and sweet pastries are the norm; freshly squeezed orange juice is also common. About 1100 they start putting out savoury fare; maybe a *tortilla*, some *ensaladilla rusa* or little ham rolls in preparation for pre-lunch snacking. It's a workers' tradition – from labourers to executives – to drop down to the local bar around 1130 for a *pincho de tortilla* (slice of potato omelette) to get them through until two.

Lunch is the biggest meal of the day for most people in Spain, and it's also the cheapest time to eat. Just about all restaurants offer a *menú del día*, which is usually a set three-course meal that includes wine or soft drink. In unglamorous workers' locals this is often as little as €8; paying anything more than €13 indicates the restaurant takes itself quite seriously. Most places open for lunch at about 1300, and stop serving at 1500 or 1530, although at weekends this can extend; it's not uncommon to see people still lunching at 1800 on a Sunday. The quality of à la carte is usually higher than the *menú*, and quantities are larger. Simpler restaurants won't offer this option except in the evenings. **Tapas** has changed in meaning over the years, and now basically refers to all bar food. This range includes free snacks given with drinks (now only standard in certain provinces), *pinchos*, small saucer-sized plates of food (this is the true meaning of *tapa*) and more substantial dishes, usually ordered in *raciones* and designed to be shared. A *ración* in Northern Spain is no mean affair; it can often comfortably fill one person, so if you want to sample a range of things, you're better to ask for a half (*media*) or a *tapa* (smaller portion, when available).

Most restaurants open for dinner at 2030 or later. Although some places do offer a cheap set *menú*, you'll usually have to order à la carte. In quiet areas, places stop serving at 2200 on week nights, but in cities and at weekends people sit down at 2230 or later. A cheap option at all times is a *plato combinado*, most commonly offered in cafés. They're usually a greasy spoon-style mix of eggs, steak, bacon and chips or similar and are filling but rarely inspiring.

Eating for pilgrims deviates slightly from these norms. In most pilgrim hostels there's a curfew of 2200 or 2300 as most *peregrinos* favour an early start. Restaurants and bars in villages along the Camino are accustomed to pilgrims' need to dine earlier, and usually offer a set evening meal for €9 or €10 that might be served from 1900 onwards. If the local hostel doesn't provide breakfast, there will likely be a local café that opens at 0700 or earlier for breakfast to take advantage of the pilgrim traffic. Bear in mind, however, that at that time you'll only be eating with other pilgrims. If you want to experience Spanish eating culture in general, you'll need to do it at lunchtime or sleep in a place with no curfew a couple of times.

Vegetarians in Spain won't be spoiled for choice, but at least what there is tends to be good. There's a small but rapidly increasing number of dedicated vegetarian restaurants, but many other places won't have a vegetarian main course on offer, although the existence of *raciones* and salads makes this less of a burden than it might be. *Ensalada mixta* nearly always has tuna in it, but it's usually made fresh, so places will happily leave it out. *Ensaladilla rusa* is normally a good bet, but ask about the tuna too, just in case. Tortilla is simple but delicious and ubiquitous. Simple potato or pepper dishes are tasty options (although beware of peppers stuffed with meat), and many *revueltos* (scrambled eggs) are just mixed with asparagus. Annoyingly, most vegetable *menestras* are seeded with ham before cooking, and bean dishes usually contain at least some meat or animal fat. You'll have to specify *soy vegetariano/a* (I am a vegetarian), but ask what dishes contain, as ham, fish and chicken are often considered suitable vegetarian fare. Vegans will have a tougher time. What doesn't have meat nearly always contains cheese or egg.

Drink

In good Catholic fashion, **wine** is the lifeblood of Spain. It's the standard accompaniment to most meals, but also features very prominently in bars, where a glass of cheap *tinto* or *blanco* can cost as little as €0.80, although it's more normally €1.20. A bottle of house wine in a restaurant is often no more than €5 or €6. *Tinto* is red (although if you just order *vino* it's assumed that's what you want); *blanco* is white, and rosé is either *clarete* or *rosado*. A well-regulated system of *denominaciones de origen* (DO), similar to the French *appelation controlée* has lifted the reputation of Spanish wines high above the party plonk status they once enjoyed. Much of Spain's wine is produced in the north, and recent years have seen regions such as the Ribera del Duero, Rueda, Navarra, Toro, Bierzo, and Rías Baixas achieve worldwide recognition. But the daddy, of course, is still Rioja.

The overall standard of Riojas has improved markedly since the granting of the higher DOC status in 1991, with some fairly stringent testing in place. Red predominates; these are mostly medium-bodied bottles from the Tempranillo grape (with three other permitted red grapes often used to add depth or character). Whites from Viura and Malvasia are also produced: the majority of these are young, fresh and dry, unlike the traditional powerful oaky Rioja whites now on the decline. Rosés are also produced. The quality of individual Riojas varies widely according to both producer and the amount of time the wines have been aged in oak barrels and in the bottle. The words *crianza*, *reserva* and *gran reserva* refer to the length of the ageing process, while the vintage date is also given. Rioja producers store their wines at the bodega until deemed ready for drinking, so it's common to see wines dating back a decade or more on shelves and wine lists.

A growing number of people feel, however, that Spain's best reds come from further west, in the Ribera del Duero region east of Valladolid. The king's favourite tipple, Vega Sicilia, has long been Spain's most prestigious wine, but other producers from the area have also gained stellar reviews.

Visiting the area in the baking summer heat, it's hard to believe that nearby Rueda can produce quality whites, but it certainly does. Most come from the Verdejo grape and have an attractive, dry, lemony taste; Sauvignon Blanc has also been planted with some success.

Galicia produces some excellent whites too; the coastal Albariño vineyards produce a sought-after dry wine with a very distinctive bouquet. Ribeiro is another good Galician white, and the reds from there are also tasty, having some similarity to those produced in nearby northern Portugal. Ribeira Sacra is another inland Galician denomination producing whites and reds from a wide range of varietals.

Among other regions, Navarra, long known only for rosé, is producing some quality red wines unfettered by the stricter rules governing production in Rioja, while Bierzo, in western León province, also produces interesting wines from the red Prieto Picudo and Mencía grapes. Other DO wines in Northern Spain include Somontano, a red and white appelation from Aragón and Toro, whose baking climate makes for full-bodied reds. Some Toro wines have achieved a very high worldwide profile.

One of the joys of Spain, though, is the rest of the wine. Order a *menú del día* at a cheap restaurant and you'll be unceremoniously served a cheap bottle of local red (sometimes without even asking for it). Wine snobbery can leave by the back door at this point: it may be cold, but you'll find it refreshing; it may be acidic, but once the olive-oil laden food arrives, you'll be glad of it. It's not there to be judged, it's a staple like bread and, like bread, it's sometimes excellent, it's sometimes bad, but mostly it fulfils its purpose perfectly. Wine is not a luxury item in Spain, so people add water to it if they feel like it, or lemonade (*gaseosa*), or cola (to make the party drink called *calimocho*). Tinto de verano is a summer slurper similar to sangría, a mixture of red wine, gaseosa, ice, and optional fruit.

Spanish **beer** is mostly lager, usually reasonably strong, fairly gassy, cold and good. On the tapas trail, many people order *cortos*, usually about 100 ml. A *caña* is a larger draught beer, usually about 200 ml. Order a *cerveza* and you'll get a bottled beer. Many people order their beer *con gas* (half beer and half fizzy sweet water) or *con limón* (half lemonade, also called a *clara*). In some pubs, particularly those specializing in different beers (*cervecerías*), you can order pints (*pintas*).

Spirits are cheap in Spain. Vermouth (*vermut*) is a popular pre-lunch *aperitif*, as is *patxarán*. Many bars make their own vermouth by adding various herbs and fruits and letting it sit in barrels; this can be excellent, particularly if its from a *solera*. This is a system where liquid is drawn from the oldest of a series of barrels, which is then topped up with the next oldest, resulting in a very mellow characterful drink. After dinner or lunch it's time for a *copa*: people relax over a whisky or a brandy, or hit the mixed drinks (*cubatas*): *gin tonic* is obvious, as is *vodka con cola*. Spirits are free-poured and large; don't be surprised at a 100 ml measure. A mixed drink costs €4-6. Whisky is popular, and most bars have a good range. Spanish brandy is good, although its oaky vanilla flavours don't appeal to everyone. There are numerous varieties of rum and flavoured liqueurs. When ordering a spirit, you'll be expected to choose which brand you want; the local varieties (eg *Larios* gin, *DYC* whisky) are marginally cheaper than their imported brethren but lower in quality. *Chupitos* are shots; restaurants will often throw in a free one at the end of a meal, or give you a bottle of *orujo* (grape spirit) to pep up your black coffee.

Juice is normally bottled and expensive; *mosto* (grape juice; really pre-fermented wine) is a cheaper and popular soft drink in bars. There's the usual range of **fizzy drinks** (*gaseosas*) available. *Horchata* is a summer drink, a sort of milkshake made from tiger nuts. **Water** (*agua*) comes *con* (with) or *sin* (without) *gas*. The tap water is totally safe to drink, but it's not always the nicest; many Spaniards drink bottled water at home.

Coffee (*café*) is usually excellent and strong. *Solo* is black, mostly served espresso style. Order *americano* if you want a long black, *cortado* if you want a dash of milk, or *con leche* for about half milk. A *carajillo* is a coffee with brandy. **Tea** (*té*) is served without milk unless you ask; herbal teas (*infusiones*) are common, especially chamomile (*manzanilla*) and mint (*menta poleo*). **Chocolate** is a reasonably popular drink at breakfast time or in the afternoon (*merienda*), served with *churros*, fried doughsticks that seduce about a quarter of visitors and repel the rest.

Festivals on the Camino de Santiago

Even the smallest village in Spain has a fiesta, and some have several. Although mostly nominally religious in nature, they usually include the works; a Mass and procession or two to be sure, but also live music, bullfights, competitions, fireworks, a funfair, concerts and copious drinking of *calimocho*, a mix of red wine and cola (not as bad as it sounds). A feature of many are the *gigantes y cabezudos*, huge-headed papier-mâché figures based on historical personages who parade the streets. Adding to the sense of fun are *peñas*, boisterous social clubs who patrol the streets making music, get rowdy at the bullfights and drink wine all night and day. Most fiestas are in summer, and if you're travelling the Camino in that period you're bound to run into one; expect some trouble finding accommodation. Details of the major town fiestas can be found in the travel text. National holidays and long weekends (*puentes*) can be difficult times to travel; shops are shut, and transport books out days ahead. If the holiday falls mid-week, it's usual form to take an extra day off, forming a long weekend known as a *puente* (bridge).

Public holidays

The holidays listed here are national or across much of Northern Spain.
1 Jan Año Nuevo, New Year's Day.
6 Jan Reyes Magos/Epifanía, Epiphany; when Christmas presents are given.
19 Mar San José/Fathers' Day, holiday in some regions
Easter Jueves Santo, Viernes Santo, Día de Pascua (Maundy Thu, Good Fri, Easter Sun).
23 Apr Public holiday in Castilla y León
1 May Fiesta de Trabajo, Labour Day.

25 Jul Día del Apóstol Santiago, Feast of St James.
15 Aug Asunción, Feast of the Assumption.
12 Oct Día de la Hispanidad, Spanish National Day (Columbus Day, Feast of the Virgin of the Pillar).
1 Nov Todos los Santos, All Saints' Day.
6 Dec Día de la Constitución Española, Constitution Day.
8 Dec Inmaculada Concepción, Feast of the Immaculate Conception.
25 Dec Navidad, Christmas Day.

Essentials A-Z

Accident and emergency
There are various emergency numbers, but the general one across the nation is now T112. This will get you the police, ambulance, or fire brigade. T091 gets just the police.

Electricity
Spain uses the standard European 220V plug, with 2 round pins.

Embassies and consulates
For embassies and consulates of Spain, see www.maec.es.

Health
Health for travellers in Spain is rarely a problem. Medical facilities are good, and the worst most travellers experience is an upset stomach, usually merely a result of the different diet rather than any bug.

The water is safe to drink, but isn't always that pleasant, so many travellers (and locals) stick to bottled water. The sun in Spain can be harsh, so take adequate precautions to prevent heat exhaustion/sunburn. Many medications that require a prescription in other countries are available over the counter at pharmacies in Spain. Pharmacists are highly trained but don't necessarily speak English. In all medium-sized towns and cities, at least one pharmacy is open 24 hrs; this is organized on a rota system; details are posted in the window of all pharmacies and in local newspapers.

Language
For travelling purposes, everyone in Northern Spain speaks Spanish, known either as *castellano* or *español*, and it's a huge help to know some. Most young people know some English, and standards are rapidly rising, but don't assume that people aged 40 or over know any at all.

Spaniards are often shy to attempt to speak English. While many visitor attractions have some sort of information available in English (and to a lesser extent French and German), many don't, or have English tours only in times of high demand. Most tourist office staff will speak at least some English, and there's a good range of translated information available in most places.

While efforts to speak the language are appreciated, it's more or less expected, to the same degree as English is expected in Britain or the USA. Nobody will be rude if you don't speak any Spanish, but nobody will think to slow their rapidfire stream of the language for your benefit either, or pat you on the back for producing a few phrases in their tongue.

The other languages you'll come across in Northern Spain are *Euskara/Euskera* (the Basque language), *Galego* (Galician), *Bable* (the Asturian dialect) and perhaps *Aragonés* (Aragonese).

Money
Check www.xe.com for exchange rates.

Currency
The euro (€) is divided into 100 *céntimos*. Euro notes are standard across the whole zone, and come in denominations of 5, 10, 20, 50, 100, and the rarely seen 200 and 500. Coins have one standard face and one national face; all coins are, however, acceptable in all countries. The coins are slightly difficult to tell apart when you're not used to them. The coppers are 1, 2 and 5 cent pieces, the golds are 10, 20 and 50, and the silver/gold combinations are €1 and €2.

ATMs and banks
The best way to get money in Spain is by plastic. ATMs are plentiful, and just about all of them accept all the major international

debit and credit cards. The Spanish bank won't charge for the transaction, though they will charge a mark-up on the exchange rate, but beware of your own bank hitting you for a hefty fee: check with them before leaving home. Even if they do, it's likely to be a better deal than exchanging cash. The website www.moneysavingexpert.com has a good rundown on the most economical ways of accessing cash while travelling.

Banks are usually open Mon-Fri 0830-1400 (and Sat in winter) and many change foreign money (sometimes only the central branch in a town will do it). Commission rates vary widely; it's usually best to change large amounts, as there's often a minimum commission of €6 or so. Nevertheless, banks nearly always give better rates than change offices (*casas de cambio*), which are fewer by the day. If you're stuck outside banking hours, some large department stores such as the *Corte Inglés* change money at knavish rates. Traveller's cheques are accepted in many shops, although they are far less common than they were.

As a pilgrim, it's important to be aware that you may be walking a few days in some areas without passing through a village that has an ATM. Pilgrim hostels don't take plastic, and nor do many cheap *pensiones* and restaurants, so make sure you're aware of how much cash you'll need for the days ahead. Obviously, with so much communal travelling and sleeping, it's a good idea to keep all your cash on your person at all times.

Tax
Nearly all goods and services in Spain are subject to a value-added tax (IVA). This is only 10% for most things the traveller will encounter, including food and hotels, but is as high as 21% on some things. IVA is normally included in the stated prices. You're technically entitled to claim it back if you're a non-EU citizen, for purchases over €90. If you're buying something pricey, make sure you get a stamped receipt clearly showing the IVA component, as well as your name and passport number; you can claim the amount back at major airports on departure. Some shops will have a form to smooth the process.

Cost of living and travelling
As a pilgrim you can travel cheaper than most thanks to the network of hostels that you can access with your *credencial* ('pilgrim passport'). A thrifty walker can spend as little as €20 a day, sleeping in hostels, preparing your own meals or contributing to communal dinners. For a more comfortable Camino, alternating hostels with cheap hotels and eating out, €50 per person per day is reasonable.

If you're going to be staying in hotels, the news isn't great for the solo traveller: single rooms tend not to be particularly good value, and they are in short supply. Prices range from 60% to 80% of the double/twin price; some establishments even charge the full rate. If you're going to be staying in 3- to 5-star hotels, booking them ahead on internet discount sites can save a lot of money.

Public transport is generally cheap; intercity bus services are quick and low-priced and trains are reasonable, though the fast AVE trains cost substantially more.

It's also worth checking if the 10% IVA (sales tax) is included in meal prices, especially in the more expensive restaurants; it should say on the menu whether this is the case.

Opening hours
Business hours Mon-Fri 1000-1400, 1700-2000; Sat 1000-1400. **Banks** Mon-Fri 0830-1400; Sat (not in Aug) 0900-1300. **Government offices** Mornings only.

Safety
Northern Spain is generally a very safe place. Tourist crime is very low in this region, but the communal nature of the pilgrim trail means, inevitably, that the odd camera, wallet, or mobile phone does disappear.

There are several types of police, helpful enough in normal circumstances. The paramilitary **Guardia Civil** dress in green and are responsible for the roads (including speed traps and the like), borders and law enforcement away from towns. They're not a bunch to get the wrong side of but are polite to tourists and have thankfully lost the bizarre winged hats they used to sport. The **Policía Nacional** are responsible for most urban crime fighting, these are the ones to go to if you need to report anything stolen, etc. **Policía Local/Municipal** are present in large towns and cities and are responsible for some urban crime, as well as traffic control and parking.

Time
Spain operates on western European time, ie GMT +1, and changes its clocks in line with the rest of the EU.

'Spanish time' isn't as elastic as it used to be, but if you're told something will happen *'enseguida'* ('straight away') it may take 10 mins, if you're told *'cinco minutos'* (5 mins), grab a seat and a book. Transport, leaves promptly.

Tipping
Tipping in Spain is far from compulsory, but much practised. Around 10% is considered extremely generous in a restaurant; 3-5% is more usual. It's rare for a service charge to be added to a bill. Waiters do not normally expect tips, but in bars and cafés people will often leave small change, especially for table service. Taxi drivers don't expect a tip, but will be pleased to receive one. In rural areas, churches will often have a local keyholder who will open it up for you; if there's no admission charge, a tip or donation is appropriate (say €1 per head; more if they've given a detailed tour).

Tourist information
The tourist information infrastructure in Northern Spain is organized by the regional governments and is generally excellent, with a wide range of information, often in English, German and French as well as Spanish. Offices within the region can provide maps of the area and towns, and lists of registered accommodation, usually with 1 booklet for hotels, *hostales*, and *pensiones*; another for campsites, and another, especially worth picking up, listing farmstay and rural accommodation, which has taken off in a big way; hundreds are added yearly.

Along the Camino, tourist offices have pilgrim-specific information sheets and brochures, with locations of hostels, and simple maps of the route through the region. There are also some volunteer-run information centres specifically for pilgrims.

Opening hours are longer in major cities; many rural offices are only open in summer. Average opening hours are Mon-Sat 1000-1400, 1600-1900, Sun 1000-1400. Offices are often closed on Sun or Mon. Staff often speak English and other European languages and are well trained. The offices (*oficinas de turismo*) are often signposted to some degree within the town or city. Staff may ask where you are from; this is not nosiness but for statistical purposes.

The regional tourist boards of Northern Spain have useful websites, the better of which have extensive accommodation, restaurant, and sights listings. You can usually order brochures online too. They are:
Aragón, www.turismodearagon.com
Castilla y León, www.turismocastillayleon.com
Galicia, www.turgalicia.es
La Rioja, www.lariojaturismo.com
Navarra, www.turismonavarra.es

Websites on the Camino
www.santiago-compostela.net Multilingual pages on the Camino, with packing tips, forums, and photos of every stage.

www.peregrinossantiago.es Run by the archdiocese of Santiago, this website has some good practical advice, particularly for those undertaking the Camino for spiritual reasons.

www.santiagoturismo.com Santiago's tourism website has good practical advice

on the pilgrimage, and details of service/tour providers that can be booked online.
www.caminodesantiago.consumer.es
If you read Spanish, this has the most comprehensive route information as well as details and recent reviews on all the pilgrim hostels.
www.caminodesantiago.me
Excellent forum for pilgrims to discuss planning, practicalities and route info.
www.jacotrans.com Backpack-transporting service along the length of the Camino Francés. Also can help with bike logistics and repairs.
www.xacobeo.es Detailed website run by the Galician government focusing on the Camino Francés and other variants in Galicia only.
www.csj.org.uk The Confraternity of St James is a British association devoted to the Camino in all its aspects. Their website is full of useful advice and links, including to similar organizations in other countries.

Other useful websites
http://maps.google.es Street maps of most Spanish towns and cities.
www.alsa.es Northern Spain's major bus operator. Book online.
www.elpais.es Online edition of Spain's biggest-selling non-sports daily paper. English edition available.
www.guiarepsol.com Excellent online route planner for Spanish roads, also available in English.
www.inm.es Site of the national metereological institute, with the day's weather and next-day forecasts.
www.movelia.es Online timetables and ticketing for several bus companies.
www.paginasamarillas.es Yellow Pages.
www.paginasblancas.es White Pages.

www.parador.es Parador information, including locations, prices and photos.
www.renfe.com Online timetables and tickets for RENFE train network.
www.spain.info The official website of the Spanish tourist board.
www.ticketmaster.es Spain's biggest ticketing agency for concerts, etc, with online purchase.
www.todoturismorural.com and **www.toprural.com** 2 excellent sites for *casas rurales*.
www.tourspain.es A useful website run by the Spanish tourist board.
www.typicallyspanish.com News and links on all things Spanish.

Visas
Entry requirements are subject to change, so always check with the Spanish tourist board or an embassy/consulate if you're not an EU citizen. EU citizens and those from countries within the Schengen agreement can enter Spain freely. UK/Irish citizens will need to carry a passport, while an identity card suffices for other EU/Schengen nationals. Citizens of Australia, the USA, Canada, New Zealand and Israel can enter without a visa for up to 90 days. Other citizens will require a visa, obtainable from Spanish consulates or embassies. These are usually issued very quickly and valid for all Schengen countries. The basic visa is valid for 90 days, and you'll need 2 passport photos, proof of funds covering your stay and possibly evidence of medical cover (ie insurance). For extensions of visas, apply to an *oficina de extranjeros* in a major city.

Weights and measures
Metric.

Camino de Santiago

Contents

26 Western Pyrenees: Camino Francés
- 27 St-Jean-Pied-de-Port to Roncesvalles
- 27 Roncesvalles and around
- 28 Pamplona/Iruña
- 34 Listings

40 Western Pyrenees: Camino Aragonés
- 41 Canfranc Valley
- 41 Jaca
- 44 Jaca to Sangüesa
- 45 Sangüesa/Zangoza and around
- 47 Sangüesa to Puente la Reina
- 47 Listings

51 Western Navarra
- 51 Puente La Reina/Gares and around
- 51 Estella/Lizarra and around
- 52 Estella to Viana
- 53 Listings

56 Route through La Rioja
- 57 Logroño
- 60 Nájera
- 61 Onwards from Najera
- 62 Santo Domingo de la Calzada
- 63 Santo Domingo to Burgos
- 64 Listings

68 Burgos
- 69 Places in Burgos
- 76 Listings

80 West from Burgos
- 80 Burgos to Carrión de los Condes
- 82 Carrión de los Condes and beyond
- 83 Sahagún and beyond
- 85 Listings

87 León
- 90 Places in León
- 93 Listings

97 West of León
- 98 Astorga and around
- 100 El Bierzo
- 102 Listings

105 Route through Galicia
- 108 Listings

110 Santiago de Compostela
- 111 Arriving in Santiago de Compostela
- 111 Background
- 113 Cathedral and around
- 117 Monasterio de San Martín Pinario and around
- 118 Around Porta do Camino
- 119 Colegiata de Santa María de Sar
- 120 Listings

Footprint features

- 29 Charlemagne and Roland
- 30 The kingdom of Navarra
- 31 Fiesta de San Fermín
- 37 Patxarán
- 42 The Holy Grail
- 59 Rioja wine
- 62 Chickens in the church
- 72 El Cid
- 81 Sasamón
- 98 The Maragatos
- 112 Saint James and the Camino de Santiago
- 118 Extension to Cape Finisterre

Western Pyrenees: Camino Francés

The principal route of the pilgrims to Santiago, the Camino Francés, starts in the French town of St-Jean-Pied-de Port, then crosses the small independent kingdom of Navarra from north to west. It has left a sizeable endowment of some of the peninsula's finest religious architecture. Entering the province above Roncesvalles, where Charlemagne's rearguard was given a nasty Basque bite, it continues to Pamplona and thence through small attractive towns such as Estella and Viana. It's not all hard work though; at one lunch stop there's a drinking fountain that spouts red wine.

This northern half of Navarra is spiritually and culturally part of the Basque lands, from the mountainous moist pastureland of the Pyrenees to the drier, gentler agricultural slopes of the west. In the midst of it all is Pamplona, a pleasant and sober town that goes berserk for nine days in July for the Fiesta de los Sanfermines, of which the best-known event is the daily *encierro*, or running of the bulls, made famous by Hemingway and more recently by thousands of wine-swilling locals and scared-looking tourists on television every year.

St-Jean-Pied-de-Port to Roncesvalles → *For listings, see pages 34-39.*

While many pilgrims start their long walk in Roncesvalles, the semi-official starting point of the Camino Francés is over the border in France, in the pretty town of St-Jean-Pied-de-Port. 'Pied de port' means 'foot of the pass' so you're not in for an easy first day's stroll as you cross the Pyrenees into Spain, but it's worth adding this extra day on to the beginning of the route. The scenery is fabulous, and there's plenty of first-day camaraderie trudging up the long ascent to the pass.

St-Jean's centre is delightful, with picturesque houses huddling along the river, spanned by a photogenic medieval bridge that is the designated starting point of the road to Santiago. The **pilgrim office** ① *39 rue de la Citadelle, T+33 5 59 37 05 09, www.aucoeurduchemin.org*, can get you sorted out with information and a *credencial* (pilgrim passport), which costs €1.50.

From here, it's a steady 13-mile uphill slog to the day's highest point, the **Collado Lepoeder**. If you had been walking this route in the late eighth century, you might have met the ragged remnants of Charlemagne's ambushed army coming the other way (see box, page 29). The route ascends 1300 m and is best taken slowly, as it's the first day of many. There are several viewpoints to stop at, as well as the pilgrim *albergue* at **Orisson** for late starters. An alternative route follows the road via the border village of **Valcarlos**; it's a lesser ascent but not as picturesque or peaceful.

Once you reach the Collado, it's all downhill. Take the slightly longer of two routes to Roncesvalles; this takes you via the **Puerto de Ibañeta** pass, where there's a modern chapel and a memorial to Roland. Some say this is where the grieving Charlemagne buried Roland; at any rate the memorial is slightly incongruous, seeing as it was the Navarrans who probably did him in. Many scholars in fact consider the valley of Valcarlos as the most likely location of the battle itself. A more recent and appropriate memorial in Roncesvalles commemorates Charlemagne's vanquishers. From the Puerto de Ibañeta it's an easy downhill run into Roncesvalles.

Roncesvalles and around → *For listings, see pages 34-39. Phone code: 948. Altitude: 924 m.*

On a misty evening the stern ecclesiastical complex at Roncesvalles resembles Colditz, but fortunately offers a distinctly warmer welcome to Santiago-bound pilgrims, for whom it is either the starting point or the first stop along the Camino Francés; it was also the last stop for many of Charlemagne's knights including the famous Roland (see box, page 29).

Roncesvalles/Orreaga is little more than the Colegiata church complex, pilgrim hostel, hotel and a couple of *posadas*. It sits just below the Puerto de Ibañeta pass that divides Spain from French Basqueland. Some 3 km closer to Pamplona through an avenue of trees, the village of **Burguete** offers more services, and has been made moderately famous by Hemingway, whose characters Jake and Bill put away several gallons of wine there on a fishing expedition before descending to Pamplona in his novel *Fiesta* (*The Sun Also Rises*).

Places in Roncesvalles

A **pilgrim hostel** was originally built in Roncesvalles in 1127. Its fame grew with the growing streams of walkers who were succoured here, and was further aided when a local shepherd discovered the Virgin of Roncesvalles. The statue is said to have been buried to protect it from Moorish raiders. The **Collegiate church** ① *T948 790 480, summer daily 0800-*

2030, winter 1500-1800, free or €4.30 including visit to the Iglesia de Santiago and the Silo, which are otherwise kept closed, guided tours 1000-1400, 1530-1900, is the highlight of the sanctuary, a simple and uplifting example of French Gothic architecture, with blue stained-glass windows and a silver-plated statuette of the Virgin taking pride of place above the altar. On her birthday, 8 September, there's a major *romería* (pilgrimage) and fiesta here. Off the cloister is the burial chapel of the Navarran King Sancho VII ('The Strong'), whose bones were transferred here in 1912. He lies with his wife under a 2.25-m 14th-century alabaster statue of himself that's said to be life size; in the stained-glass depiction of him battling the Moors at the scene of his greatest triumph, Navas de Tolosa, he cuts an imposing figure. A **war hammer** leaning nearby is predictably said to have been Roland's. The small **museum** ⓘ *daily 1000-1400, 1500-1800 (1900 summer, closed afternoons in Jan)*, attached to the complex is less impressive, but has a few interesting manuscripts, as well as a blue-embossed reliquary known as 'Charlemagne's chess set'.

A few paces away from the church complex are two further buildings, the tiny 14th-century **Iglesia de Santiago** and the 12th-century funerary structure known as the **Silo of Charlemagne** ⓘ *see Collegiate church, above for both*. Legend maintains that the Silo was built on the site where Charlemagne buried Roland and his stricken rearguard. Underneath it is a burial pit holding bones of various origins; some may well have been pilgrims for whom the hard climb over the Pyrenees had proved to be a step too far; the bear and wolf population likely also took a toll.

Opposite the complex, there's a **visitor centre** ⓘ *1100-1330, 1600-1900, €1*, which is half an excuse for a shop to keep the steady flow of visitors happy. There's also a small exhibition and audiovisual display on Navarra and the Roncesvalles area.

The Roncesvalles **tourist office** ⓘ *Mon-Sat 1000-1400, 1530-1900 (1500-1800 winter), Sun 1000-1400, T948 760 301*, is attentive and helpful, although queues can be long.

Roncesvalles to Pamplona

You can walk the 42 km from Roncesvalles to Pamplona in a day, but it's a long haul and most pilgrims choose to break the journey halfway, in the village of **Zubiri**, a not-especially attractive spot surrounded by lovely rolling, forested hills. From Roncesvalles to here, it's a comparatively easy day with gentle rises and falls, before a longer, spectacular descent as you approach Zubiri. The following day to Pamplona is less attractive, but a flattish, easy walk.

Pamplona/Iruña → *For listings, see pages 34-39. Phone code: 948. Population: 198,491. Altitude: 444 m.*

Pamplona, the capital of Navarra, conjures images of wild drunken revelry and stampeding bulls. And rightly so, for that is exactly what happens for nine days every July during Los Sanfermines. Love it or hate it, if you're around you have to check it out. At other times Pamplona is quite a subdued but picturesque city, its high-walled old town very striking when approached from below. It's a good place to stop over, with plenty of good accommodation and eating options; you can do *pinchos* Basque-style or sit down to a huge Castilian roast.

Arriving in Pamplona

Getting around Walking around Pamplona is the best option; the only time you might want to use the city buses is to reach the Hospitales district where the stadium,

Charlemagne and Roland

Taking the crown of the Franks in AD 768 at the age of 26, Charlemagne embarked on a lifelong campaign to unite and bring order to western Europe, which resulted in an empire that included France, Switzerland, Belgium, Holland, much of Italy and Germany, as well as the 'Spanish March', a wedge of territory stretching down to the Ebro River. Or so he thought; the locals weren't so sure. Allowing him to pass through their territory to battle against the Moors, the local Basques were outraged at Charlemagne's conduct: he destroyed Pamplona's fortifications after taking it; and accepted a bribe from the city of Zaragoza to return to France. As the army ascended the Ibañeta Pass above Roncesvalles on their way home, their rearguard and baggage train was ambushed and slaughtered by locals. Among the dead was Hrudoland, or Roland, governor of the marches of Brittany, a shadowy historical figure immortalized in the later romantic account of the event, *Le Chanson de Roland*, which blamed the attack on the Moors.

planetarium and several hotels and *pensiones* are located. Numerous buses plough up and down Avenida Pío XII connecting the Hospitales district with the centre. You can get on them at Avenida Carlos III, near Plaza del Castillo. The **RENFE** train station is inconveniently situated a couple of kilometres north of town, but is connected every 10 minutes by bus.

Orientation Pamplona is an easy city to get the hang of: the walled old town perches over the plain above the Río Arga. To the south and west stretch the Ensanches, the newer town, which radiates outwards along avenues beginning near the Ciudadela, a large bastion turned public park.

Tourist information Pamplona has an excellent **tourist office** ⓘ *Av Roncesvalles 4, T848 420 420, www.turismo.navarra.es, Nov-Apr Mon-Fri 1000-1700, Sat-Sun 1000-1400, May-Jun, Sep-Oct, Mon-Sat 1000-1400, 1600-1900, Sun 1000-1400, Jul-Aug Mon-Fri 0900-1900, Sat 1000-1400, 1600-1900, Sun 1000-1400.*

Background
The Pamplona area was probably settled by Basques, who gave it the name Iruña/Iruñea, but the city's definitive founding was by the Roman general Pompey, who set up a base here around 74 BC while campaigning against the renegade Quintus Sertorius, who had set himself up as a local warlord. No shrinking violet, Pompey named the city after himself (Pompeiopolis). The city flourished due to its important position at the peninsula's doorstep, but was sacked time and again by Germanic tribes. After a period of Visigothic control, it was taken by the Moors in AD 711, although the inhabitants were allowed to remain Christian. There was more territorial exchange and debate before the final emergence of the Kingdom of Pamplona in the ninth century. Sacked and destroyed by the feared caliph of Córdoba Abd-al-Rahman in AD 924, the city only gradually recovered, hampered by squabbling between its municipalities.

Pamplona's rise to real prominence ironically came when Navarra was conquered by Castilla; Fernando built the city walls and made it the province's capital. After a turbulent 19th century, Pamplona expanded rapidly through the 20th century, necessitating the development of successive *Ensanches* (expansions) south and west of the old centre.

The kingdom of Navarra

While the area has been populated for millennia, the historical entity of Navarra emerged in the ninth century after periods of Basque, Roman, Visigothic, Moorish and Frankish control as part of the Reconquista, the Christian battle to drive the Moors southwards and out of the peninsula. Under the astute rulership of King Sancho III in the early 11th century, Navarra was unified with Castilla and Aragón, which meant that Sancho ruled an area extending from the Mediterranean right across to Galicia; not for nothing is he known as 'the Great'. After his death things began to disintegrate, and provinces were lost left, right but not centre until 1200, when it had roughly the boundaries it has today, but including Basse-Navarre, now in France. In 1512, King Fernando of Aragón (Regent of Castilla following his wife's death) invaded Navarra and took it easily.

In the 19th century, after centuries of relative peace, things kicked off, first with Napoleon's invasion, then with the rise of the liberal movement and Carlism. These events were always likely to cause schisms in the province, which already had natural divisions between mountains and plains, and families who were Basque, French, or Spanish in alignment. Navarra became the centre of Carlism and suffered the loss of most of its rights as a result of that movement's defeat. During the Civil War, the Carlists were on Franco's side; the province was favoured during his rule, in contrast to the other Basque provinces, which had taken the Republican side.

Today, as a semi-autonomous province, the divisions continue; many Basques are striving for the union of Navarra with Euskadi, but the lowland towns are firmly aligned with Spain. Navarra's social and political differences are mirrored in its geography; it is (to use a cliché) a land of contrasts. The northern and eastern parts of the province are dominated by the Pyrenees and its offshoots, and are lands of green valleys and shepherd villages, which are culturally very Basque. The baking southern and central plains seem to reflect the dusty days of the Reconquista and are more Castilian Spanish in outlook and nature.

Places in Pamplona

Plaza del Castillo At the southern entrance to the old town is the pedestrianized Plaza del Castillo, centre of much of the city's social life. Before the Plaza de Toros was built, the bullfights were held in this square. Behind the square to the east is the famous cobbled **Estafeta**, the main runway for the bulls during Los Sanfermines; it's lined with shops and bars. It's amazing how narrow it can look when six bulls are charging down it towards you. At the famous corner where the bulls turn into Estafeta, the new **Museo del Encierro** ⓘ *C Mercaderes 17, T948 225 413, daily 1100-1400, 1600-2000, €8*, has history and photos of the running of the bulls, as well as several audiovisual exhibits including simulators that give you some of the idea of the *encierro* itself.

Cathedral and around The quiet, seemingly deserted part of town east of the Plaza del Castillo is dominated by the **cathedral** ⓘ *T948 212 594, www.catedraldepamplona.com, summer Mon-Sat 1000-1400, 1600-1900, winter Tue-Fri 1030-1700, Sat 1030-2000, Sun 1030-1400, €5 (€3 for pilgrims), including entry to the Diocesan museum*. Don't be daunted by the rather austere 18th-century façade, as the interior is a masterpiece of delicate Gothic work. Facing the front, the entrance is up the street to your right. First stop is the gorgeous cloister,

Fiesta de San Fermín

Better known in English as the 'running of the bulls', the nine-day Fiesta de San Fermín lays a serious claim to being the biggest party in Europe. The city goes completely *loca*, and the streets and bars burst with locals and tourists clad traditionally in white with red neckscarves, downing beer and wine with abandon while dancing to the music pumping from a dozen different sources.

It's quite possible to lose a week of your life here and never set eyes on a bull, but it's the *encierros* (bull-runnings) that add the spice. It's difficult to imagine any other country allowing over three tons of bullflesh to plough through a crowd of drunken citizens, but it happens here at 0800 every morning of the fiesta. The streets are barricaded and six bulls are released to run from their *corral* to the Plaza de Toros. If they keep in formation and don't get panicked or distracted they'll only take three minutes to cover the course, but if they find a buttock or two to gore along the way, they can be on the streets for 10 minutes or more. Rockets are let off; the first is single and signals the release of the bulls; the next, a double, means that they've all left the *corral*; and the triple is fired after they've arrived at the bullring and have been safely penned. For good measure, a few cows (with covered horns) are then released into the ring. They always toss a few people, to the amusement of the large crowd. That evening the bulls are fought in the daily *corrida*.

The festival kicks off each year on 6 July at the Ayuntamiento, with a rocket (*El Chupinazo*) fired at midday and cries of '¡Viva San Fermín!'. The saint himself was a Roman convert to Christianity who became the first bishop of Pamplona. The day proceeds with a procession of larger than life papier mâché headed figures (*cabezudos y gigantes*) who parade through town. 7 July is the biggest day with the first *encierro*, but there are plenty of things going on all week, with live bands, processions, street performers, fireworks and more. Especially noticeable are the *peñas*, large social clubs that travel Spain to find a party. Boisterous and with their own brass section, their colourful parades are a feature of the week.

When you come to Los Sanfermines, give it a little time. It can be overwhelming, and there's plenty to dislike: the stench of stale beer and urine, crowds, inflated prices ... but it's enjoyable and addictive. It's also easy to get away from the hectic atmosphere – walk a few streets into the new town, and you can mix with jovial locals enjoying an equally good-natured, but more civilized, party.

One of the best aspects of the festival is that it's still a fiesta with a strong local flavour. While things are busiest from 1900, it's great to wander around during the day, seeking out little pockets of good time in the quiet backstreets. It's a time for family and friends to get together too; you'll see long tables set up in unlikely places for massive alfresco meals.

Animal rights campaigners have correctly highlighted that the *encierro*, with its crowds and noise, is a stressful experience for the poor beasts involved. As an alternative, PETA (People for the Ethical Treatment of Animals) organize a festive protest on the 5 July. **The Running of the Nudes** (www.runningofthenudes.com) is exactly what it sounds like – a light-hearted clothing-optional fun run with an anti-bullfighting agenda.

The festival finally ends at midnight on 14 July, again at the Ayuntamiento, with a big crowd chanting the '*Pobre de mí*' (poor me), mourning the end of the fiesta.

Pamplona/Iruña

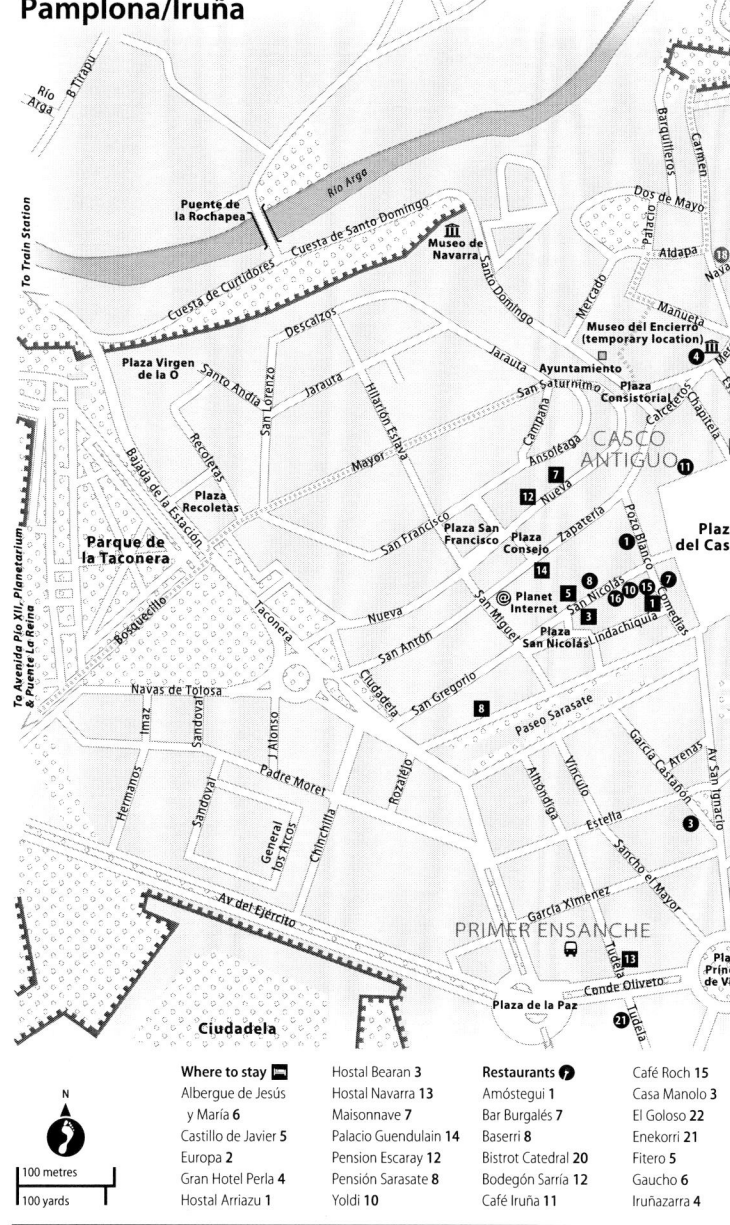

Where to stay
Albergue de Jesús y María 6
Castillo de Javier 5
Europa 2
Gran Hotel Perla 4
Hostal Arriazu 1

Hostal Bearan 3
Hostal Navarra 13
Maisonnave 7
Palacio Guendulain 14
Pension Escaray 12
Pensión Sarasate 8
Yoldi 10

Restaurants
Amóstegui 1
Bar Burgalés 7
Baserri 8
Bistrot Catedral 20
Bodegón Sarría 12
Café Iruña 11

Café Roch 15
Casa Manolo 3
El Goloso 22
Enekorri 21
Fitero 5
Gaucho 6
Iruñazarra 4

32 • Camino de Santiago Western Pyrenees: Camino Francés

a superb space full of delicate harmony with excellent carved reliefs on some of the doorways leading off it. The cathedral itself, which is similarly impressive, houses the tombs of Carlos III ('the noble') of Navarra and his queen. The **Diocesan museum** is located in what used to be the larder, kitchen and dining room, and now holds a reasonably interesting selection of artefacts.

Behind the cathedral, past the shady **Plaza de San José**, is the tranquil corner of **El Caballo Blanco**, named after the inviting bar that looks over the ramparts. Walking down the east wall from here you'll reach the **Plaza de Santa María la Real**, another peaceful spot, overlooked by the archbishop's palace.

Plaza Consistorial and around The centre of town is occupied by the small Plaza Consistorial, seat of the pretty baroque **Ayuntamiento**, where the crowd gathers to watch the start of Los Sanfermines. Down the hill from here, near the market, is the impressive **Museo de Navarra** ① *Tue-Sat 0930-1400, 1700-1900, Sun 1100-1400, restricted opening during Los Sanfermines, €2, free for pilgrims and free on Sat afternoon and Sun*, set in a stately former convent hospital. The museum contains a wide range of material, from prehistoric remains on the ground floor through to modern Navarran art at the top. There are a few Goyas, as well as much religious art that has been gathered from the many provincial churches and monasteries.

Primer Ensanche The Primer Ensanche, the city's earliest expansion, lies immediately to the south of Plaza del Castillo. The Avenida de San Ignacio has a statue depicting the saint, founder of the Jesuit order, wounded while defending the city; the wounds more or less led to his conversion. This avenue ends at the busy **Plaza Príncipe de Viana**; a short way to the west, the bus station stands on the offbeat **Plaza de la Paz**. Beyond the old town, in the Primer Ensanche, stretches

Camino de Santiago Western Pyrenees: Camino Francés • 33

the pentagonal wall of the **Ciudadela**, a low military bastion constructed by Felipe II; it houses a chapel and a small arms exhibition. The newer parts of town south of here are blessed with plenty of green space.

Back on the edge of the old town, the **Plaza de Toros** is the first thing you see after winding up the Bajada de Labrit into town from the Puente de la Magdalena, where the pilgrims cross the river. It's no exaggeration to say that Hemingway's novel *Fiesta* (*The Sun Also Rises*) has had a massive impact on Pamplona's prosperity over the years, so it's fitting that there's a bust of him in front of the ring – the street outside is also named after him.

Pamplona to Puente la Reina

Pamplona is separated from the western Navarran farmland by a hill, the **Alto del Perdón**, which you'll soon see looming ahead as you leave the city. It's a steady rather than heartbreaking ascent up a path through shrubby terrain. Descending, you meet the Camino Aragonés at **Obanos** before walking into **Puente la Reina**, one of the Camino's iconic stops.

Western Pyrenees: Camino Francés listings

For hotel and restaurant price codes and other relevant information, see pages 12-19.

Where to stay

St-Jean-Pied-de-Port *p27*

€€ Gite Azkorria, 50 Rue de la Citadelle, T+33 559 370 053, www.hebergements-pays-basque.fr. This attractive, colourful and friendly modern place makes the perfect place to rest your bones in comfort before embarking on a long walk. Home-cooked dinners and good breakfasts available.

€ Refuge Municipal, 55 Rue de la Citadelle, T+33 559 370 509, www.aucoeurduchemin.org. Comfortable pilgrim hostel that includes breakfast in the €8 fee. Book in at the pilgrim office at number 39.

Roncesvalles/Orreaga and around *p27*

There are plenty of *casas rurales* around Burguete/Auritz should you fail to find a bed.

€€ Hotel Loizu, Av Roncesvalles 7, Burguete/Auritz, T948 760 008, www.loizu.com. Closed mid-Dec to mid-Mar. The most upmarket of the places to stay in this area, this is a decently modernized old house in Burguete with reasonable rooms with TV and heating, which can be much needed both in summer and winter. The nicest rooms are on the top floor use stripped-back stone to great decorative effect.

€€ Hotel Roncesvalles, Roncesvalles s/n, T948 760 105, www.hotelroncesvalles.com. Occupying an 18th-century building that's part of the Roncesvalles complex, this cosy modern hotel offers comfortable rooms, and good-value apartments. They offer discounts for pilgrims.

€ Albergue de Peregrinos de Roncesvalles, Roncesvalles s/n, T948 760 000, www.roncesvalles.es. Huge, commodious and spotless pilgrim hostel with modern dorm beds for €10. Pilgrim passport available here.

€ Hostal Burguete, C San Nicolás 71, Burguete/Auritz, T948 760 005, www.hotelburguete.com. Closed mid-Dec to mid-Mar. The place where Ernest used to hang out, and the base for Jake and Bill's expedition in *Fiesta* (*The Sun Also Rises*). On the main (only) street through Burguete; this is a place with plenty of character and decent double rooms.

€ La Posada, Roncesvalles s/n, T948 760 225, www.laposadaderoncesvalles.com. It feels like an old travellers' inn and it is one, dating from 1612. The best place to stay in Roncesvalles itself with snug, heated en suite rooms. There's also a log fire and a more than decent cheap restaurant.

Camping
Camping Urrobi, Ctra Pamplona–Valcarlos Km 42, T948 760 200, www.campingurrobi.com. Open Apr-Oct. Just below Burguete, this campsite is reasonably equipped and also has bungalows and cheap dormitory beds.

Roncesvalles to Pamplona *p28*
€ Albergue Zaldiko, Puente de la Rabia 1, Zuribi, T609 736 420, www.alberguezaldiko.com. This compact place is slightly pricier than the official pilgrim hostel but is worth it for its greater comfort and warm welcome.

Pamplona *p28, map p32*
There are scores of budget options around the old town and along Av Pío XII in the Hospitales district; look for signs saying '*camas*' above bars and restaurants. The codes given here do not apply for San Fermín, when prices treble at least. At other times, finding accommodation is never a problem.

€€€€ Gran Hotel Perla, Plaza del Castillo 1, T948 223 000, www.granhotellaperla.com. Where Hemingway lay his bearded head when he came to town, the Perla is right on the square and has recently been converted from dilapidation to a most elegant 5-star hotel, beautifully lit at night. Rooms all have balconies looking out on to Estafeta, another street, and/or the plaza, and are most spacious, with elegant period furniture. The helpful staff are particularly welcoming and there's an excellent restaurant.

€€€€ Palacio Guendulain, C Zapatería 53, T948 225 522, www.palacioguendulain.com. In the heart of old Pamplona, this noble old palace has been recently converted into a plush boutique hotel, with period furnishings and a selection of handsome carriages. Service is excellent, with little details normally absent in larger, more impersonal places. The rooms are spacious, with super-comfortable beds and luxurious bathrooms. Recommended.

€€€ Maisonnave, C Nueva 20, T948 222 600, www.hotelmaisonnave.es. A sleek but friendly modern hotel with comfortable furnishings, a decent café and a sauna among other amenities. The a/c rooms are equipped with every comfort and are pretty good value for this type of facility, with some good out-of-season specials.

€€€ Tres Reyes, C Taconera s/n, T948 226 600, www.hotel3reyes.com. This giant hotel towers over the edge of the old town and its rooms offer plenty of natural light and great views from their lofty position. Its mostly geared for conferences, which, for the leisure traveller translates to excellent facilities, plenty of staff on call, and weekend rates that are very good value, up to 50% cheaper with advance booking.

€€ Hostal Arriazu, C Comedias 14, T948 210 202, www.hostalarriazu.com. Offering more than your average *hostal*, this is a boutique option close to the Plaza del Castillo. Prices are high, but you get rooms that have polished parquet floors and firm beds. It sometimes feels more like a homestay, and you have the run of the sitting room area.

€€ Hostal Bearan, C San Nicolás 25, T948 223 428, www.hostalbearan.es. One of the better equipped of the several *hostales* on this street, this has spacious doubles with good heating and decent bathrooms. The rooms have simple but modern furnishings, and with the location, are reasonable value, though not for single travellers. Facilities include hairdryers and free Wi-Fi though it doesn't work in all rooms. Ask in the bar next door if there's nobody around.

€€ Hostal Navarra, C Tudela 9, T948 225 164, www.hostalnavarra.com. Bright modern *hostal* with hotel-standard rooms just around the corner from the bus station and a short walk from the old town. There's free Wi-Fi and helpful management. No lift.

€€ Hotel Castillo de Javier, C San Nicolás 50, T948 203 040, www.hotelcastillodejavier.com. This hotel has a great central location. It's decorated with a light modern touch; the rooms are smallish but comfortable, with funky modern art on the walls. There

Camino de Santiago **Western Pyrenees: Camino Francés listings** • 35 are several nice touches throughout, and rooms have TV and telephone; for a little more cash you can have a hydromassage shower in the bathroom. Downstairs there's a café/bar and 1 room is equipped for disabled travellers.

€€ Hotel Europa, C Espoz y Mina 11, T948 221 800, www.hoteleuropapamplona.com. If there's a hint of the self-satisfied about this place, they have good reason – it is a small and superbly located hotel just off the Plaza del Castillo, with balconies overlooking C Estafeta (the main drag of the bull-running). The restaurant is also one of the better ones in town.

€€ Hotel Leyre, C Leyre 7, T948 228 500, www.hotel-leyre.com. Although furnished in fairly unimaginative 3-star standard style, this hotel is close to the bullring and offers plenty of comfort and facilities. It's handy for both the old and new towns, and offers very good and notably friendly service.

€€ Hotel Yoldi, Av San Ignacio 11, T948 224 800, www.hotelyoldi.com. Hemingway stayed here after his friend Juanito Quintana lost his hotel, La Perla, during the Civil War. It happily offers modern comforts with surprisingly reasonable prices. The rooms are a/c and spacious, if a little unimaginatively furnished. They have good facilities.

€ Albergue de Jesús y María, C Compañia 4, T948 222 644. Spacious modern pilgrim's rest in a characterful old building near the cathedral. Closed during Sanfermines.

€ Pensión Escaray, C Nueva 24, T948 227 825. This simple little place is a likeable basic budget option. Run by a solicitous mother-son combination, it has clean and fairly unadorned rooms with shared bathroom. There's a fair difference in quality between the rooms on the 2 different floors.

€ Pensión Sarasate, Paseo Sarasate 30, T948 223 084, www.pensionsarasate.es. A small, quiet and friendly *pensión* with well-cared-for rooms in the heart of things. This is one of Pamplona's best budget options. The rooms vary; some have balcony; all are decorated in a cheerful and homely style.

Restaurants

Roncesvalles/Orreaga and around
p27

While the Posada and Sabina in Roncesvalles do fine fare with cheap pilgrim menus, there's better eating in Burguete, 3 km down the road.

€€ Loizu, Av Roncesvalles 7, Burguete/Auritz. T948 760 008. This hotel restaurant serves up good warming mountain food with a touch of class. There's a *menú* for €17.50.

€ Burguete, C San Nicolás 71, Burguete/Auritz, T948 790 488. If you've read *Fiesta* you'll be eating here. The piano that Bill played to keep warm is *in situ* in the dining room and, while they may have forgotten how to make rum punch, there is a *menú* that is good value and includes trout, as it should. Pictures of the bearded writer adorn the room but it's thankfully far from being a shrine.

Pamplona *p28, map p32*

€€€ Amóstegui, C Pozo Blanco 20, T948 224 327. A traditional and central upstairs restaurant that serves excellent Navarran cuisine. Try some fresh asparagus or artichokes if they're in season, but only go for the fresh foie gras if you fancy something seriously rich. Other specialities of the house include pigeon and *zarzuela* (fish stew). Politely formal service.

€€€ Enekorri, C Tudela 14, T948 230 798, www.enekorri.com. One of Pamplona's gourmet temples, this is modishly lit and a place to be seen hereabouts. Tuna with cherry gazpacho was a taste sensation last time we passed by, but the meats are beautifully treated and presented too. It's haute cuisine without too much frippery. Recommended.

€€€ Josetxo, Plaza Principe de Viana 1, T948 222 097, www.restaurantejosetxo.com. Closed Sun and Aug. One of Pamplona's most refined restaurants, with wines to match. The *txangurro* (spider crab) stuffed in its own shell is one of a number of

Patxarán

One of Navarra's most emblematic products is this liqueur, usually taken as a *digestivo* after a meal. Although there are *patxaranes* made from a variety of berries and fruits, the traditional Navarran one, which now has its own DO (*denominación de origen*), is made from sloe berries macerated in an aniseed liquor. Usually served on ice, the taste can range from the sweet and superbly delicate to medicinal. The name comes from the Euskara word for sloe, *basaran*. Some folk like to mix it: a *San Fermín* is *patxarán* and *cava* (sparkling wine), while a *vaca rosa* (pink cow) is a blend of the liqueur with milk. Adding cinnamon or coffee is another option.

---

outstanding dishes that focus on Navarran tradition rather than current fashions.

€€ Bistrot Catedral, C Navarrería 20, T948 210 152, www.bistrotcatedral.com. The artistic modern design of this small place near the cathedral, all CDs, cable curtains and cork chairs and tables, isn't let down by the food, which features exquisitely presented *pinchos* and *raciones*: try the sauteed vegetables and mushrooms with egg yolk. It's also a good place for a *copa*: the G&Ts stand out.

€€ Casa Manolo, C García Castañón 12, T948 225 102, www.restaurantecasamanolo.com. A dependable 2nd-floor restaurant proudly presenting Navarran specialities like *pichón estofado con pochas* (braised pigeon with beans). Good service.

€€ El Goloso, C Aoiz 12, T948 291 973. It's worth seeking out this stylish modern new town tapas bar for its relaxed but modish decor, buzzy atmosphere, and excellent array of plates, from tiny snacks to substantial portions of succulent meat and fish, all beautifully presented. Great value.

€€ Otano, C San Nicolás 5, T948 227 036, www.casaotano.com. Popular, attractive and central, this upbeat restaurant has tables overlooking one of Pamplona's livelier weekend streets. It specializes in its roast meats, but if there's *rodaballo* (turbot) about, definitely consider it. There's a good-value *menú* that's also served in the evenings midweek and a long list of scrumptious desserts. The bar downstairs is great, with friendly service and tasty *pinchos*. The *tortilla* is superb. Recommended.

€€ San Nicolás, C San Nicolás 13, T948 221 319. On one of Pamplona's main eat streets, this bistro-style set-up has a small but attractive back dining area where you can chow down on tasty French-inspired Basque fare at fair prices. Good mixed salads, rich duck confit, and good-value Navarran wines make this a worthwhile experience.

€ Bar Burgalés, C Comedias 5, T948 225 158. Recently refurbished, this spot has a fair bit of history behind it. A long curving bar now supports some rather untraditional fare, with elaborate gourmet creations alongside more typical fritos and rolls. It's all delicious.

€ Baserri, C San Nicolás 32, T948 222 021, www.restaurantebaserri.com. This popular chess-board patterned restaurant serves a good value *menú del día* daily except Sun and nightly except Fri and Sat. A more elaborate menu is served at other times. The bar does a good range of *pinchos*.

€ Bodegón Sarría, C Estafeta 52, T948 227 713, www.bodegonsarria.com. Rows of quality ham hanging from the ceiling; you can try *pinchos* at the bar or sit at the wooden tables and snack on *raciones*, which also include tripe and stews.

€ Fitero, C Estafeta 58, T948 222 006, www.barfitero.es. Award-winning bites on the main drag, which include an excellent spinach and prawn *croqueta* among other fancy delights.

€ Gaucho, C Espoz y Mina 7, T948 225 073, www.cafebargaucho.com. A buzzy little corner bar with good *pinchos* and strong coffee. It's always busy; there's a great variety of beautifully elaborate fare on the bar. Recommended.

€ Iruñazarra, C Mercaderes 15, T948 225 167, www.irunazarra.org. This spacious and convivial Basque tavern has been going for ages. It's a top spot to eat cheap *raciones* at tables at the back; you can accompany them with cider poured from a big barrel. A cheerful mixture of young and old.

€ Monasterio, C Espoz y Mina 11, T948 212 859. Next door to **Gaucho**, this lacks nothing by comparison; it's longer, more brightly lit and more modern in feel but has equally fine snacks, all labelled.

Cafés

Café Iruña, Plaza del Castillo 44, T948 222 064, www.cafeiruna.com. This marvellous spot on the square is a beautifully refurbished Pamplona classic with its magnificent belle epoque interior. It's got everything; reasonably priced coffee, tasty *pinchos*, a to-be-seen-on terrace, and a good restaurant serving traditional Navarran food and wine.

Café Roch, C Comedias, T948 222 390, www.caferoch.com. Well over a century old, this is a down-to-earth Navarran spot with a real mix of people dropping by throughout the day. Venerable floorboards and a buzz of chatter add to the atmosphere, and little fried morsels vanquish any hunger pangs.

Bars and clubs

Pamplona *p28, map p32*
The streets in the western part of the old town are full of bars, while C Calderería, C Carmen and around have a vibrant Basque social scene.

Caballo Blanco, Rincón del Caballo Blanco s/n, T948 211 504. Closed Jan/Feb. Pamplona's nicest spot, a fantastic location tucked into a quiet corner of the city walls with views over the ramparts. The bar's in a beautiful stone building, but the beer garden is the place to hang out. Peaceful.

La Barbacoa, C Carmen 2, T948 224 315. This corner spot on the infamous 'Mussel Bar' square is an excellent place for a glass of wine or a *copa*, with an attractive interior, all soft greys and beiges and exposed brick. It's the sort of place where everybody knows each other by name and everybody stays a bit longer than they thought they would.

Toki Leza, C Calderería 5, T948 229 584. Long and simple, this wood and brick bar is one of the liveliest around. It's Basque, and has live music every Sun.

Entertainment

Pamplona *p28, map p32*
For bull running, see box, page 31.

Cinema and theatre

Cines Carlos III, C Cortes de Navarra, T948 225 595. Handiest cinema for the old town.

Teatro Gayarre, Av Carlos III 3, T948 220 139, www.teatrogayarre.com. This noble old theatre doesn't see as much action as in its heyday, but still has regular shows.

Football

Pamplona's football team, **Osasuna**, www.osasuna.es, are a hardworking and passionately supported club; it's one of the nicer places to go and see a game in Spain, but wrap up well. They play at **Reyno de Navarra** (formerly El Sadar) stadium south of the city; you can get there by taking bus No 5 from Av Carlos III near Plaza Castilla. Tickets are €30-50 and are on sale office hours at the stadium a couple of days before the match, as well as 2 hrs before kick-off.

Festivals

Pamplona *p28, map p32*
See **San Fermín** box, page 31.

Shopping

Pamplona/Iruña *p28, map p32*
Foto Auma, Plaza del Castillo. During Los Sanfermines, this photography shop has excellent photos of that day's *encierro*.
Librería Abarzuza, C Santo Domingo 29, T948 213 213. Sells decent maps of the city.

What to do

Pamplona *p28, map p32*
Bideak, www.bideak.es. An association of tour operators who will find the company that does what you want done, from architectural tours to canoeing and horse trekking.
Novotur, C Dra Juana García Orcoyen 1, T948 383 755, www.novotur.com. One of several outfits doing guided tours of the city. The tourist office has a full list.

Transport

St-Jean-Pied-de-Port *p27*
There are trains to St-Jean-Pied-de-Port from **Bayonne** (€9.40, 1¼ hrs), and summer buses from **Pamplona**. Otherwise, you can get a taxi from **Roncesvalles**.

Roncesvalles/Orreaga and around
p27
Artieda, T948 300 287, www.autocares artieda.com, run 1 bus from **Pamplona** to Roncesvalles at 1800 Mon-Fri, 1600 on Sat (€6), with an extra bus at 1000 Mon-Sat in Jul and Aug. The trip is just over 1 hr and the bus can accommodate bikes.

Pamplona *p28, map p32*
Bus Pamplona is the hub for buses in the area. It's easily reached from **Madrid** (Conda and PLM, 12 daily, €21-28, 5-6 hrs), **Zaragoza** (Conda, 6-8 daily, €14-15, 2-2½ hrs), **Bilbao** (La Burundesa, 5-6 daily, €13.40, 2 hrs) or **San Sebastián** (La Roncalesa, 12 daily, €7, 1 hr) among other places.

Train 4 fast trains daily from **Madrid** (3 hrs 10 mins, €59) and 5 services to **Zaragoza** (1¾-2¼ hrs, €15-23), some continuing to **Barcelona**.

Directory

Pamplona *p28, map p32*
Internet Kuria Net, C Curia 15, T948 223 077, 1000-2200, €3 per hr.
Medical services Hospital de Navarra, C Irunlarrea s/n, T948 422 100/948 422 212 (emergencies). **Police** Main police station at C Chinchilla, T112 (emergencies).
Post office Paseo de Sarasate s/n.
Telephone *Locutorio* next to the bullring at Paseo Hemingway s/n, 1000-2230.

Western Pyrenees: Camino Aragonés

Although on a world scale the Pyrenees are no giants, their awesome ruggedness is mightily impressive; they are a formidable natural barrier between the peninsula and the rest of Europe. They gain steadily in height from west to east and here, in Aragón, are accessed by a series of north–south valleys; just to the south of these, Jaca is the effective capital of the region, a fun-loving outdoorsy place that acts as a supply centre to holiday favourites, such as Sallent de Gállego, and top ski resorts, such as Candanchú or Astún. Pilgrims on the Camino Aragonés have their first taste of Spain in this area, which also harbours the stunning carved capitals of San Juan de la Peña.

Descending from the mountains, pilgrims on this route usually make Sangüesa their first stop in Navarra. It's a fine little town with more than its fair share of quirky buildings, and within reach are a few other interesting places.

Canfranc Valley → *For listings, see pages 47-50.*

The most popular starting point for pilgrims on this route is the top of the **Puerto de Somport** (Somport pass), where you can stand amid splendid Pyrenean scenery with France on one side of you and Spain on the other. Apart from the dramatic vistas, the Canfranc Valley isn't Spain's most vibrant, except in winter, when two important ski resorts liven things up.

From the hostel at the top of Somport, it's a long downhill day to Jaca, following the path of the Río Aragón.

Candanchú and Astún

The ski resort of Candanchú sits amid pretty mountains 1 km below the border, and just off the Camino. An ugly place, it's nevertheless equipped with excellent facilities, a variety of accommodation, and a full range of runs, as well as a cross-country circuit. Check the website www.candanchu.com for further information. Nearby, at just 4 km distance, Astún is a smaller but equally professional centre, with a range of high-end accommodation.

Canfranc and Canfranc-Estación

The village of Canfranc was destroyed by fire in 1944 and plays second fiddle to its neighbour up the valley, Canfranc-Estación, where most of its residents settled after the blaze. Between the two is a small but impressive moated defensive tower built by Felipe II. It now functions as an information centre for the **Somport tunnel** linking France and Spain, which was finally opened in 2003 despite much opposition from environmentalists. Canfranc-Estación's main feature is, sure enough, its railway station, inaugurated in 1928 in a spirit of Franco-Hispanic cooperation. A massive edifice with a platform of prodigious length, it will look familiar to fans of the film *Dr Zhivago*, in which it featured. Since France closed the rail link in the 1970s, it's been a sad, derelict place but is finally undergoing rehabilitation that should see it transformed into a cultural centre and possibly a hotel by 2014 or so.

Villanúa

The first large settlement in the Canfranc Valley is Villanúa, whose main attraction is a limestone cave, **La Cueva de las Güixas** ① *T974 378 465, www.villanua.net/pdf/cuevas.pdf, the opening schedule is impossibly complex but it's basically summer daily 1000-1330, 1630-2000, rest of the year weekends only; morning visit at 1230 and evening one at 1730, €6.* Formerly a home for prehistoric man, it has some calcified formations and an underground river. The tour takes about one hour. The Camino passes close to the caves before arriving at Villanúa.

Jaca → *For listings, see pages 47-50. Phone code: 974. Population: 13,396. Altitude: 820 m.*

A relaxed spot in northern Aragón, Jaca is far from being a large town but it ranks as a metropolis by the standards of the Pyrenees, for which it functions as a service centre and transport hub. The town has enthusiastically bid for three Winter Olympics, most recently for the 2010 event, but with no luck so far. Most visitors to this part of the Pyrenees are in Jaca at some point, and its also the major stop on the Camino Aragonés pilgrim route, so there's always plenty of bustle about the place.

Jaca's **tourist office** ① *Plaza San Pedro 11, T974 360 098, oficinaturismo@aytojaca.es, Mon-Sat 0900-1330, 1630-1930, mid-Jul-Aug Mon-Sat 0900-2100, Sun 0900-1500, 1700-2000,* is down the side of the cathedral in the heart of town.

The Holy Grail

Relics have always been big in Spain. Fragments of the true cross, feathers from the archangel Gabriel's wings, half-pints of the Virgin's milk, the last breath of San Sebastián in a bottle ... But the daddy of them all is the Holy Grail, the cup used to knock back the bevvy at the Last Supper. Several Aragonese monasteries have held this over the years although, irritatingly for Northern Spain, it's now in Valencia. St Peter thoughtfully took the goblet with him after dinner, and brought it to Rome, where it was in the possession of pope after pope until things got dicey and it was handed to a Spanish soldier, who took it home to Huesca in the third century.

When the Moors got too close for comfort, the local bishop took to the hills, and hid the Grail in the monastery of Siresa. After a century or so it was transferred to safer Jaca, where it sat in the cathedral awhile before monks took it to nearby San Juan de la Peña, where it was guarded by Templar knights. The Aragonese King Martino V thought it would look nice on his sideboard, however, and took it to his palace in Zaragoza in 1399. The monks weren't too happy, but he managed to fob them off with a replica (a replica of the replica is still there; the original replica was destroyed in a fire). When the king died, the Grail showed up in Barcelona. When Alfonso V, King of Valencia, acceded to the Aragonese throne, he took it home with him, and it was eventually placed in the cathedral, where you can see it today.

Spoilsport art historians have revealed that it has been embellished in the ninth, 15th and 16th centuries, but its heart is an agate cup dating from Roman times, so you never can tell.

Background

Jaca was the centre of the Aragonese kingdom in the early Middle Ages under Ramiro I and his son Sancho Ramírez, who established the *fueros*. It was a crucial base in the Reconquista after having been under Moorish control in the eighth century, and a Roman base before that. The city sits on a high plateau above the rivers Aragón and Gállego.

Places in Jaca

"It does exist, love for a building, however difficult it may be to talk about. If I had to talk I would have to explain why it should be this particular church that, when I can no longer travel, I will want to have been the last building I have seen." Cees Nooteboom, Roads to Santiago.

Jaca's treasure is its delightful Romanesque **cathedral** ① *1130-1330, 1600-2000*, which sits moored like a primitive ship, surrounded not by boats but buildings. Neither majestic nor lofty, it was built in the late 11th and early 12th centuries, although the interior owes more to later periods. The main entrance is a long open portico, which approaches a doorway topped by lions and the Crismon symbol. The idea was perhaps that people had a few paces to meditate on their sins before entering the house of God.

The south door has a wooden porch and fine, carved capitals depicting Abraham and Isaac, and Balaam with the angel. These were beautifully carved by the 'Master of Jaca'. The interior is slightly less charming; the most ornate of the chapels is that of San Miguel, which contains a fanciful 16th-century *retablo* and a carved portal. Next to this is a 12th-century figurine of a wide-hipped virgin and child, dedicated to Zaragoza's Virgin of the Pillar. The main altar is recessed, with an elaborately painted vaulted ceiling. The cathedral is usually dark; a coinbox just inside the main door takes half-euro pieces, each of which provides light for five minutes.

Worthy of a quick peek is the **Iglesia del Carmen**, with its interesting façade and scaly columns and a Virgin seemingly flanked by a pair of mandarins.

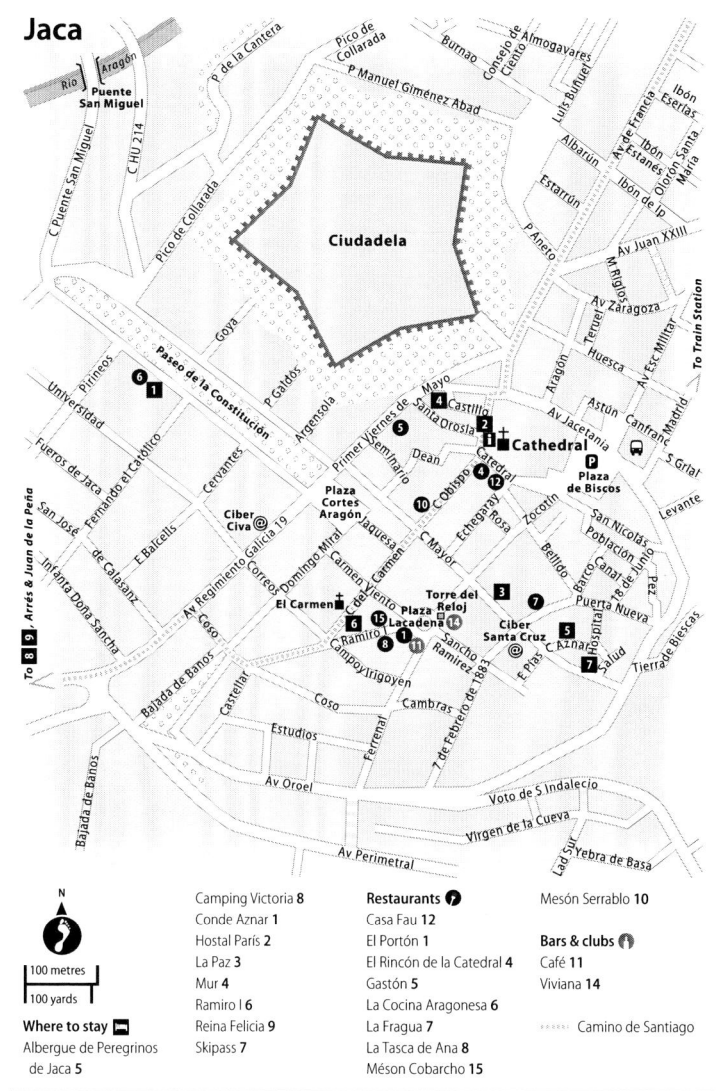

Jaca

Where to stay
Albergue de Peregrinos de Jaca 5
Camping Victoria 8
Conde Aznar 1
Hostal París 2
La Paz 3
Mur 4
Ramiro I 6
Reina Felicia 9
Skipass 7

Restaurants
Casa Fau 12
El Portón 1
El Rincón de la Catedral 4
Gastón 5
La Cocina Aragonesa 6
La Fragua 7
La Tasca de Ana 8
Méson Cobarcho 15
Mesón Serrablo 10

Bars & clubs
Café 11
Viviana 14

···· Camino de Santiago

In the cathedral cloister is the **Diocesan Museum** ⓘ *Sep-Jun Tue-Fri 1000-1330, 1600-1900, Sat 1000-1330, 1600-2000, Sun 1000-1330, Jul-Aug Tue-Sun 1000-1330, 1600-2000, €6 (€3 pilgrims)*, which houses a superb collection of Romanesque and Gothic frescoes, taken from other churches in the area and cleverly reconstructed. The best is an awesome 11th-century set from Bagües, depicting an abbreviated history of the old and new Testaments, comic-strip style. Another highlight is the apse paintings from Riesto, featuring some marvellously self-satisfied 12th-century apostles. Of the paintings, a prim Saint Michael is standing, as is his habit, on a chicken-footed demon who is having a very bad time of it; a wood-carved Renaissance assembly of figures around the body of Christ is also impressive.

Jaca's **citadel** ⓘ *www.ciudadeladejaca.es, guided visits only Wed-Mon 1100-1400, 1600-1900 (summer 1700-2000); wait at the red line for a guide to arrive, €10*, is still in use by the military. A low but impressively large star-shaped structure, it was constructed during Felipe II's reign. The garrison here rose against the monarchy in 1930, before the rest of the Republican movement was ready for action: two young officers who decided to march on Zaragoza were arrested and executed. Their deaths were not in vain, though, as the indignation caused boosted feeling against the monarchy – the Republic was proclaimed shortly afterwards, and the king went into exile. The tour takes about an hour (including a museum of lead soldiers); it's only €6 to enter if you bypass this and the temporary exhibitions.

Built over the foundations of the old Royal Palace is the **Torre del Reloj**, an attractive Gothic affair that is now HQ to a Pyrenean taskforce. It sits in Plaza Lacadena, an attractive spot at night, with several bars and a floodlit fountain.

Walking down **Paseo de la Constitución**, the town comes to an abrupt end in a slope down to the **Río Aragón**. A path leads to the river, a bathing spot, which is traversed by a medieval bridge.

Jaca to Sangüesa → *For listings, see pages 47-50.*

Stock up on cash in Jaca, as there are no ATMs until Sangüesa, three days' walk hence. It's 25 km of gentle downhill gradients from Jaca until a moderate climb into the village of **Arrés**. But you might find yourself overnighting elsewhere, as there's a highly recommended detour that takes you up a difficult half-day climb to the fabulous monastery of San Juan de la Peña, one of the highlights of the Camino. From here you can descend the road for an hour and bit to **Santa Cruz de la Serós**, where there is cheap accommodation, and rejoin the Camino (5 km further on) the next day.

Monasterio de San Juan de la Peña

ⓘ *mid-Oct to Feb 1000-1530, Mar to May and Sep to mid-Oct 1000-1400, 1530-1900, Jun to mid-Jul 1000-1400, 1500-2000, mid-Jul to Aug 1000-2000, €7 visitor, €4 pilgrim old monastery only, €8.50/4.50 including one of the exhibitions in the new monastery, €11/6 including both. All tickets include entry to the monastery at Santa Cruz de la Serós, 6 km further north.*

This famous monastery allegedly came into being when a noble named Voto was chasing a deer on horseback. The despairing creature took the Roman option and leaped to its death over a cliff. Voto's horse was unable to stop itself from following. Still in the saddle, Voto launched a quick prayer to John the Baptist and, to his amazement, landed safely outside a small cave. Investigating, he found the body of a hermit and a small shrine to the saint. He was so moved by his salvation that he decided to continue the hermitage and settled here with his brother, who was equally impressed by the tale. The monastery became an important centre on the Pilgrim Route to Santiago in the Middle Ages and today constitutes two separate buildings.

The new monastery is an impressive brick baroque structure which houses a hotel as well as two modern displays, one on the kingdom of Aragón, another on the history and architecture of the old monastery.

It's the older monastery that draws visitors, spectacularly wedged into the cliff 1 km down the hill. Built around bedrock, the lower part consists of a spooky 11th-century church and dormitory, with fragmentary wall paintings and the tombs of several early abbots. Upstairs is a pantheon, where nobles could (with a hefty donation) be buried; it's decorated with the characteristic *ajedrezado jaqués* chessboard pattern that originated in these parts.

The high church features three apses, one of which holds a replica of the Holy Grail, see box, page 42, and a martial funerary chapel that holds the remains of the Aragonese kings Pedro I and Ramiro I. It's the open remains of the cloister that inspire most awe; the columns are decorated with superbly carved Romanesque capitals under the conglomerate cliff. Scenes from the life of Christ and the book of Genesis are superbly portrayed; Cain takes on Abel with a particularly fearsome sledgehammer.

Arrés to Sangüesa

Roughly paralleling the N240 main road, but on the south side of the Río Aragón, this two-day stretch takes you out of the fertile Pyrenees zone and into the drier hills and valleys of Zaragoza province. It's an up-and-down first day to **Ruesta**, set beside the sky-blue **Embalse de Yesa** reservoir. Ruesta is a curious place, for it was abandoned in 1960 when the dam was built, for fear of flooding, and partly repopulated as part of a reconstruction project in more recent times. It's a pretty hilltop village dominated by a castle dating mostly from the 11th century.

The next day takes you past the picturesque ruined chapel Ermita de Santiago before a steady climb up to **El Alto** at 850 m, where you are rewarded with great views over the reservoir and surrounding countryside. Once you've made this point, it's a fairly easy descent and traverse of flattish countryside into Navarra and the town of **Sangüesa**. Just after crossing the Navarran border, a side trip leads to the worthwhile **Monasterio de San Salvador de Leyre** (see below), which can also be visited from Sangüesa.

Sangüesa/Zangoza and around → *For listings, see pages 47-50.*

Originally founded by Romans on a nearby hill, Sangüesa served its apprenticeship as a bastion against the Moors before quieter times saw it moved down to the banks of the cloudy green Río Aragón. Most notable among several impressive structures is the Iglesia de Santa María by the bridge. Sweaty pilgrims trudging into town will be happy to know that in Sangüesa the stench from the nearby paper mill makes all bodily odours fade into insignificance. After an hour or so, it's actually not too bad – plenty of locals swear they miss it when they're out of town.

The **tourist office** ⓘ *opposite the church of Santa María, T948 871 411, Apr-Oct Mon-Sat 1000-1400, 1600-1900, Sun 1000-1400, Nov-Mar Tue-Sun 1000-1400*, is helpful.

Iglesia de Santa María
ⓘ *T620 110 581, tours of this and other churches, summer Mon-Sat 1000-1400, 1600-1800, winter Mon-Sat 1000-1400, €1.95 church only, €4 whole town.*

The church's elaborately carved portal takes Romanesque sculpture to heights of delicacy and fluidity seldom seen elsewhere, although some of the themes covered stray a fair way from lofty religion. The inside is less interesting and annoyingly only accessible by guided tour (the office is at the back of the building). This goes for most of the other buildings in town. The church can be visited independently just before Mass, which is at 1900 in winter and 2000 in summer.

Palacio de Vallesantoro
Sangüesa's town hall is based in the outrageous Palacio de Vallesantoro. The doorway is flanked by two bizarre corkscrew (Solomonic) columns, but it's the macabre overhanging eaves that draw even more attention. They make the building look like a Chinese pagoda, designed after a night of bad dreams. Leering dogs, lions and asses alternate with tortured human figures along the black overhang.

Iglesia de Santiago
ⓘ *The church is only opened at Mass times or on the town's guided tour.*
A couple of streets back is the church of Santiago, a late Romanesque building with an impressive fortified tower and several good Gothic sculptures, including one of Saint James himself. He also appears in colour on the building's façade, flanked by two pilgrims who look as though they might have made the journey from the Australian outback.

Off the main street, an elegant arched arcade points the way to the Palacio Príncipe de Viana, formerly a residence of kings of Navarra, while on Calle Alfonso el Batallador, not far from the Ayuntamiento, is a working iron forge that uses fairly traditional methods and specializes in forging individualized tokens for pilgrims. Across the river is a statue of St Christopher, patron saint of travellers, which explains the cut-out of a car that's been strangely attached to it.

Monasterio de San Salvador de Leyre
ⓘ *T948 884 150, Mon-Fri 1015-1400, 1530-1900, Sat 1015-1400, 1600-1900, €2.10; the monks chant offices at 0730, 0900, 1900 and 2110 in the church.*
Off the N240 northeast of Sangüesa, a road winds 4 km through fragrant hills to the Monasterio de San Salvador de Leyre. A monastery was first founded here as early as the eighth century AD, but the beautiful, rugged spot – the name means 'eagerness to overcome' in Euskara – had been a favourite haunt of hermits before that. Nothing but foundations remain from that period – the older parts of today's structure date from the 11th and 12th centuries, when the Navarran monarchs took a liking to the spot and made it the seat of their kingdom. The centre flourished with religious and secular power and became extremely wealthy before an inevitable decline began. The abbey was abandoned in the 19th century after loss of monastic privileges and was not re-used until 1954, when it was colonized by Benedictines from the Monasterio de Santo Domingo de Silos.

The church itself is of mixed styles but preserves much simplicity and tranquillity inside, above all when it's filled with the Gregorian chanting of the monks during offices. The structure is remarkably off-kilter – lovers of symmetry and proportion will be appallingly ill-at-ease. The portal is a fascinating 12th-century work, filled with Romanesque scenes. While the main groups are of the Last Judgement, Christ and the Evangelists, the sculptors let their fancy run a bit freer elsewhere – you can spot several interesting demons and nightmarish animals, Jonah getting swallowed, and some lifelike prowling lions. Inside, the centrepiece is the Virgin of Leyre, while the adult Christ is relegated to his customary Spanish place in the wings. A large chest on one wall contains the bones of no fewer than 10 Navarran kings, seven queens and two princes – these were exhumed and boxed in 1915 – their feelings on the matter unrecorded. A small side chapel has a *retablo* in a pleasingly rustic style.

The crypt, accessed from the ticket office, is a weird space, whose stone altar and ram-horned columns suggest darker ritual purposes. The columns all vary and are tiny – it's strange to have the capitals at waist height. Next to the crypt is a tunnel leading to an image of San Virila – a former abbot. This dozy chap wandered up to a nearby stream and was so enchanted by the song of a bird that he didn't make it back for vespers for another three centuries. If you fancy some time out too, follow his lead and head up to the spring, which is signposted five minutes' walk above the complex. If you like the spot, you might consider staying in the attached *hospedería* (see Where to stay, below).

Sangüesa to Puente la Reina → *For listings, see pages 47-50.*

Pilgrims usually take two days from Sangüesa to Puente la Reina, where the Camino Aragonés merges with the Camino Francés.

The first day features some fairly steep climbing on the main route, but a worthwhile deviation eliminates some of the steeper gradients and also allows you to take in one of the area's scenic highlights, the **Foz (Hoz) de Lumbier**. This is a fashionably petite designer gorge, with gurgling stream, overhanging rock walls and a large vulture population circling lazily above, in the vain hope that a walker might drop dead from the significant summer heat.

After the gorge, from the town of Lumbier, head for Nardués and Aldunate before rejoining the main Camino. If you want to make Puente la Reina in two days, it's worth pushing on to **Monreal** for the night.

The second day is a long one, with plenty of up-and-down to take a toll on your legs. The rolling hills are picturesque but tiring, but a succession of Navarran villages offer chances for recuperation. The Camino meets the Camino Francés at the village of Obanos, near the usual overnighting stop of Puente la Reina. Before you get here, you pass one of the Camino's, and Spain's, most unusual constructions, the octagonal Romanesque chapel of **Eunate**. It's surrounded by a stone 'fence' of arches.

Western Pyrenees: Camino Aragonés listings

For hotel and restaurant price codes and other relevant information, see pages 12-19.

Where to stay

Canfranc Valley *p41*
€ Albergue Aysa, T974 373 023, www.albergueaysa.com. With a spectacular mountain setting at the top of the Somport pass on the French border, this is the most popular overnighting spot before starting the long walk to Santiago. It's a typical Spanish mountain hostel, with filling meals available and a convivial spirit. Essential to book ahead in summer.

Candanchú and Astún *p41*
€€ Hotel Candanchú, T974 373 025, www.hotelcandanchu.com. Closed Oct-Nov and May-Jun. One of the more characterful of the hotels, an old-style Spanish winter hotel with rustic decor, views and a terrace, with a good restaurant. The tariff rises sharply (**€€€**) over a few of the crucial ski

weekends, but this is compensated for by attractive full-board rates. In summer it's much cheaper. The restaurant is good.

Canfranc and Canfranc-Estación *p41*
There are several *albergues* and hotels.
€€€ Hotel Santa Cristina, Ctra Candanchú Km 669, T974 373 300, www.santacristina.es. You can't miss this massive hotel, a couple of kilometres beyond Canfranc-Estación. The rooms are spacious and warm and decorated with more subtlety than the exterior would suggest. All facilities for skiers are present, and there's a lively bar and restaurant. The views are great when it's clear.
€ Pepito Grillo, T974 373 123, www.pepitogrillo.com. This simple mountain hostel has friendly management, dorm beds, and simple doubles and rooms for groups. It's a lively hub for hillwalkers and pilgrims. Closed 2nd half Oct and Nov.

Jaca *p41, map p43*
It's worth booking accommodation ahead here in both high summer and high winter.
€€€ Hotel Reina Felicia, Paseo Camino de Santiago 16, T974 365 333, www.pronihoteles.com. This hotel in a new suburb a couple of kilometres from the centre stands out for its avant-garde modern design. Rooms are comfortable, with dark chocolate colours and swish bathrooms. Facilities include a spa and pool complex, but it's a little disappointing that they cost extra. There's a good breakfast buffet.
€€ Hotel Conde Aznar, Paseo de la Constitución 3, T974 361 050, www.condeaznar.com. A charming hotel whose rooms show their age but offer significant value. The doubles vary substantially in size; some are quite small. For a little more money, you can procure one with a hydromassage unit, or a 'special', which is part way to being a suite. At peak times, they may only take bookings on a half-board basis; no hardship, as the restaurant is the best in town. Excellent service. Recommended.
€€ Hotel La Paz, C Mayor 41, T974 360 700, www.alojamientosaran.com. A very decent place run by decent folk. The rooms are standard modern Spanish, with TV, tiled floors and bathrooms. Some have balconies. Various apartments are also available.
€€ Hotel Mur, C Santa Orosia 1, T974 360 100, www.hotelmur.com. This is a historic Jaca hotel with a good feeling about it. Bedrooms are airy and have full facilities; the best overlook the citadel, so you can watch the top-secret manoeuvres of the Spanish army.
€€ Ramiro I, C del Carmen 23, T974 361 367, www.hotelramirojaca.es. Closed Nov. Middle-of-the-road hotel with courteous management and fairly simple but spacious enough rooms. The restaurant is uninspiring but decent value.
€ Albergue de Peregrinos de Jaca, C Conde Aznar 7, T974 360 848. Spacious and spotless municipal pilgrim hostel, efficiently and cordially run. Closed Nov-Feb.
€ Hostal París, Plaza San Pedro 5, T974 361 020, www.hostalparisjaca.com. A good option near the cathedral with clean doubles with excellent modern shared bathrooms. The doors are locked at night until about 0700, so be sure to make some arrangement if you've got an early start.
€ Skipass Hostal, C Mayor 57, T974 363 954, www.skipasshostal.com. Good-value place on the main street with unadorned but comfortable rooms at a low price. Rates include Wi-Fi and breakfast.

Camping
Camping Victoria, Ctra Jaca–Pamplona, T974 357 008, www.campingvictoria.es. A year-round site with bungalows that's got less campervan traffic than many, and only 15 mins' walk from town.

Jaca to Sangüesa *p44*
€ Hospital de Peregrinos, El Portillo s/n, Arrés, T974 348 643. Small, sociable pilgrim shelter where you're guaranteed to make friends and feel something of the 'spirit of the Camino'.

San Juan de la Peña *p44*
€€ Hospedería San Juan de la Peña, T974 374 422, www.touractive.com. This hotel occupies the southern wing of the upper monastery and adds plenty of modern comforts to the historic building. The rooms are attractive and spacious, with polished wooden floors; some are appealing duplexes that cost some €35 more. Wi-Fi, gym, and other business-standard facilities are present, but the isolated location and short wander down the path to the ancient cloister under the overhang are the real reasons to stay here. The restaurant isn't up to much.

Arrés to Sangüesa *p45*
€ Albergue de Ruesta, Ruesta s/n, T948 398 082. Set in 2 reformed houses in this attractive village, this guarantees a warm welcome. Dinner and breakfast available.

Sangüesa *p45*
€€ Hostal JP, Paseo Raimundo Lumbier 3, T948 871 693, www.hostalruraljp.es. A clean, fresh and good option (if slightly hospital-like) just across the river from the Iglesia de Santa María. The rooms are modern and pleasant enough, and have a good bathroom and cable TV. There are also apartments (and, in summer, pilgrim dorm beds) available.
€ Albergue de Peregrinos, C Enrique de Labrit, T659 068 769. Small but decently equipped place that tends to fill fast. Free washing and drying facilities and one of the cheaper *albergues* on the Camino at €5 a bed.

Camping
Camping Cantolagua, Paseo Cantolagua s/n, T948 430 352, www.campingcantolagua.com. A good site by the riverside, with a swimming pool and tennis courts. There are also bungalows, caravans and rooms available at good cheapish rates.

Monasterio de San Salvador de Leyre *p46*
€€ Hospedería de Leyre, Monasterio de Leyre, T948 884 100, www.hotelmonasterioleyre.com. With great views over the plains and the reservoir below, and some very nice walks in the scented hills, this monastery hotel offers much more than monastic comfort, as well as some very good meals. The rooms are simple but welcoming; some are larger than others.

Sangüesa to Puente la Reina *p47*
€ Albergue de Peregrinos, C de la Corte s/n, Monreal, T948 362 057. Small and simple pilgrim hostel offering decent comfort. Fills fast but they put mattresses on the floor if there's no room.

Restaurants

Jaca *p41, map p43*
€€€ El Portón, Pl Marqués de la Cadena 1, T974 355 854. This elegant rustic restaurant sits in Jaca's most attractive square. Quality ingredients are prepared and served with some style, and the waiting staff are polite and helpful. They're at their best here with traditional Aragonese plates given modern flair.
€€€ La Cocina Aragonesa, Paseo de la Constitución 3, T974 361 050, www.condeaznar.com. Jaca's best, a friendly spot serving up classy Aragonese cuisine with a distinctly French touch. Part of the **Hotel Conde Aznar**. There's a *menú del día*, but it's not really representative of the quality on offer. There's a lovely covered and heated terrace; a contrast to the, cosier interior.
€€€ Mesón Cobarcho, C Ramiro I 2, T974 363 643. There are several spots in town that specialize in grilled and roast meats, but this spacious and inviting restaurant might just be the best. Truly excellent ox *entrecots* come sizzling, juicy, tasty, and sizeable, and salads or grilled vegetable platters balance out the meal. Recommended.

€€ **Gastón**, Av Primer Viernes de Mayo 14, T974 361 719. This upstairs establishment offers a €18 set menu that features good home-style cooking. On the main menu, the *lenguado* (sole) in cava is excellent.

€€ **La Fragua**, C Gil Berges 4, T974 360 618. A good hearty *asador*, popular with locals at weekends for its excellent *chuletón de buey* (ox steaks) and other hearty meat dishes. All portions are enormous.

€€ **Mesón Serrablo**, C Obispo 3, T974 362 418. An attractive and delicious restaurant in an antique-style stone building. 2 levels, and a good weekend *menú* for €18. The value-for-money is high here.

€ **Casa Fau**, Plaza de la Catedral 3, T974 361 594. This is a great place by the cathedral, with a homely wooden atmosphere perfect after a day on the slopes; or a sunny terrace for warmer weather. The bar proudly displays an array of tasty *pinchos*, including a tasty terrine from across the border, and the service comes with a smile. Recommended.

€ **El Rincón de la Catedral**, Plaza de la Catedral 4, T974 355 920. The place to sit and admire the soft Romanesque lines of the cathedral. Large range of French-style meals, salads, and gourmet *montaditos* costing around €2.

€ **La Tasca de Ana**, C Ramiro I 3, T974 364 726. An indispensable stop on the Jaca food trail with a very large variety of quality hot and cold tapas, great salads, good wine and more. The only problem is that it's so good, it can be tough to get in the door.

Sangüesa *p45*

€€ **Mediavilla**, C Alfonso el Batallador 15, T948 870 212. A hospitable *asador* with filling *menús* for €19 and €24. There's a range of very tasty roast meat, but plenty of lighter dishes to accompany it.

€ **Bar Ciudad de Sangüesa**, C Santiago 4, T948 871 021. There are several bars on this street – this bar does good cheap meals and is popular with locals. The quality is very high for the price, and the style is traditional, with hearty country food.

€ **El Pilar**, C Mayor 87, Sangüesa, T948 870 027. The posh place in town to come for a drink or a coffee, this also offers a selection of gourmet *pinchos*, such as a little pastry basket with local wild mushrooms. There's a terrace in summer.

Bars and clubs

Jaca *p41, map p43*

Café, Plaza de Lacadena s/n. Unremarkable-looking spot, this is actually one of Jaca's best bars, with a great collection of vinyl and a good vibe to boot.

Viviana, Plaza de Lacadena s/n. With a mixed selection of Asian prints on the walls, a pool table, and drum 'n bass sounds, this is one of Jaca's most frequented bars. Stick to beer here though: the mixed drinks aren't great.

Transport

Jaca *p41, map p43*
Bus
Jaca's bus station is conveniently located on Plaza Biscos in the centre of town. 5-10 daily buses run between Jaca and **Huesca** (1 hr, €7). These connect in Huesca with buses to **Zaragoza** (€8.30). There are 2 buses daily to Pamplona (1 hr 40 mins, €8.60).

There are 5 daily buses from Jaca up the **Canfranc Valley**. They go as far as the **Puerto de Somport** (35 mins).

Train
The trains are neither as handy nor as useful as the buses and the station in Jaca is to the east of town. A shuttle bus links to it from outside the bus station. 3 daily trains head down to **Huesca** and on to **Zaragoza**. There are also trains to **Canfranc**.

Sangüesa *p45*
Bus
La Veloz Sangüesina, T948 870 209, runs buses to and from **Pamplona**, 3-5 daily, 1 on Sun (30 mins, €3.80).

Western Navarra

The two main branches of the Camino de Santiago, the Camino Francés (which has come through Roncesvalles and Pamplona) and the Camino Aragonés (which has tracked through Aragón and Sangüesa) meet near Puente La Reina and continue westwards together. This part of the province is one of Navarra's nicest; towns such as Estella and Viana are joys for the pilgrim or casual traveller to discover. Off the main route, too, are some perfect little villages, while, to top things off, some of Navarra's best wine is made in the area.

Puente La Reina/Gares and around → *For listings, see pages 53-55.*

"And from here all roads to Santiago become only one." While this, inscribed on the monument at the entrance to the village, is not completely true, the two principal pilgrim routes converge in the village of Obanos (famous for its biennial staging of a mystery play based on a legend of the Camino) before reaching the famous medieval bridge that Puente la Reina is named for and grew around. It's a long and beautiful Romanesque span that emerges from an arched entrance and speaks of many kilometres to come under a beating sun.

The town is small, and a good place to stop for a night if you're inclined. Arriving from the east, on the outskirts, you'll see the strange monument to pilgrims, a wild-eyed and gaunt bronze figure who might provoke more anxiety than comfort in passing *peregrinos*. One of the main pilgrim hostels isn't much further, and stands next to the 12th-century **Iglesia del Crucifijo**.

In the heart of town is another **church** ⓘ *Mon-Sat 1000-1330, 1700-2000, Sun 0845-1400*, dedicated to Santiago himself. The so-called Matamoros ('Moor killer') might not be too impressed to notice that his doorway looks remarkably Muslim in style with its horseshoe notched recessed portal. Opposite is the fine façade of the **Convento de la Trinidad**. The peaceful centre of the town, the **Plaza Julián Mena**, houses the Ayuntamiento and **tourist office** ⓘ *Tue-Sat 1000-1400, 1530-1830 (1700-2000 summer), Sun 1100-1400*.

Puente la Reina to Estella

This is one of the Camino's most interesting sections. A few kilometres after leaving Puente la Reina, there's a short but lung-stretching climb. Then the route passes through picturesque wine-making villages set among rolling farmland.

Estella/Lizarra and around → *For listings, see pages 53-55.*

The major town of western Navarra, Estella is a very likeable place to stay a while. The town likes to dust off the moniker 'the Toledo of the North'; this is a little over-the-top, but its crop of historic buildings is certainly interesting.

Estella's history as a town goes back to 1052 when King Sancho Ramírez, taking ruler and pencil to the burgeoning pilgrim trail, established it as a new stop on the official route.

On a hill, close to the Puente de la Cárcel, on the western bank, the older part of town, is the towering grey bulk of the **Iglesia de San Pedro de la Rúa** ⓘ *summer daily 1000-1330, 1830-2030, winter Mon-Fri 1800-1945, Sat 1100-1330, 1830-2045, Sun 1100-1330, €3.40, €2.90 pilgrims*, with its crusty façade and indented Romanesque portal. The highlight inside is the semi-cloister. It was here that the Castilian kings used to swear to uphold the Navarran *fueros* after the province was annexed; it was a promise honoured in varying degrees by different monarchs.

Opposite is the **Palacio de los Reyes** ⓘ *Tue-Sat 1100-1300, 1700-1900, Sun 1100-1330, free*, another Romanesque edifice, which now houses a museum devoted to the early 20th-century painter Gustavo de Maeztu, who was influenced by the art nouveau movement and lived his later years in Estella.

Across the river, the **Iglesia de San Miguel** is also set above the town on a hillock. Its most endearing feature is the Romanesque portal, richly carved with a scene of Christ in Majesty surrounded by his supporting cast. It's an impressive work. Like San Pedro, the church is only open by guided tour or about an hour before 2000 Mass (1900 in winter).

The newer part of town centres around the large **Plaza de los Fueros**, overseen by the **Iglesia de San Juan**, a mishmash of every conceivable style. Nearby is the quiet **Plaza de Santiago**, in whose centre four horrible creatures spill water from their mouths into a fountain.

Estella's **tourist office** ⓘ *T948 556 301, Easter-Oct Mon-Sat 1000-1400, 1600-1900, Sun 1000-1400, Nov-Easter Mon-Fri 1000-1700, Sat and Sun 1000-1400*, is next to the Palacio de los Reyes; guided tours of the town depart from here.

Around Estella

There are numerous **wineries** in the Estella area which are happy to show visitors around. The tourist office provides a list of bodegas (phone beforehand to arrange a visit). One of the quality labels is **Palacio de la Vega** ⓘ *T948 527 009*, in the small town of Dicastillo, south of Estella. The bodega, whose home is a striking 19th-century palace, is a modern producer that has been at the forefront of the successful establishment of French varietals like Cabernet Sauvignon and Merlot in Navarra. A more traditional producer of quality wines is **Bodegas Sarría** ⓘ *based by Puente La Reina, T948 202 200, www.bodegadesarria.com*.

Estella to Viana → *For listings, see pages 53-55.*

Though most pilgrims do a long day from Estella to Torres del Río, and then a shorter second day to Logroño via Viana, it's worth taking an extra day over it to give yourself an overnight stop in Viana, perhaps spending the first night at the *albergue* at Los Arcos.

A couple of kilometres after leaving Estella, you reach the **Monasterio de Irache** ⓘ *Tue 0900-1330, Wed-Sun 0900-1330, 1700-1900 (1630-1800 winter)*, the oldest of the original Navarran pilgrim refuges. The light and airy church features an inscrutable Virgin and a bony bit of San Veremundo in a reliquary by the altar.

The monastery is famous for its palatable red table wine, and pilgrims might be tempted to linger on the way here a little: there's a tap at the back of the bodega that spouts red wine for the benefit of travellers on the road, a sight to gladden the heart!

After leaving the monastery, there's a long but not too steep climb to the village of **Villamayor de Monjardín**, surrounded by vineyards. Once you descend from here, it's flat all the way to **Los Arcos**, and on to **Torres del Río**. The last of Navarra's hills, topped by a chapel, awaits you on the other side before you begin a slow descent to **Viana** and on to the Riojan capital of Logroño.

Viana

One of Navarra's loveliest towns, Viana is the last stop before the Camino descends into the oven of La Rioja. Fortified to defend the kingdom's borders against Castilla, it still preserves sections of its walls, rising above the surrounding plains. The **Iglesia de Santa María** has a monumental façade and a high Gothic interior, whose sober interior is enlivened by a great number of ornate baroque *retablos*.

In front of the church is the gravemarker of an unexpected man; Cesare Borgia, a 15th-century Italian noble who could rightly be described as Machiavellian – *The Prince* was largely based on his machinations. Son of a pope, after becoming a cardinal he most probably had his elder brother murdered as part of his scheme, one of a number of opportunistic assassinations he masterminded while conquering significant swathes of Italian territory. It all went pear-shaped for Borgia, though; after having been imprisoned in Spain, Borgia was placed under the protection of the King of Navarra, and he ended up as a minor noble in Viana. He was then elected constable of the town, but was killed in a siege by Castilian forces in 1507, aged, would you believe, only 30.

The atmospheric ruined Gothic church of **San Pedro** sheltered French troops during the Peninsular War before it collapsed in 1844. Viana has a **tourist office** ⓘ *summer Mon-Sat 0900-1400, 1700-1900, Sun 1000-1400, winter Mon-Sat 0900-1400.*

Western Navarra listings

For hotel and restaurant price codes and other relevant information, see pages 12-19.

Where to stay

Puente La Reina/Gares and around
p51
Puente has a couple of excellent lodging choices. It's close to Pamplona, so prices soar during Los Sanfermines.
€€€ El Peregrino, C Irunbidea s/n, T948 340 075, www.hotelelperegrino.com. An impressively individual and classy hotel and restaurant on the approach to town. Packed with arty objects and quirky architectural kinks, but with a comfortable stone-and-wood feeling. Lovely pool and surrounding terrace. The restaurant is of a very high standard.
€€ Bidean, C Mayor 20, T948 341 156, www.bidean.com. A charming hotel in the centre of town with welcoming staff and an old-fashioned homely feel.
€ Albergue de los Padres Reparadores, C Crucifijo 1, T948 340 050. One of a few pilgrim hostels, this is by the church on your way in to town and is recommendable for its friendly vibe and excellent grassy patio garden to relax in.

Estella *p51*
€€€ Hotel Tximista, C Zaldu 15, T948 555 870, www.hoteltximista.com. A converted flour mill holds this, Estella's most upmarket option. The building's unusual form lends itself to offbeat rooms, which are decorated in crisp modern fashion. The peaceful waterside location adds to the charm.
€€ Hotel Yerri, Av Yerri 35, T948 546 034, www.hotelyerri.es. This hotel is a reliable Estella option, situated near the bullring. The rooms are modern and have cable TV, good bathroom and telephone, but are fairly blandly decorated. Parking available.
€ Cristina, C Baja Navarra 1, T948 550 772. A well-positioned *hostal* in Estella's liveliest part. Nearly all the rooms have a balcony to watch the world go by; those rooms overlooking the Plaza de los Fueros can get a bit noisy. All rooms are en suite.
€ Hospital de Peregrinos, C La Rúa 50, T948 550 200. Recommended pilgrim stop with a great kitchen, convivial atmosphere and friendly proprietor.

€ Pensión San Andrés, Plaza Santiago 58, T948 554 158. This is a very good, cheap option on a quiet square in the heart of town. The management is very friendly, and the rooms homely and comfortable. They come with or without bathroom. Location is excellent.

Estella to Viana *p52*
€ Albergue Casa de la Abuela, Plaza Fruta 8, Los Arcos, T948 640 250. This warmly welcoming hostel specializes in making pilgrims feel right at home. Breakfast and private rooms available.

Viana *p53*
€€ Palacio de Pujadas, C Navarro Villoslada 30, T948 646 464, www.palaciodepujadas.com. This lovely hotel is set in an historic old-town *palacio*. The interior is a lesson in combining modern comfort while staying true to the original building; the rooms are a delight with stately tasteful furniture. There's free internet access for guests.
€ Albergue Parroquial de Viana, Plaza de los Fueros s/n, T948 645 037. Next to the Santa María church, this simple hostel will have you sleeping on mattresses on the floor but is worth it for the atmosphere, sociable communal meals and friendly hosts.
€ Casa Armendáriz, C Navarro Villoslada 19, T948 645 078. This, a good choice for lodging, has clean and proper rooms with or without bathroom – the latter are pretty basic – as well as cheerful dining in an old wine cellar.

Restaurants

Puente La Reina/Gares and around *p51*
€€€ El Peregrino (see Where to stay, above). The hotel's high-class restaurant offers excellent fare in small portions at high prices.
€ Restaurante Joaquin, C Mayor 48, T948 340 931. This is a decent lunchtime option with a *menú del día* for €10. The food is typically Navarran, with fine trout and other hearty dishes.

Estella *p51*
Estella's signature dish is *gorrín*, another name for roast suckling pig, a heavy but juicy meal seeded with a potent dose of garlic.
€€€ La Cepa, Plaza de los Fueros 15, T948 550 032, www.restaurantecepa.com. One of Estella's best, this restaurant makes up for its dull decor with imaginatively prepared Navarran dishes. They prepare a fine *gorrín* but also work with more subtle ingredients like local truffles.
€€ Astarriaga, Plaza de los Fueros 12, T948 550 802, www.asadorastarriaga.com. An *asador* offering a decent *menú del día*, and doing the usual good steaks, but also some traditional Navarran offerings. Good *pinchos* and a terrace on the square. It's also just about the most popular spot for afternoon coffee.
€€ Katxetas, Estudio de Gramática 1, T948 550 010, www.restaurantekatxetas.es. This cheerful spot is a Basque cider house tucked into what was once the city walls and serving challengingly large portions. The traditional *menú* is delicious but extremely filling.

Festivals

Estella *p51*
Mid-Jul Medieval week, with troupes of *jongleurs* and crumhorn-players roaming the streets, which are enlivened by flaming torches, bales of straw and chickens and rabbits in cages.
Aug Estella's fiesta starts on the first Fri of the month, with *encierros* (bull-runnings), *corridas* and more.

Viana *p53*
Late Jul Viana goes wild for the joint fiesta of **Mary Magdalene** and **St James**; there are 2 *encierros* daily.

⊖ Transport

Puente La Reina/Gares and around *p51*
Bus
La Estellesa (T948 222 223) runs frequent buses from **Pamplona** to Puente la Reina (20 mins); the buses continue to **Logroño**.

Estella *p51*
Bus
La Estellesa (T948 222 223) runs 10 buses a day to and from **Pamplona** (1 hr, €4). A similar number go to **Logroño**.

Viana *p53*
Bus
La Vianesa (T948 446 227) run to both **Pamplona** and **Logroño** a few times daily.

Route through La Rioja

The province of La Rioja is known above all for its red wines. The Río Ebro runs down a wide, shallow valley of enormous fertility, which also produces important cereal, fruit and vegetable crops. The region was well known by the Romans, who produced and exported much of the good stuff from here; they referred to the zone as Rioiia; the name comes from the Río Oja, a tributary of the Ebro.

La Rioja is Spain's smallest mainland region, given semi-autonomous status for the same political reasons as Cantabria: it was felt that if it was just one more province of Castilla, the people would be more easily swayed by whisperings from separatist movements in Euskadi and Navarra, of which the territory was historically a part. In truth, though, it feels very conservative and Spanish, particularly when the summer sends temperatures soaring over 40°C.

For those heading to Santiago, the stretch from Logroño is often completed under baking sun, but there are a couple of characterful towns in which to stop and find some shade. Nájera and Santo Domingo de la Calzada are appealing places, and the imposing monasteries of San Millán merit a detour. The area prides itself on being the birthplace of the Spanish language; the earliest known texts in that idiom derive from here.

The cuisine is wholly unsuited to the heat, being designed more for the chilly winters. Riojan dishes include hearty stews of beans, or large roasts of goat and lamb, perfect with a local red. In recent years, Spanish wineries have finally woken up to the potential of tourism. The major bodegas have competed with each other erecting ever-more ambitiously designed modern wineries, and dozens of them offer excellent guided visits and tasting sessions.

Logroño → *For listings, see pages 64-67. Phone code: 941. Population: 152,107. Altitude: 379 m.*

The capital of La Rioja province is a pleasant, small city with plenty of plane trees and opportunities for leisurely outdoor life. It's also an important stop on the Camino de Santiago. If you've got transport it makes an excellent base for exploring the area's bodegas, and, happily, has several excellent restaurants with Riojan cuisine that's a suitable match for the region's reds and a great old-town zone packed with tapas bars.

Arriving in Logroño
Getting there and around Logroño is a good transport hub, with connections to most of Northern Spain. Bus services run from the station on Avenida España. The train station is just south of the bus station. ▶▶ *See Transport, page 67.*

Tourist information The **tourist office** ⓘ *T941 291 260, www.lariojaturismo.com, Oct-May Mon-Fri 1000-1400, 1600-1900, Sat-Sun 1000-1400, 1700-1900; Jun-Sep Mon-Fri 0900-1400, 1700-2000, Sat 1000-1400, 1700-2000, Sun 1000-1400, 1700-1900*, is on the western side of the old town and has details of wineries you can visit in the region.

Background
Logroño emerged in history in Visigothic times, and later, along with much of Northern Spain, became part of the Navarran kingdom until it was annexed by Castilla in 1076 under the name *illo gronio*, meaning 'the ford'. The town prospered as pilgrims flooded through on their way to Santiago, but the city's development was plagued throughout history by fighting; the rich agricultural lands of the region were a valuable prize. The city's name rose when it mounted a legendary defence against a French siege in 1521 and when it became an important tribunal of the Inquisition. In more peaceful times, with Rioja wine drunk all over the world, it has prospered significantly.

Places in Logroño
Logroño's Casco Antiguo sits on the south bank of the Ebro, while the newer town's boulevards stretch west and south to the train station, a 10-minute walk away. Centred around its elegant Renaissance cathedral, not all the old town is actually very old, but it's a pleasant space with arcades and outdoor tables at which to bask in the summer sun.

Logroño's outdoor life is centred around its cathedral, **Santa María de la Redonda** ⓘ *Mon-Sat 0800-1300, 1830-2045, Sun 0900-1400, 1830-2045, free*, a handsome structure, with an ornate gilt *retablo* and elaborate vaulting. The impressive baroque façade still has a faded inscription proclaiming the glory of the Nationalist rising and the *Caudillo*, Franco.

West of the cathedral, along the arcaded Calle Portales, you'll come to **Plaza de San Agustín**, with its impressive post office and the **Museo de la Rioja**. It's a typical provincial museum, the usual mixed bag of archaeological finds and art; the highlight here is a portrait of Saint Francis by El Greco. At time of research it was closed temporarily for a facelift.

The **Iglesia de Santiago** is a bare and atmospheric Gothic edifice with a sizeable *retablo* of carved polychrome wood. There's an inscription outside to the Falangist leader José Antonio Primo de Rivera, but the front is dominated by a statue of Santiago Matamoros trampling some Moorish heads onboard a monster stallion. The **Iglesia de San Bartolomé** is worth a visit for its intricate Gothic portal and *mudéjar*-influenced tower.

Wineries

Most bodegas have set visiting hours, but you'll nearly always have to phone in advance to arrange a tour or tasting. The tourist office has an excellent book, *Datos Enoturismo*, with a list of various bodegas in the region that welcome visitors. It's in Spanish and English. A smaller pamphlet carries the vital details too.

One of the closest bodegas to Logroño is **Marqués de Murrieta de Ygay** ⓘ *Ctra Zaragoza Km 5, T941 271 370, www.marquesdemurrieta.com, phone or email to arrange a visit, closed Aug, the cost of the tour depends on which wines you choose to taste; tours*

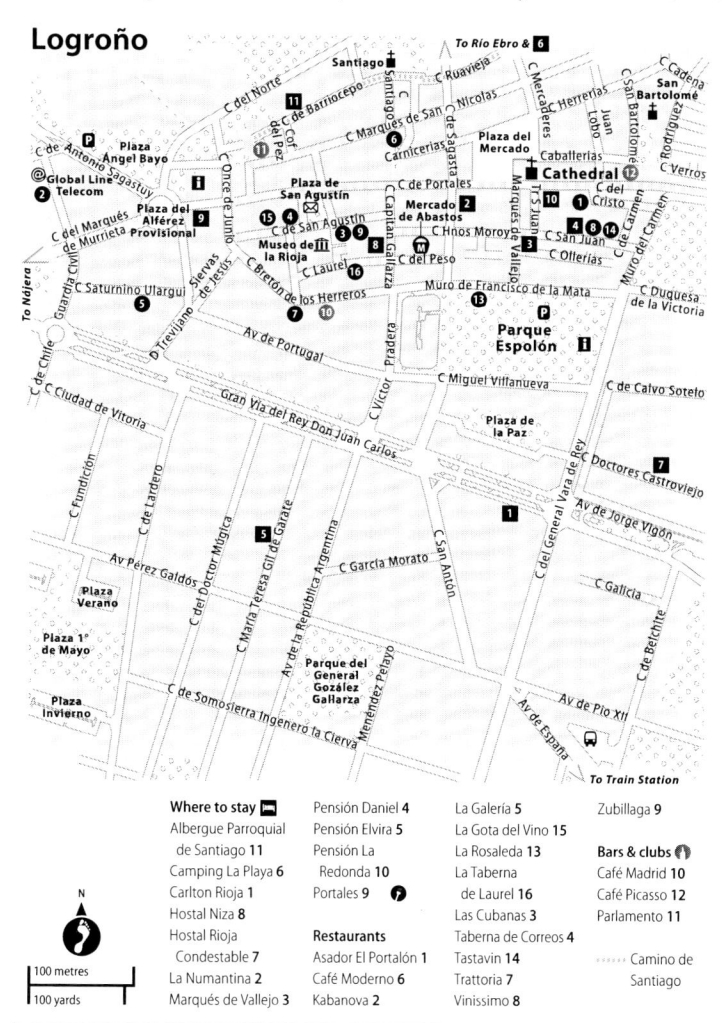

Logroño

Where to stay	Pensión Daniel 4	La Galería 5	Zubillaga 9
Albergue Parroquial de Santiago 11	Pensión Elvira 5	La Gota del Vino 15	
Camping La Playa 6	Pensión La Redonda 10	La Rosaleda 13	**Bars & clubs**
Carlton Rioja 1	Portales 9	La Taberna de Laurel 16	Café Madrid 10
Hostal Niza 8		Las Cubanas 3	Café Picasso 12
Hostal Rioja Condestable 7	**Restaurants**	Taberna de Correos 4	Parlamento 11
La Numantina 2	Asador El Portalón 1	Tastavin 14	
Marqués de Vallejo 3	Café Moderno 6	Trattoria 7	······ Camino de Santiago
	Kabanova 2	Vinissimo 8	

58 • Camino de Santiago Route through La Rioja

Rioja wine

Spain's most famous wine-producing area is not solely located in the province of the same name, but extends into Basque Alava and a small part of Navarra. The Ebro Valley has been used for wine production since at least Roman times; there are numerous historical references referring to the wines of the Rioja region.

In 1902 a royal decree gave Rioja wines a defined area of origin, and in 1926 a regulatory body was created. Rioja's DO (*denominación de origen*) status was upgraded to DOC (*denominación de origen calificada*) in 1991, with more stringent testing and regulations in place. Wine was formerly produced in bodegas dug under houses; the grapes would be tipped into a *lagar* (fermentation trough) and the wine made there; a chimney was essential to let the poisonous gases escape. Techniques changed with the addition of French expertise in the 19th century, who introduced destalking and improved fermentation techniques. Now, the odd wine is still made in the old underground bodegas, but the majority of operations are in large modern buildings on the edges of towns, with ever more striking edifices designed by heavyweights of the architecture world.

Rioja's reputation worldwide is now thriving. Sales are around the 250 million litre mark, about a quarter of which is exported, mostly to the UK, USA, Germany, Scandinavia, and Switzerland.

By far the majority of Riojas are red (85-90%); white and rosé wines are also made. There are four permitted red grape varieties (with a couple of exceptions), these being Tempranillo, which is the main ingredient of most of the quality red Riojas, Garnacha (grenache), Mazuelo, and Graciano. Many reds are blends of two or more of these varietals, which all offer a wine something different. Permitted white varieties are Viura (the main one), Malvasia, and Garnacha Blanca.

The region is divided into three distinct areas, all suited to producing slightly different wines. The Rioja Alavesa is in the southern part of the Basque Country and arguably produces the region's best wines. The Rioja Alta is in the western part of Rioja province and its hotter climate produces fuller-bodied wines, full of strength and character; parts with chalkier soil produce good whites. The Rioja Baja, in the east of Rioja province, is even hotter and drier, and favours Garnacha; wines from here don't have the same long-term ageing potential. Most of the best Rioja reds are produced from a combination of grapes from the three regions.

Oak ageing has traditionally been an important part of the creation of Rioja wine; many would say that Riojas in the past have been over-oaked but younger styles are currently more in fashion. The quality of individual Riojas varies widely according to both producer and the amount of time the wines have been aged in oak barrels and in the bottle. Riojas are classified according to the amount of ageing they have undergone. The words *crianza*, *reserva* and *gran reserva* refer to the length of the ageing process, while the vintage date is also given. Rioja producers store their wines at the bodega until ready for drinking, so it's common to see wines dating back a decade or more on shelves and wine lists.

Many bodegas accept visitors, but arrange the visit in advance. The best bases for winery visiting are Briones and Haro in the Rioja Alta, and beautiful Laguardia in the Rioja Alavesa.

available in Spanish and English. An attractive traditional winery, Murrieta has one of the best reputations for quality in the entire Rioja region. Its reds, though complex, are remarkably smooth for a wine with such lengthy ageing potential. To get there, it's about 45 minutes' (unpleasant) walk or €10 in a taxi on the Zaragoza road.

A little closer to town, **Ontañón** ⓘ *Av de Aragón 3, T941 234 200, Mon-Sat 1230 and 1730, Sun 1230; ring to book a tour (€6 including tasting)*, is just a bottling and ageing point; the actual winemaking is done elsewhere. The Bacchanalian sculptures and paintings by a local artist are impressive.

Also within walking distance of the centre is the spectacular, modern **Bodega Juan Alcorta** ⓘ *Camino Lapuebla 50, T941 270 900, www.bodegasjuanalcorta.com, tours (English and French available) Mon-Fri 1100, 1300, 1600, Sat 1100, 1300, must be pre-booked, €5*, where the reliable mass-produced Campo Viejo reds are made. On a hill overlooking the Ebro, this low, modern masterpiece is a great example of innovative design, and includes a giant cellar.

Nájera → *For listings, see pages 64-67.*

A longish day of fairly gentle climbing takes pilgrims through the rosé wine centre of Navarrete before ending up in the town of Nájera. It doesn't seem as large as its population of 7000 would suggest; most are housed in the modern sprawl close to the highway, leaving the river and careworn but attractive old town in relative tranquillity. The town's name derives from an Arabic word meaning 'between rocks', referring to its situation, wedged among reddish crags that jut over the buildings of the centre. These rocky walls are riddled with caves, some of which were used extensively in medieval times and were dug through to make a series of interconnecting passageways. These can be accessed to the south of the town's imposing highlight, the Monasterio de Santa María la Real.

In former times Nájera was an important medieval city and a capital of many Navarran kings; under Sancho the Great in the early 11th century most of Northern Spain was ruled from here. In the 14th century, Nájera was the site for two important battles of the Hundred Years War, both won by Pedro the Cruel, while a famous short-term resident was Iñigo de Loyola, waiting on the Duke of Navarra during the period immediately before his wounding at Pamplona and subsequent conversion from dandy to saint.

The impressive **Monasterio de Santa María la Real** ⓘ *Mon-Sat 1000-1300, 1600-1730 (1900 summer), Sun 1000-1230, 1600-1730 (1830 summer), €3*, is a testament to this period's glories. It was originally founded by Sancho's eldest son, King García, who was out for a bit of falconry. His bird pursued a dove into a cave; following them in, García found them sitting side by side in front of a figure of the Virgin Mary with a vase of fresh lilies at her feet. After his next few battles went the right way, he decided to build a church over the cave; the rest, as they say, is history. Today the figure is in the main *retablo*, still with fresh lilies at her feet, and the cave holds a different Virgin. The present monastery church is a much-altered Gothic construction, which was heavily damaged during the Peninsular War and later, when much looting followed the expulsion of the monks by government order in 1835. Heavy investment in restoration has restored many of its glories. The cloister is entered via an elaborate door crowned by the coat of arms of Carlos V, who donated generously to monastery building projects. Above is an elaborately painted dome. The cloister is pleasant, although many of the artistic details have been destroyed. The church itself is a fairly simple three-naved affair. The *retablo* features the statue of Mary; to either side kneel King García and his queen. Most impressive is the rear of the church, where elaborately carved tombs flank the entrance to the original cave. The tombs hold the mortal remains of several 10th to 12th-century dukes, Navarran kings and other worthies, but were made several centuries later. The exception is the sepulchre of Doña Blanca, a beautifully carved Romanesque original with Biblical reliefs and funerary scenes. Above in the gallery the *coro* (choir), although damaged, is a superb piece of woodwork, an incredibly ornate late Gothic fusion of religious, naturalistic, and mythological themes adorning the 67 seats.

Around the corner is the moderately interesting **Museo Arqueológico** ⓘ *Plaza Navarra, Mon-Sat 1000-1400, 1700-2000, Sun 1000-1400, €1.20*, with a range of finds from different periods mostly garnered from volunteer excavations. The area was inhabited by prehistoric man and later by a succession of inhabitants, including Romans, Visigoths and Moors.

The **Iglesia de Santa Cruz** is smaller and simpler than La Real and dates from the 17th century. It seems to be the preferred home for the town's stork population, which have built some unlikely nests in its upper extremities.

The **tourist office** ⓘ *Plaza San Miguel 10, T941 360 041, summer Tue-Sat 1000-1400, 1600-1900, Sun 1030-1400, Oct-Jun Tue-Sat 1000-1330, 1600-1800, Sun 1030-1400, also open Mon in Aug*, will provide a map of the town.

A half-hour walk from Nájera takes you to **Tricio**, famous for its peppers and the **Ermita de Santa María de Arcos** ⓘ *Sat 1030-1330, 1630-1930, Sun 1030-1330, also open Tue-Fri in summer*, which is worth a look. Built over extensive Roman remains, some of it dates to the fifth century AD; it's a curious architectural record and a peaceful little place.

Onwards from Nájera → *For listings, see pages 64-67.*

The main pilgrim route heads from Nájera straight to Santo Domingo de la Calzada, but an extra day's detour takes you into the Riojan hills to investigate the monasteries of San Millán de Cogolla. It adds an extra 16km to your route but is a very worthwhile side-trip.

San Millán de Cogolla

ⓘ *Suso: visits must be booked in advance, T941 373 082, Easter-Sep Tue-Sun 0930-1330, 1530-1830, Oct-Easter Tue-Sun 0930-1330, 1530-1800, €3; Yuso: www.monasteriodeyuso.org, Easter-Sep Tue-Sun 1000-1330, 1600-1830, Oct-Easter Tue-Sat 1000-1300, 1530-1730, Sun 1000-1300, open Mon in Aug, €5, admission by guided tour only.*

Some 18 km into the hills is the village of San Millán de Cogolla, which grew up around its two monasteries. The original is the **Monasterio de Suso**, tucked away in the hills a kilometre or so above town. It was started in the sixth century to house the remains of San Millán himself, a local holy man who lived to be 101 years old. It feels an ancient and spooky place, with low arches and several tombs. Mozarabic influence can be seen in the horseshoe arches and recessed chapels. The saint himself was buried in a recessed chapel off the main church but was dug up by Sancho the Great, who built a solemn carved cenotaph in its place. The bones were taken down the hill and another monastery was built around them, **Monasterio de Yuso** (the word means 'low' in a local dialect; *Suso* means 'high'). The current structure is on a massive scale and is a work of the 16th century, far more ornate and less loveable than Suso. Still an active monastery, the highlight is the galleried library, an important archive, some of whose volumes can barely be lifted by one person. San Millán finds himself in an ivory-panelled chest in the museum; this ascetic hermit would also be surprised to see himself depicted over the main entrance door astride a charger with sword in hand and enemies trampled underhoof. There's also

Chickens in the church

A buff 18-year-old German by the name of Hugonell was heading for Santiago with his parents in the Middle Ages when they stopped in Santo Domingo de la Calzada for the night.

The barmaid at the inn liked what she saw but got a terse '*nein*' from the boy. In revenge she cunningly replaced his enamel camp-mug with a silver goblet from the inn and denounced him as a thief when the family departed. Finding the goblet in his bags, the boy was taken before the judge, who had the innocent teenager hanged outside town. The parents, grief-stricken, continued to Santiago.

On their way back months later, they passed the gallows once again, only to find Hugonell still alive and chirpy; the merciful Santo Domingo had intervened to save his life.

The parents rushed to the judge and told the story, demanding that their son be cut down. The judge laughed sardonically over his dinner and said "Your boy is about as alive as these roast chickens I´m about to eat". At that, the chickens jumped off the plate and began to cluck. The boy was duly cut down.

In memory of this event, a snow-white cockerel and hen have been kept in an ornate Gothic henhouse inside the cathedral ever since. They are donated by local farmers and changed over monthly.

---

a **tourist office** in the grounds of Yuso. A minibus makes the ascent from Yuso to Suso during visiting hours.

The monastery has styled itself the 'birthplace of Spanish', as the first known scribblings in the Castilian language were jotted as marginal notes by a 10th-century monk in a text found in Yuso's library. A couple of centuries later, the nearby village of **Berceo**, which you'll pass through on your way to rejoin the main Camino route, produced a monk, Gonzalo, who penned the first known verse to have been written in the language.

Santo Domingo de la Calzada → *For listings, see pages 64-67.*

Santo Domingo is a lovely town, worth a stop for anyone passing through the area. It has a curious history, mostly connected with the man for whom it is named. Born in 1019, Domingo dedicated his young life to the pilgrims. He built a hospice, a bridge and generally improved the quality of the path; it's no wonder he's the patron saint of road workers and engineers in these parts. He made himself a simple tomb by the side of the Camino before dying at the ripe old age of 90, but admirers later had him transferred to the cathedral, which was built in the town that grew up around his pilgrims' rest stop.

The **cathedral** ⓘ *daily 1000-1930, €3.50*, with its ornate free-standing tower, is the town's centrepiece. Time and the elements haven't quite rubbed off the fascist slogans on the façade, but inside it's pleasant and light. There's much of interest after you've made it through the officious bureaucracy at the entrance. Santo Domingo himself is in an elaborate mausoleum with a small crypt underneath it. Around it are votive plaques and offerings from various engineering and road maintenance firms. An attractive series of 16th-century paintings tell some incidents from the saint's life. One of these concerns his 'miracle of the wheel': a weary pilgrim foolishly had a nap on the road and was run over and killed by an oxcart; Santo Domingo prayed on his behalf and he rose again. In memory of this event a cartwheel is hung in the cathedral every 11 May.

Otherwise, the chooks are the main attraction in their ornate coop, punctuating the pious air with the odd cock-a-doodle-doo (see box, opposite). There's a 16th-century *retablo* with a few nasty fleshy relics of various saints in small cases and a museum around the cloister. Climb onto the roof for some fresh air and a good view over the many narrow streets below. The guided visit includes the cloister and the small museum of religious artefacts.

There are several admirable buildings in the old town, which basically consists of three parallel streets, and the northwest section of the old walls is still intact; pilgrims who have passed through Puente la Reina may experience a bit of déjà vu. Not far from the cathedral, on the main pedestrian street (Calle Mayor), is an exhibition on the Camino de Santiago.

The **tourist office** ⓘ *C Mayor 44, T941 341 230, www.santodomingodelacalzada.org, Mon-Sat 1000-1400, 1600-2000, Sun 1100-1430*, is on the main street.

Some 12 km south of Santo Domingo, the **convent church of Cañas** ⓘ *C Real 2, Cañas, T941 379 083, Tue-Sat 1030-1330, 1600-1800, Sun 1100-1330, 1600-1800, to 1900 summer, €3.50*, is worth visiting if you've got transport. Founded in the 12th century by Cistercian monks, it's now an austere but noble spot. The visit progresses around the cloister, off which is entered the fine Gothic church, with a beautiful apse with double row of alabaster-paned windows; the altar and retable have been removed to the other end to allow the majesty of the architecture full rein. The adjacent chapterhouse has carved tombs of former abbesses, with that of Beata Urraca López still preserving traces of original colour, a particularly fine example of Gothic funerary sculpture. A display of church treasures includes skulls of some of St Ursula's alleged 11,000 virgin martyrs; an atmospherically lit exhibition of religious art rounds out the visit.

Santo Domingo to Burgos → *For listings, see pages 64-67.*

It's 75 km from Santo Domingo across the Castilian plateau to Burgos, and weather conditions can be extreme: baking hot summer days and freezing winds and snow in spring and autumn. It's a journey that most pilgrims divide into three days; with hostels in most villages, it's a matter of choice where you stop for the night.

Belorado is a common choice for the first night's rest; it's a a fairly typical Castilian village centred on its church and plaza.

The next day is a slow climb up to a height of 1150 m, where there's a Francoist memorial to the Civil War dead. A peaceful place to spend the last night before Burgos is at **San Juan de Ortega**. In the green foothills north of the N120, it's nothing more than a church and *albergue*, and has been a fixture of the Camino ever since Juan, inspired by the good works of Santo Domingo de la Calzada up the road, decided to do the same and dedicate his life to easing the pilgrims' journey. He started the church in the 12th century; the Romanesque apse survives, although the rest is in later style. It's a likeable if unremarkable place. San Juan is buried here in an ornate Gothic tomb. Pilgrims stay at the hospital that he founded.

From San Juan, you pass through the village of **Agés**, then **Atapuerca**, near which are the excavations that forced a fundamental rethink of prehistoric hominids' population of Europe (see page 75 for visiting details). Then it's a climb up to a large wooden cross at 1070 m, and a slow gentle 18 km descent into Burgos.

Route through La Rioja listings

For hotel and restaurant price codes and other relevant information, see pages 12-19.

Where to stay

Logroño *p57, map p58*
As many visitors to Logroño are on expenses-paid wine-buying junkets, the hotel accommodation is overpriced.

€€€ Hotel Carlton Rioja, Gran Vía 5, T941 242 100, www.hotelcarltonlogrono.com. One of Logroño's better hotels, though overpriced, located in the new town, 5 mins from the old centre. The interior doesn't quite live up to the smart façade, and the rooms vary significantly in size. Good service and discount for internet bookings.

€€ Hostal Niza, C Gallarza 13, T941 206 044, www.hostalniza.com. A good choice right in the centre of the old town, perfect for tapas time. The rooms have been touched up with a bit of style, and feature exposed brick and stone design, comfortable beds and clean spacious bathrooms.

€€ Hostal Rioja Condestable, C Doctores Castroviejo 5, T941 247 288, www.hostalriojacondestable.com. This clean and modern *hostal* has a slightly cramped, lugubrious feel but offers good-value rooms on a a pedestrian street. The owners are welcoming and thoughtful.

€€ Hotel Portales, C Portales 85, T941 502 794, www.hotelsercotelportales.com. Right in the centre, with parking available, this is an excellent, modern hotel. The clean lines of the rooms feel almost Nordic, and the fair prices, with free Wi-Fi and breakfast often included, make this the best choice in town.

€€ La Numantina, C Sagasta 4, T941 251 411, www.hostalnumantina.com. This *hostal* is rather faded but still very comfortable. The rooms are all doubles, with en suite bathroom and the location is great, in the heart of the old town.

€€ Marqués de Vallejo, C Marqués de Vallejo 8, T941 248 333, www.hotelmarquesdevallejo.com. This friendly old town hotel is very sleek and stylish, with dark wood parquetry and grey and white minimalism. The renovated rooms are very comfortable and there's a curious modern suite with the bed in the middle of the room. Business lounge with internet access, free Wi-Fi, and underground parking close by.

€ Albergue Parroquial de Santiago, C Barriocepo 8, T941 209 501, www.santiagoelreal.org. The pilgrim hostel of the Santiago El Real church is a place with a tradition of pilgrim hospitality where you pay by donation. Meals available.

€ Pensión Daniel, C San Juan 21, T941 252 948, www.pensiondaniel.com. One of 3 *pensiones* in the same building, right in the middle of town. This is the best of them; it offers comfort at a low price.

€ Pensión Elvira, C María Teresa Gil de Garate 20, T941 240 150, www.pensionelvira.galeon.com. This *pensión*, situated in the new town, is smart and has good-value rooms.

€ Pensión La Redonda, C Portales 30, T941 272 409. In the heart of town, this cute spot offers simple but correct rooms; try and get the one that looks out at the cathedral.

Camping

Camping La Playa, T941 252 253, www.campinglaplaya.com. By the River Ebro on the opposite bank from town, this is a good place to stay, and relatively handy for town. There are several cabins available.

Nájera *p60*
€€ Hostal Ciudad de Nájera, C Calleja San Miguel 14, T941 360 660, www.ciudaddenajera.com. A modern *hostal* decorated with verve in bright colours. The delightful owners have equipped the good-value rooms superbly, with excellent bathrooms, TVs and piped music. There's also a cheery guest lounge and downstairs bodega.

€€ Hotel Duques de Nájera, C Carmen 7, T941 410 421, www.hotelduquesdenajera.com.

Right in the attractive centre of town, this hotel fulfils its mission by supplying very comfortable, modern rooms backed up by lofty standards of cleanliness and service.

€ Albergue Puerta de Nájera, C Ribera del Najerilla 1, T941 362 317, www.alberguedenajera.com. This recently opened private pilgrim hostel is one of the Camino's best, with a super-welcoming host, great facilities, and a tranquil riverside location.

San Millán de Cogolla p61
€€€ Hospedería Monasterio San Millán, T941 373 277, www.sanmillan.com. An atmospheric place to stay, this is set in a wing of Yuso monastery and offers excellent, spacious rooms, a heavy Spanish decor, and willing service. There are often exceptional special offers, so it's always worth phoning. Opposite is an *asador*, which is a decent place to eat, if a little oversized.

Santo Domingo de la Calzada p62
€€€ Parador de Santo Domingo de la Calzada, Plaza del Santo 3, T941 340 300, www.parador.es. Right next to the cathedral, this mostly modern parador is built around the saint's old pilgrim hospital and is an attractive place with facilities and charm, backed up by a decent restaurant. Another parador, **Bernardo Fresneda**, with 3-star facilities in a converted monastery, offers similar comfort. It's a hospitality training school, so service is exceptionally willing.
€€ Hostal Rey Pedro I, C San Roque 9, T941 341 160, www.hostalpedroprimero.es. Pushing the boundaries between *hostal* and hotel, this modern place offers plenty of comfort and conveniences, including appealing rooms with free Wi-Fi.
€€ Hotel El Corregidor, C Mayor (Zumalacárregui) 14 Av Calahorra 17, T941 342 128, www.hotelelcorregidor.com. Bright and breezily decorated modern hotel (although the pink curtains in the rooms are a bit sugar sweet) in the old town; it's a friendly and comforting spot to stay.

€ Albergue Casa del Santo, C Mayor 38, T941 343 390, www.alberguecofradiadelsanto.com. Formidably equipped with facilities, modern and spacious, this is a fabulous hostel run by a religious brotherhood keen on keeping Santo Domingo's pilgrim-caring spirit alive.
€ Hostal Miguel, C Juan Carlos I 23, T941 343 252, www.pensionmiguel.com. On the main road around town, this *pensión* has rooms that are noisy but not overly so. The en suite ones are significantly nicer than the ones without bathroom.

Santo Domingo to Burgos p63
€ Albergue A Santiago, C Redoña s/n, Belorado, T947 562 164, www.a-santiago.es. Not too many pilgrims' rests on the Camino have a swimming pool, but you get one here, as well as a grassy garden to have a siesta in.
€ Albergue de San Juan Ortega, San Juan Ortega, T947 560 438. Though it's not the most modern or comfortable of hostels, this place is part of the Camino's history, and the tranquility of this hamlet might entice you to linger. If you don't like it, you can push on to Agés, under 4 km away.

Restaurants

Logroño p57, map p58
Logroño has a busy tapas scene; the place to head for is **Calle Laurel**, which proudly claims to have the highest concentration of bars per square metre in Northern Spain (although there are several pretenders to this throne). Order *cosechero* if you want the young, cheap local wines, or *crianza* for older, oak-aged reds. Nearby **C San Agustín** has several good restaurants. The central market near here is a great place to buy fresh meat, fruit and vegetables.
€€€ Kabanova, C Benemérito Cuerpo de la Guardia Civil 9, T941 212 995, www.kabanova.com. Just outside the old town, this stylish but reasonably priced restaurant has interesting nouvelle Riojan cuisine. The menu is short but features delicacies such as pigs' feet stuffed with foie and

pear. There are various set menu options including a well-priced degustation.

€€€ La Galería, C Saturnino Ulargui 5, T941 207 366, www.restaurantelagaleria.com. This restaurant is one of the Rioja's best places to eat. Local Riojan vegetables, delicately treated fish, and juicy meat are presented in innovative ways without detracting from their natural flavours. The best way to go here is to let the owners pick a tasting menu for you. Recommended.

€€€ Las Cubanas, C San Agustín 17, T941 220 050, www.lascubanas.net. A historic Logroño restaurant, this is an upmarket spot serving variations on traditional dishes as well as delicious avant-garde creations. The €30 lunch *menú* is popular with local wine execs.

€€ Asador El Portalón, C Portales 7, T941 241 334, www.asadorelportalon.es. While this *asador* does excellent heavy roast meat, it also has a very nice line in salads to balance out a meal. It's one of several worthwhile *asadores* around the centre.

€€ La Gota del Vino, C San Agustín 14, T941 210 146. The tapas bar of a successful restaurant, this is a simple, smart and minimalist spot with shell-like chairs and a high metallic bar. There are several wines to choose from at the bar which has excellent and artistic *pinchos* and *cazuelitas* (small pots of stew).

€€ Trattoria, C Bretón de los Herreros 19, T941 202 602. Modern and stylish, this is an excellent Italian restaurant with a split-level interior and a €12 *menú del día*.

€€ Vinissimo, C San Juan 23, T941 258 828. A good choice, with a €10 *menú*. There's a slightly North African flavour, with dishes like couscous and tagine featuring on the menu, but it's a place to learn about the local wine too. You can book a tutored tasting session in English (€15) as well as purchase bottles.

€€ Zubillaga, C San Agustín 3, T941 220 076. A wide mix of northern Spanish cuisine, with many tasty fish dishes – try the *merluza con setas*, a tasty dish of hake and wild mushrooms. There are also hearty roast meats, as well as more delicate fare, such as crêpes.

€ La Taberna del Laurel, C Laurel 7, T941 220 143. This narrow spot is a C Laurel classic. It's very famous around here for its *patatas bravas*: fried potatoes with lashings of tomato and garlic sauce.

€ Taberna de Correos, C San Agustín 8. This excellent place does regular specials on good local wines and specializes in a range of great hot *pinchos*: 'La Pluma' is a delicious mini brochette of succulent pork for just €1.80. Recommended.

€ Tastavin, C San Juan 25, T941 262 145. Bright and modern, this is one of a few bars on this old-town street. Delicious gourmet *pinchos* are arranged along the bar, using quality ingredients and a dash of flair. There's a good choice of well-poured wine too.

Cafés

Café Moderno, Plaza Martínez Zaporta 7, T941 220 042. A very popular local spot lavishly decorated in swish neo-baroque style with bright lights and black and white photos. It's popular for a pre- or post-cinema drink, but also does tapas and a cheap *menú del día*.

La Rosaleda, Parque Espolón s/n, T941 220 053. open summer only. An outdoor café with heaps of tables in the park. A great place to while away the hot afternoon.

Nájera *p60*

€ El Buen Yantar, C Mártires 19, T941 360 274. This *asador* does a very good *menú* with hearty Riojan bean dishes washed down by tasty grilled meat and decent house wine.

€ La Taberna de Manu, C Mayor 21, T941 410 428. Much the best tapas bar in town, this spot is decked out with slightly bizarre original paintings, and signed shirts of notable handball players. The bar snacks include plump *tigres* (mussels topped with bechamel sauce and grilled) as well as the local speciality, fried sheep's ears, a waste-not-want-not Riojan dish.

Santo Domingo de la Calzada *p62*

There's good, cheap eating in Santo Domingo; although it might be wise to stay off the roast chicken.

€€ Casa Amparo, C San Roque 17, T941 343 016. Sporting a comfortably traditional dining room, this friendly restaurant might be just what you need after the long trudge along the Camino. Typical Riojan dishes play a big part here, and the €11 *menú del día* is one of the best in town.

€€ El Rincón de Emilio, Plaza Bonifacio Gil 7, T941 340 527. Tucked away in a tiny plaza, this is a charming chessboard of a place with good Riojan stews and meats.

Bars and clubs

Logroño *p57, map p58*

There are a number of British-type pubs popular with young Riojans; many of these cluster around C Siervas de Jesús, C Saturnino Ulargui and Av de Portugal.
Café Madrid, C Bretón de los Herreros 15. Many of Logroño's young meet here for an evening coffee or large drink. On weekend nights, it becomes a disco-bar.
Café Picasso, C Portales 4, T941 247 992. A cool café-bar with imported beers fronted by a sleek grey parrot. It's cheerful, open-minded, and there's always some local banter.
Parlamento, C Barriocepo s/n, T941 212 836. Lively café-bar with a small stone-faced interior and a terrace. It's opposite the Riojan parliament but often filled with folk much younger than your average politician.

Entertainment

Logroño *p57, map p58*

Cines Moderno, Plaza Martínez Zaporta. A conveniently central cinema.
Teatro El Bretón, C Bretón de los Herreros, T941 207 231. A theatre but also occasionally shows *versión original* (subtitled) English-language films.

Festivals

Logroño *p57, map p58*

11 Jun San Bernabé, which is used to commemorate the town's defence against the French. Free fish and wine are given out to the multitudes.
21 Sep Harvest Festival. The most enjoyable time to be in La Rioja is during harvest time. The festival coincides with the feast day of San Mateo.

Santo Domingo de la Calzada *p62*

12 May The town celebrates the anniversary of the Santo Domingo's death in style, with a series of processions for a couple of weeks prior to the fiesta.

Transport

Logroño *p57, map p58*
Bus

For bus station information: T941 235 983.
  Numerous buses go daily to **Nájera** and **Santo Domingo de la Calzada**, and there are 2 services to **San Millán de Cogolla**. **Pamplona** is served 6 times daily (€8.20, 1 hr 40 mins), and there are good connections to other Spanish cities.

Train

Trains run regularly east to **Zaragoza** (8 daily, 1¾ hrs, €14-23). There are fewer services to **Vitoria**, **Burgos**, **Bilbao** and **Haro**.

Nájera *p60*
Bus

Frequent services run from the bus terminal by the Hotel San Fernando to **Logroño** and **Santo Domingo**, and 3 or 4 daily go to **Burgos** and **Zaragoza**. There are 2 daily to **San Millán**.

Santo Domingo de la Calzada *p62*
Bus

Buses leave from Plaza Hermosilla just south of the old town. There are regular buses to **Logroño**, stopping in **Nájera**; to **Burgos**, and to **Bilbao** via **Haro** and **Vitoria**.

Burgos

"They have very good houses and live very comfortably, and they are the most courteous people I have come across in Spain." Andrés Navagero, 1526.

This Venetian traveller's comment on 16th-century Burgos could equally apply today to the city where courtesy and courtliness still rule the roost. Formerly an important and prosperous trading town, Burgos achieved infamy as the seat of Franco's Civil War junta and is still a sober and reactionary town, the heartland of Castilian conservatism. But Burgos is far from being stuck in the past: the fantastic new Museum of Human Evolution sits on the Arlanzón river; a committed programme of inserting cycleways along every major road is way ahead of its time in Castilla, and the S-4 urbanization project has turned heads in the architecture world.

Burgos's collection of superb Gothic buildings and sculpture, as well as its position on the Camino de Santiago, make it a popular destination, but the city copes well with the summer influx. Just don't come for gentle spring sunshine; Burgos is known throughout Spain as a chilly city, the epitome of the saying *'nueve meses de invierno, tres meses de infierno'* (nine months of winter, three months of hell). The chills can be banished with the traditionally hearty local cuisine and Ribera reds from the south of the province.

Arriving in Burgos → *Phone code: 947. Population: 178,966. Altitude: 860 m.*
Getting there Burgos is roughly in the centre of Northern Spain and easily accessed from most parts of the country by bus or train. There are regular services from Madrid and the Basque country as well as Santander and all Castilian towns. ▸▸ *See Transport, page 79.*

Getting around As usual, the old centre is fairly compact, but you may want to use the local bus service to access a couple of the outlying monasteries, the new train station and the campsite.

Best time to visit Burgos has a fairly unpleasant climate with short, hot summers and long, cold winters (it often snows) punctuated by the biting wind that 'won't blow out a candle but will kill a man'. The most moderate weather is found in May, June and September.

Tourist information There is a **municipal office** ⓘ *Plaza del Rey San Fernando 2, T947 288 874, www.turismoburgos.org, summer daily 1000-2000*, across from the cathedral; and also a **regional office** ⓘ *Plaza Alonso Martínez 7, T947 203 125, oficinadeturismodeburgos@jcyl.es, mid-Sep-Jun Mon-Sat 0930-1400, 1600-1900, Sun 0930-1700, summer daily 0900-2000*. There are **city tours** and a rather tacky **tourist train** ⓘ *daily in summer and at weekends Oct-Jun, €4*, which rolls around the sights, leaving from outside the cathedral square tourist office.

Background
Burgos is comfortably the oldest city in Europe, if you count the nearby cave-dwellers from Atapuerca, who were around over a million years ago. That aside, the city's effective foundation was in the late ninth century, when it was resettled during the Reconquista. Further honours soon followed; it was named capital of Castilla y León as early as the 11th century.

The city's position at the northern centre of the Castilian plain, near the coastal mountain passes, made it a crucial point for the export of goods. Burgos flourished, becoming a wealthy city of merchants and beasts of burden; in the 16th century its mule population often exceeded the human one, as bigger and bigger convoys of wool made their way over the mountains and by ship to Flanders.

The Consulado de Burgos, a powerful guild-like body, was created to administer trade, and succeeded in establishing a virtual monopoly; Burgos became one of three great 16th-century Spanish trading cities, along with Sevilla and Medina del Campo. The strife in Flanders hit the city hard, though, and other towns broke into the market. Burgos' population declined by 75% in the first half of the 17th century, and the city lapsed into the role of genteel provincial capital, apart from a brief and bloody interlude: during the Civil War the Nationalist junta was established here; the city had shown its credentials with a series of atrocities committed on Republicans after the rising.

Places in Burgos → *For listings, see pages 76-79.*

Cathedral
ⓘ *www.catedraldeburgos.es, mid-Mar to Oct daily 0930-1930, Nov to mid-Mar 1000-1900, last entry an hour before, €7, €3.50 for pilgrims (includes museum). Some of the chapels are only accessible on guided tours; the guides are independent and prices vary. Before entering the cathedral, you must buy a ticket in the reception office on the square below.*

Burgos's famed cathedral is a remarkable Gothic edifice whose high hollow spires rise over the city. Its beauty is an austere and solemn one, and the technical excellence of its stonework has to be admired. It also houses a collection of significant artwork.

The current structure was begun in 1221 over an earlier church by Fernando III and his Germanic wife, Beatrice of Swabia, with the bishop Maurice overseeing things. Beatrice

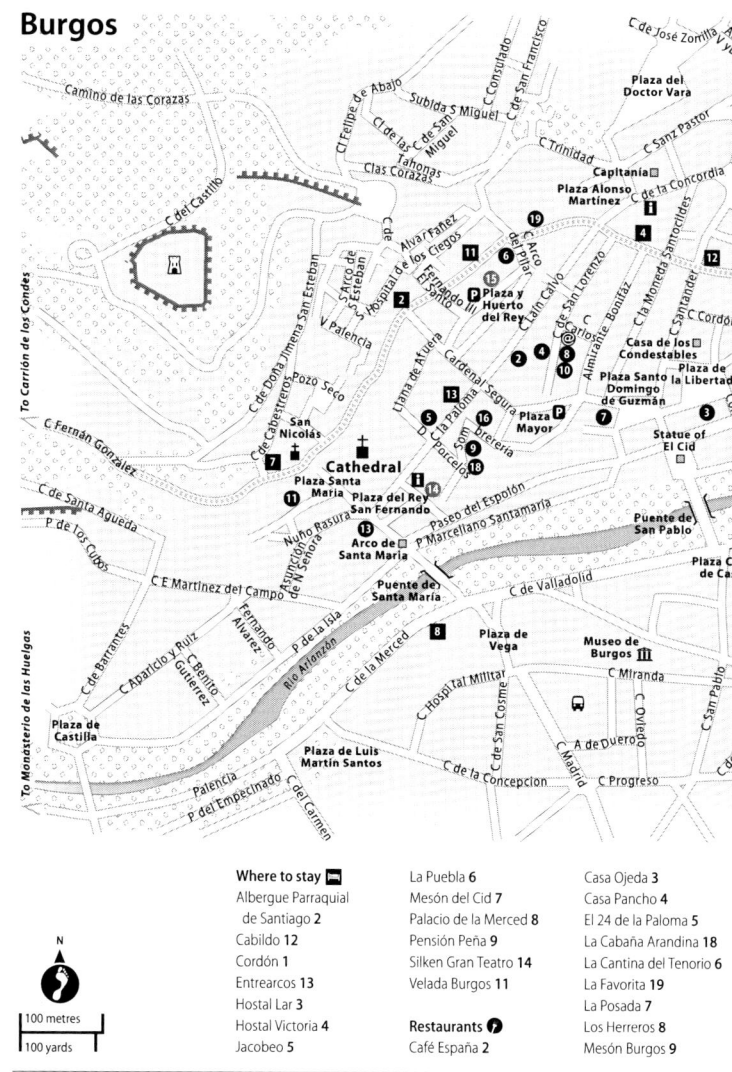

Burgos

Where to stay
Albergue Parroquial de Santiago **2**
Cabildo **12**
Cordón **1**
Entrearcos **13**
Hostal Lar **3**
Hostal Victoria **4**
Jacobeo **5**
La Puebla **6**
Mesón del Cid **7**
Palacio de la Merced **8**
Pensión Peña **9**
Silken Gran Teatro **14**
Velada Burgos **11**

Restaurants
Café España **2**
Casa Ojeda **3**
Casa Pancho **4**
El 24 de la Paloma **5**
La Cabaña Arandina **18**
La Cantina del Tenorio **6**
La Favorita **19**
La Posada **7**
Los Herreros **8**
Mesón Burgos **9**

70 • Camino de Santiago Burgos

brought him with her from Swabia, and the northern influence didn't stop there; Gil and Diego de Siloé, the top sculptors who are responsible for many masterpieces inside and throughout the province, originated from those parts, while the towers were designed by master builder Hans of Cologne.

Entering through the western door, under the spires (only completed in the 19th century), one of the strangest sights is in the chapel to the right. It's reserved for private prayer, but the figure you see through the glass is the **Christ of Burgos**. Made from buffalo hide and sporting a head of real hair, the crucified Jesus wears a green skirt and looks a little the worse for wear. The limbs are movable, no doubt to impress the 14th-century faithful with a few tricks; apparently the Christ was once so lifelike that folk thought the fingernails had to be clipped weekly. Opposite, high on the wall, the strange figure of Papamoscas strikes the hours, the closest thing to levity in this serious building.

Like those of many Spanish cathedrals, the **choir** is closed off, which spoils any long perspective views. Once inside, admire the Renaissance main *retablo* depicting scenes from the life of the Virgin. Underfoot at the crossing are the bones of El Cid and his wife Doña Jimena, underwhelmingly marked by a simple slab. The remains were only transferred here in 1927 after being reclaimed from the French, who had taken them from the monastery of San Pedro de Cardeña during the Peninsular War. They lie under the large octagonal tower, an elaborate 16th-century add-on. The choir itself is incredibly elegant and intricate – you could spend hours examining the carved wooden images; Bishop Maurice's tomb is in the centre of it.

There's a wealth of side chapels, many unfortunately shielded by *rejas* (grilles), although if an attendant is around they are happy to open them up. The chapels date from different architectural periods; some of the Renaissance ones feature stunningly fine stonework around the doorways. The **Capilla de Santa Teresa** sports a riotous Churrigueresque ceiling, while the soaring

Mesón La Amarilla 10
Mesón La Cueva 11
Mesón San Lesmes 12
Puerta Real 13
Taberna Pecaditos 16

Ram Jam Club 17

···· Camino de Santiago

Bars & clubs
Fox Tavern 14
La Negra Candela 15

Camino de Santiago Burgos • 71

El Cid

Although portrayed as something of a national hero in the 12th-century epic *El Cantar de Mío Cid* (Song of the Cid), the recorded deeds of Rodrigo Díaz de Vivar certainly give the devil's advocate a few sharp darts in the fight for places in the pantheon of Spanish heroes. Born just outside Burgos in AD 1043, El Cid (the Boss) was in fact a mercenary who fought with the Moors if the price was right.

His ability to protect his own interests was recognized even by those who sought to idolize him. The Song of the Cid recounts that, on being expelled from Burgos, the great man wrapped up his beard to protect it from being pulled by irate citizens angry at his nefarious dealings.

Operating along the border between Christian and Muslim Spain, the Cid was a man of military guile who was able to combine a zeal for the Reconquista with a desire to further his own fortune. The tawdry moment when he swindled two innocent Jewish merchants by delivering a chest filled with sand instead of gold is celebrated with gusto in Burgos cathedral where his mortal remains now lie.

Banished by Alfonso VI for double dealing, his military skills proved indispensable and he was re-hired in the fight against the Almoravids. The capture of Valencia in 1094 marked the height of his powers and was an undoubted blow to the Moors. If having his own city wasn't reward enough, the Cid was given the formidable Gormaz castle as a sort of fortified weekend retreat.

By the standards of his own time where the boundaries, both physical and cultural, between Christian and Moorish Spain were flexible, the Cid's actions make perfect sense. It is only later ages (preferring their heroes without ambiguity) that felt the need to gloss over the actual facts. By the time of his death in 1099 the Cid was well on his way to national hero status.

The Cid's horse, Babieca, has her own marked grave in the monastery of San Pedro de Cardeña. The Cid himself was buried here for 600 years until Napoleon's forces, perhaps fearing a re-appearance by the man himself, removed the body to France. He was reburied in Burgos in the 1930s.

---

late Gothic *retablo* in the **Capilla de Santa Ana** and the painted Romanesque tombs in the **Capilla de San Nicolás** are also striking.

The grandest, however, is at the very far end of the apse, the **Capilla de los Condestables**. The Velasco family, hereditary Constables of Castilla, were immensely influential in their time, and one of the most powerful, Don Pedro Fernández, is entombed here with his wife. Few kings have lain in a more elaborate setting, with a high vaulted roof, fabulous stonework and three *retablos*, the most ornate of which, the central one, depicts the purification of Mary. The alabaster figures on the sepulchre itself are by another German, Simon of Cologne, and his son. The room, oddly asymmetrical, is a memorable shrine to earthly power and heraldry. Just outside, around the ambulatory, a series of sensitive alabaster panels depicts Biblical scenes.

The **museum**, set around the top of the two-tiered tomb-lined cloister, is reasonably interesting. After passing through the baroque sacristy, the first stop is the chapterhouse, where, high on the wall, hangs a coffer that belonged to the Cid; possibly the one that was involved in a grubby little deed of his, where he sneakily repaid some Jews with a coffer of sand, rather than the gold that he owed them. In the adjacent chamber is a pretty red *mudéjar* ceiling. A 10th-century Visigothic Bible is the highlight of the next room, as well as the Cid's marriage contract, the so-called *Letter of Arras*. Finally, the museum has an excellent collection of well-restored 15th-century Flemish paintings. They are full of life and action – the mob mentality of the Crucifixion is well portrayed. There are several reliquaries holding various bits of saints (including Thomas Becket) and nothing less than a spine from the crown of thorns. A *retablo* depicts Santiago in Moor-slaying mode.

Iglesia de San Nicolás
ⓘ *Jun-Sep Mon-Sat 1000-1400, 1700-1900, Oct-May Mon-Sat 1200-1330, 1700-1900, €1.50, free Mon.*
This small church above the cathedral has a superb *retablo*, a virtuoso sculptural work, probably by Simon and Francis of Cologne. It's a bit like looking at a portrait of a city, or a theatre audience, so many figures seem to be depicted in different sections. The main scene at the top is Mary surrounded by a 360° choir of angels. The stonework is superb throughout; have a look for the ship's rigging, a handy piece of chiselling to say the least. There's also a good painting of the Last Judgement in the church, an early 16th-century Flemish work, only recently rediscovered. The demons are the most colourful aspect; one is trying to tip the scales despite being stood on by Saint Michael.

The old town is entered across one of two main bridges over the pretty Río Arlanzón, linked by a leafy *paseo*. The eastern of the two, the **Puente de San Pablo**, is guarded by an imposing mounted statue of El Cid, looming Batman-like above the traffic, heavy beard flying. The inscription risibly dubs him "a miracle from among the great miracles of the creator". The other, **Puente de Santa María**, approaches the arch of the same name, an impressively pompous gateway with a statue of a very snooty Carlos V. East of here is the **Plaza Mayor**, which is normally fairly lifeless. The **Casa Consistorial** has marks and dates from two of Burgos's biggest floods; it's hard to believe that the friendly little river could ever make it that high.

Other interesting buildings in the old centre include the **Casa de los Condestables**, with a massive corded façade. Felipe I (Philip the Fair) died here prematurely in 1506; it was also here that the Catholic Monarchs received Columbus after he returned from his second voyage. The ornate neo-Gothic **Capitanía** was the headquarters for the Nationalist *junta* in the Civil War.

Museo de la Evolución Humana and around
ⓘ *T902 024 246, www.museoevolucionhumana.com, Tue-Fri 1000-1430, 1630-2000, Sat 1000-2000, Sun 1000-1500, €6 (€4 for pilgrims). You can combine your visit with a trip to the excavation site at Atapuerca (see page 75) by prior reservation. This includes transport from the museum and costs €18, including entry to this museum, the interpretation centre at Atapuerca, and a visit to the excavations themselves.*
The excavations in the caves and galleries of the Atapuerca site near Burgos in recent years have completely changed ideas about the presence of prehistoric hominids in western Europe, and this excellent new museum brings together the information gleaned from here and other sites around the globe about our ancestors and distant cousins. Set on the riverbank in a striking building with limitless space and light, the display gives an overview of finds at Atapuerca and a comprehensive picture of our current knowledge of the numerous members of the 'homo' genus, as well as background on evolutionary theory and the voyage of the Beagle.

While Neanderthal man and homo sapiens both used the Atapuerca area, it is two earlier occupations that are most of interest here. Cosmogenic nuclide dating has put the oldest (so far) remains here at 1.3 million years old; they are sufficiently different to have been named as a new species, homo antecessor. There is evidence of their presence at Atapuerca until about 800,000 years ago. Later, Homo heidelbergensis, likely ancestors of the Neanderthals, lived here from around 600,000 years ago. The Atapuerca site is responsible for some 83% of excavated hominid material from this period, the middle-Pleistocene.

All panels are translated – perfectly – into English, as are the audiovisual features. While there are a few interactive exhibits, it's mostly a fairly serious archaeological and palaentological display, so the kids might get restless.

Not far away, and attractively set around the patioed **Casa Miranda** sections of the **Museo de Burgos** ⓘ *Tue-Sat 1000-1400, 1600-1900 (1700-2000 summer), Sun 1000-1400; €1.20, free at weekends*, are prehistoric finds from Atapuerca (see page 75), Roman finds from Clunia, religious painting and sculpture, and some more modern works by Burgalese artists.

Above the town, a park covers the hilltop, which is crowned by the **Castillo de Burgos** ⓘ *T947 288 874, Oct-Mar phone for weekday visits, Sat-Sun 1100-1400, Apr-Jun phone for weekday visits, Sat-Sun 1100-1400, 1600-1900, Jul-Sep daily 1100-1400, 1700-2030, €3.70, €2.60 without tunnels*. Heavily damaged by being blown up by the French in the Napoleonic Wars, it's recently been renovated and can be visited. A new museum summarizes some of the town and fortress's history, and the visit includes the sturdy ramparts and a claustrophobic trip into a system of tunnels dug deep into the hillside. It's a nice place to come on a sunny day, with excellent views down over the cathedral and plenty of woods to stroll in, and there are a couple of bars up here to enjoy a coffee or a drink at night.

Monasterio de las Huelgas

ⓘ *Tue-Sat 1000-1300, 1600-1730, Sun 1030-1400, €7, €4 for pilgrims, free Wed and Thu afternoons; bus Nos 5, 7 and 39 run here from Av Valladolid across the river from the old town.*
A 20-minute walk through an upmarket suburb of Burgos, the Monasterio de las Huelgas still harbours some 40 cloistered nuns, heiresses to a long tradition of power. In its day, the convent wielded enormous influence. The monastery was founded by Eleanor of England, daughter of Henry II and Eleanor of Aquitaine, who came to Burgos to marry Alfonso VIII in 1170. The Hammer of the Scots, Edward I, came here to get hitched as well; he married Eleanor, Princess of Castilla, in the monastery in 1254. Las Huelgas originally meant 'the reposes', as the complex was a favourite retreat for the Castilian monarchs. Here they could regain strength, ponder matters of state – and perhaps have a bit on the side; several abbesses of Las Huelgas bore illegitimate children behind the closed doors.

To keep the nuns separate from the public, the church was partitioned in the 16th century, and the naves separated by walls. The public were just left with a small aisle, where the visit starts. In here are a couple of curios: a moving pulpit that enabled the priest to address both the congregation and the separated nuns; and a strange statue of Santiago, sword in hand. Part of the coronation ceremony of the kings of Castilla used to involve them being knighted; as they judged no-one else in the land fit to perform the task, a statue of the saint with moveable arms used to perform the deed; this is probably one of those. There's also a retablo by the tireless Diego de Siloé in here.

The real attractions are on the nuns' side of the barricade. The church contains many ornate tombs of princes and other Castilian royals. These were robbed of much of their contents by Napoleon's soldiers. All were opened in 1942 and, to great surprise, an array of superb royal garments remained well preserved 700 years on, as well as some jewellery from the one tomb the French had overlooked. In the central nave are the tombs of Eleanor and Alfonso, who died in the same year. The arms of England and Castilla adorn the exquisite tombs. They lie beneath an ornate Plateresque *retablo*, which is topped by a 13th-century crucifixion scene and contains various relics.

Around a large cloister are more treasures; a *mudéjar* door with intricate wooden carving, a Moorish standard captured from the famous battle at Navas de Tolosa in 1212, and a postcard-pretty smaller cloister with amazing carved plasterwork, no doubt Moorish-influenced. For many, the highlight is the display of the clothing found in the tombs: strange, ornate, silken garments embroidered with gold thread. The colours have faded over the centuries, but they remain in top condition, a seldom-seen link with the past that seems to bring the dusty royal names alive.

Cartuja de Miraflores

ⓘ *Mon-Tue and Thu-Fri (closed Wed)1015-1500, 1600-1800 (1900 summer), Sat-Sun 1100-1500, 1600-1800 (1900 summer), free. Catch bus No 26 or 27 from Plaza de España and get off at the Fuente del Prior stop; the monastery is a 5-min walk up a marked side road. Otherwise, it's a 50-min walk through pleasant parkland from the centre of town.*

This former hunting lodge is another important Burgos monastery, also still functioning and populated by silent Carthusians. Juan II de Castilla, father of Isabel (the Catholic monarch), started the conversion and his daughter finished it. Like so much in Burgos, it was the work of a German, Hans of Cologne. Inside, the late-Gothic design is elegant, with elaborate vaulting, and stained glass from Flanders depicting the life of Christ. The wooden choir stalls are carved with incredible delicacy, but attention is soon drawn by the superb alabaster work of the *retablo* and the tombs that lie before it. These are all designed by Gil de Siloé, the Gothic master and they are the triumphant expression of genius. The central tomb is star-shaped, and was commissioned by Isabel for her parents; at the side of the chamber rests her brother Alonso, heir to the Castilian throne until his death at the age of 14. The *retablo* centres on the crucifixion, with many saints in attendance. The sculptural treatment is beautiful, expressing emotion and sentiment through stone. Equally striking is the sheer level of detail in the works; a casual visitor could spend weeks trying to decode the symbols and layers of meaning.

Monasterio de San Pedro de Cardeña

ⓘ *www.cardena.org, Tue-Sat 1000-1300, 1600-1800, Sun 1215-1300, 1615-1800; €2; wait in the church for a monk to appear; accommodation available at the monastery.*

Close to the city, at a distance of 10 km, the Monasterio de San Pedro de Cardeña is worth a visit, especially for those with an interest in the Cid. The first point of interest is to one side, in front of the monastery, where a gravestone marks the supposed burial site of the Cid's legendary mare, Babieca. The monastery has a community of 24 Cistercians; a monk will show you around the church, most of which dates from the 15th century. In a side chapel is an ornate tomb raised (much later) over the spot where the man and his wife were buried until Napoleon's troops nicked the bones in the 19th century; they were reclaimed and buried in Burgos cathedral. The *mudéjar* cloister dates from the 10th century and is the most impressive feature of the building, along with a late Gothic doorway in the *sala capitular*.

Atapuerca

ⓘ *T902 024 246, www.visitasatapuerca.com, 6 for the excavation areas, €5 for the thematic park. You can enter the area via Ibeas, 13 km east of Burgos on the N120, or the village of Atapuerca – take the N1 towards Vitoria, turn off at Olmos de Atapuerca and follow the signs. The Camino Francés passes through the village of Atapuerca. There's a visitor centre at both*

Ibeas and Atapuerca. Shuttle buses run from these visitor centres into the park, and also run from the Museo de Evolución Humana in Burgos. Check the museum's website for details and times of tours, as they vary greatly throughout the year.

Some 13 km east of Burgos, an unremarkable series of rocky hills have been the site of incredibly significant palaeontological and archaeological finds. Prehistoric human remains dated to over a million years were found here in 2008; the oldest known physical evidence of humans in Europe. Several fossilized remnants of Homo heidelbergensis have also been discovered here; dating has placed the bones from 500,000 to 200,000 years old. It's a crucial link in the study of hominid evolution; Neanderthals seemed to evolve directly from these Heidelbergers. A tour takes you round some of the most important excavation sites, and also to the thematic park, where there are some reconstructions and demonstrations of elements of the prehistoric hominid skillset, such as fire-making and bowmanship.

Burgos listings

For hotel and restaurant price codes and other relevant information, see pages 12-19.

Where to stay

Burgos *p68, map p70*

€€€ Hotel Cabildo, Av del Cid 2, T947 257 840, www.hotelcabildo.com. Well located, modern, and comfortable, this makes a reliable, if not spectacular, central base. Good facilities are allied with the suave contemporary decor, and helpful staff round out the experience.

€€€ Hotel La Puebla, C La Puebla 20, T947 200 011, www.hotellapuebla.com. An intimate hotel in the centre of Burgos with classy modern design, good facilities, and comfortable furnishings. Rooms are compact but comfortable, but the price seems a little elevated in high season. Parking available.

€€€ Hotel Mesón del Cid, Plaza Santa María 8, T947 208 715, www.mesondelcid.es. Superbly located opposite the cathedral, this hotel and restaurant is an excellent place to stay, with spacious, quiet and modern rooms and helpful staff. There are larger rooms and apartments available for families.

€€€ Hotel Velada Burgos, C Fernán González 6, T947 257 680, www.veladahoteles.com. Set in a beautifully converted old *palacio* in the heart of town, this stylish spot features sweet rooms with small bathrooms; most are duplex, with the sleeping area accessed via a staircase. Rooms are mostly quiet despite the noisy streets around here at weekends. You can get some good prices on their website.

€€€ Palacio de la Merced, C La Merced 13, T947 479 900, www.nh-hoteles.com. Attractively set in a 16th-century *palacio*, this hotel successfully blends minimalist, modern design into the old building, whose most charming feature is its cloister in Isabelline Gothic style. The rooms are comfortable and attractively decked out in wood. Extras such as breakfast and parking are overpriced. Recommended.

€€€ Silken Gran Teatro, Av Arlanzón 8, T947 253 900, www.hoteles-silken.com. Although primarily aimed at business visitors, this hotel makes a sound choice a short walk from the historic centre and right across a pedestrian bridge from the evolution museum. Rooms are quiet and comfortable, and, as is often the case with this chain, staff are excellent. There are good rates to be found online.

€€ Hotel Cordón, C La Puebla 6, T947 265 000, www.hotelcordon.com. A central, reasonable option, geared up for business travellers. Nothing stunning about the rooms, but there are very reasonable weekend rates if you book ahead. Free internet; Wi-Fi in some rooms.

€€ **Hotel Entrearcos**, C Paloma 4, T947 252 911, www.hotelentrearcos.com. Under the arcades on the main pedestrian street very near the cathedral, this makes a fine modern base in the heart of town. Rooms are compact but shiny and new, with free Wi-Fi that actually works, and helpful service to back it up. Prices are more than fair, especially off-season.

€€ **Hotel Jacobeo**, C San Juan 24, T947 260 102, www.hoteljacobeo.com. This smallish central hotel is well managed and features good en suite rooms with comfortable new beds in a pretty old building. Recently renovated, it features free Wi-Fi and DVD players in the rooms. It's pretty good value, particularly outside of the summer months.

€ **Albergue Municipal de Burgos**, C Fernán González 28, T947 460 922. One of the better municipal pilgrim hostels you'll find, this is spacious, modern and clean with comfortable bunks and a great location by the cathedral.

€ **Hostal Lar**, C Cardenal Benlloch 1, T947 209 655, www.hostallar.es. This quiet and decent place has well-priced en suite rooms with TV. The management is friendly; and despite pocket-sized bathrooms it's a good all-round budget option.

€ **Hostal Victoria**, C San Juan 3, T947 201 542. A good choice with friendly management, this *hostal* is central and relatively quiet, and the rooms with shared bath are comfortable and fairly spacious.

€ **Pensión Peña**, C Puebla 18, T947 206 323. An excellent cheapie, well located and maintained on a pedestrian street. The rooms are heated and have good shared bathrooms. It's often full, however, so don't hold your breath.

Restaurants

Burgos *p68, map p70*
Burgos is famous for its *morcilla*, a tasty black pudding filled with rice. Roast lamb is also a speciality here.

A popular new zone for tapas and late-night bars, known as Las Bernardillas, can be found around Plaza de Roma, in the spread-out Gamonal district northeast of the centre off the road to Vitoria. Bus No 1 will get you there from near the Puente de San Pablo.

€€€ **Casa Ojeda**, C Vitoria 5, T947 209 052, www.restauranteojeda.com. One of Burgos' better-known restaurants, backing on to Plaza de la Libertad. Traditional cuisine a bit on the heavy side, but good. Oven-roasted meats are the pride of the house, and the homemade foie is excellent. There's cheaper food available in the bar-café.

€€€ **El 24 de la Paloma**, C Paloma 24, T947 208 608, www.restauranteel24dela paloma.com. A smart restaurant near the cathedral with a range of succulent dishes like *cigalas* in tempura with cherry ketchup, or de-boned suckling pig. There's a degustation menu for €48, or a lunchtime one for €27 that includes roast lamb. They run regular themed Spanish wine tastings.

€€€ **Puerta Real**, Plaza Rey San Fernando s/n, T947 265 200, www.puertareal.es. On the cathedral square, this smart *asador* specializes in succulent roast meats, with lamb foremost among them. There's a set menu for €30, which includes that, as well as the other Burgos speciality *morcilla* and a decent Ribera wine. They also show a confident touch with fish dishes. Service here is excellent.

€€ **La Favorita**, C Avellanos 8, T947 205 949, www.lafavoritaburgos.com. This large barn-like spot is modern but feels traditional with its hanging hams, rows of wine bottles and wooden fittings. There's plenty of space to enjoy tasty *pinchos* – try the grilled foie gras or chopped ham with garlic mayonnaise for a rich treat – or *raciones* of traditional products. There's an attractive dining room out the back for sit-down meals. Recommended.

€€ **La Posada**, Plaza Santo Domingo de Guzmán 18, T947 204 578, www.restaurante laposada.net. This central spot is a likeable restaurant with a cheery downstairs bar that spills onto the street, and comforting and delicious home-style cooking in the upstairs *comedor*. Dishes, including soups and stews, are prepared to perfection.

€€ Mesón Burgos, C Sombrerería 8, T947 206 150, www.mesonburgos.com. Downstairs is one of Burgos' better tapas bars, famous for its *patatas bravas*. This is complemented by a friendly upstairs restaurant with good, if unexceptional fare. The service is good and the decor traditional and comfortable.

€€ Mesón La Cueva, Plaza de Santa María 7, T947 205 946, www.restaurante-lacueva.es. A small dark Castilian restaurant with good service and a traditional feel. The *menestra de verduras* is tasty and generous, and the roast meats are good.

€ Casa Pancho, C San Lorenzo 13, T947 203 405. One of several good options on this street, Casa Pancho is large, warm, light and stylish, with an array of excellent *pinchos* adorning the bar, and cheerful service. Anything involving prawns or mushrooms is a good bet.

€ La Cabaña Arandina, C Sombrerería 12, T947 261 932, www.lacabanaarandina.com. This spot near the cathedral is a Burgos favourite. It's cheery and light and there's plenty of competition to sit at the wooden tables and enjoy *raciones* of cheeses, *revueltos* or *morcilla*; or stand at the bar and sample the delicious tapas. Recommended.

€ La Cantina del Tenorio, C Arco del Pilar 10, T947 269 781, www.lacantinadeltenorio. es. This delicatessen and bar is a buzzy and cosy retreat from the Burgos wind. A range of delicious fishy bites and small rolls is strangely complemented by baked potatoes, given a Spanish touch with lashings of paprika. Characterful and friendly.

€ Los Herreros, C San Lorenzo 20, T947 202 448, www.mesonlosherreros.es. This old favourite is an excellent tapas bar with a big range of hot and cold platelets for very little; its popularity with Burgos folk speaks volumes.

€ Mesón La Amarilla, C San Lorenzo 26, T947 205 936. A good sunken bar serving some decent *tapas*, some seeming to use a whole jar of mayonnaise. There's a good cheap restaurant upstairs too, with a €12 *menú del día*.

€ Mesón San Lesmes, C Puebla 37, T947 205 956. This likeable little corner place offers cheerful cheap eats in a gregarious downmarket bar. Simple *raciones* of things like *callos* (tripe), calamari and mixed salad cost €5-10 and are filling and satisfying. Or you could weigh down the checked tablecloth with a monster *chuletón* steak.

€ Taberna Pecaditos, C Sombrerería 3, T947 278 573. The Burgos answer to the credit crunch: this upbeat little bar uses good-quality produce from its deli opposite and offers a range of tasty snacks and drinks, all at €1. Fill in your order using the forms at the bar.

Cafés

Café España, C Laín Calvo 12, T947 205 337. There's a sepia tinge to this venerable old-style café in the heart of Burgos. Warm in winter and with a terrace in summer, it's friendly and specializes in liqueur coffees.

Bars and clubs

Burgos *p68, map p70*
During the week, nightlife is poor, but it picks up at weekends, when on C Huerta del Rey the bars spill out onto the street.

Fox Tavern, Paseo del Espolón 4, T947 273 311. Impossible to miss, this is a decent pub that doesn't push the Irish theme too far. Comfy seats including a terrace looking up at the cathedral; the food is nothing special.

La Negra Candela, C Huerta del Rey 18, T947 202 844. One of the best options in this busy weekend drinking zone, warm and dark.

Ram Jam Club, C San Juan 29, T607 7 84 339. A popular basement bar with a good vinyl selection, mostly playing British music from the 1970s and 1980s. It's always filled with interesting people. The decor changes regularly; there's live music fairly often here too.

Entertainment

Burgos *p68, map p70*
Teatro Principal, Paseo del Espolón s/n, T947 288 873, on the riverbank.

Festivals

Burgos *p68, map p70*
Jan 30 Fiesta de San Lesmes, Burgos' patron saint.
Mar/Apr Semana Santa (Easter week) processions are important in Burgos, with a fairly serious religious character.
End Jun Fiesta de San Pedro, Burgos' main festival of the year.

Transport

Burgos *p68, map p70*
Burgos is a transport hub, with plenty of trains and buses for all parts of the country.

Bus
The bus station is handily close to town, on C Miranda just across the Puente de Santa María. All buses run less often on Sun.

Within the province buses run to **Aranda de Duero** 6-7 a day (1 hr 15 mins, €8), **Miranda** 3 a day, 0645, 1315, 2030, **Santo Domingo de Silos** 1 a day, 1730 Mon-Thu, 1830 Fri, 1400 Sat, none on Sun, **Roa** 1 a day Mon-Fri, 1800 (1 hr 30 mins), **Sasamón** 1 a day, 1830, none on Sun, **Castrojeriz** 2 a day, 1445, 1830, **Oña** 3 a day, 0645, 1300, 1830.

There are regular services roughly paralleling the Camino to **Logroño** (from €6, 2 hrs) and **León** (€15, 2 hrs) with intermediate stops. Burgos is also well connected with other Spanish cities such as **Madrid** and **Santander**.

Trains
The swish new Burgos train station is a long way from the centre in the northeast of town, and is connected by buses to the centre. There are several trains daily to **Madrid** (2½-4½ hrs, €33-43) via **Aranda**, 4 west to **León** via **Palencia** (2 hrs), and services east to **Vitoria**, **Logroño**, **San Sebastián** and **Zaragoza**. You can also buy tickets at a central booking office at C de la Moneda 19.

West from Burgos

For many people, Castilla is the image of Spain: a dry, harsh land of pious Inquisition-ravaged cities, ham, wine and bullfighting. Visitors tend to love or hate the dusty *meseta* with its extremes of summer and winter temperatures; it's a bleak, almost desert landscape in parts.

The main route to Santiago crosses the heart of the region and is dignified by numerous churches and monasteries in noble Romanesque or Gothic.

Burgos to Carrión de los Condes → *For listings, see pages 85-86.*

It's a flat, treeless 84-km trudge across the Castilian plateau from Burgos to Carrión de los Condes, and weather conditions – whether extreme heat or biting cold and wind – can make it an arduous one. Most pilgrims break the walk into three days. Nearly every village has a pilgrim *albergue*, so you can be fairly flexible as to where you stop. A long first day could take you as far as Hontanas via typical Castilian pueblos like Tardajos (from where there's a detour to Sasamón; see box, opposite) and Hornillos.

Castrojeriz and beyond

Some 9 km on from **Hontanas**, and also a popular overnight stop, Castrojeriz was formerly a Celtic settlement, and the *castro* hilltop structure has been preserved. There are three churches, linked by Calle Real. The **Church of San Juan** is the village's main attraction; it's a clean, if over-restored Gothic building influenced by the Burgos German tradition and features a nice double-columned cloister. As well as the bare ruin of a castle on the hill, there are a couple of other impressive buildings in the town, most notably the **Casa de Gutiérrez Barona**, a large knightly residence. This predates Castrojeriz's only moment in the spotlight. During the *comunero* revolt this town was deemed unlikely to rebel so the Council of Castilla took up residence here, and the place briefly buzzed with noblemen.

After Castrojeriz there's a short but killer climb rewarded by great views across the Castilian wheat belt. After you descend, it's more flat walking through landscape that changes little, crossing the Pisuerga river, passing through the village of Boadilla and then crossing the famous **Canal de Castilla** to reach Frómista. It's a long day but it's worth getting this far, for Frómista is one of the architectural highlights of the Camino.

Frómista

In northern Palencia, Frómista, as well as lying on the Camino de Santiago, is a compulsory stop on the Romanesque circuit. The reason is the **Iglesia de San Martín** ⓘ *winter 1000-1400, 1530-1800, summer 0930-1400, 1630-2000, €1, €1.50 with San Pedro*, a remarkable 11th-century Romanesque church, one of the purest and earliest, derived almost wholly from the French model that permeated the peninsula via the Pilgrim Route. From the outside it's beautiful, an elegant gem standing slightly self-satisfied in the sunlight. The church managed to survive the Gothic and baroque eras without being meddled with,

Sasamón

A little-walked but interesting detour is to follow the N120 from Tardajos, turn right at Olmillos de Sasamón and spend the first night out of Burgos in Sasamón, a few kilometres north of the main Camino. You can rejoin it the next day at Castrojeriz by following the BU404 via Villasandino.

The **Iglesia de Santa María la Real** ⓘ *daily 1100-1400, 1600-1900 (ask in the bar opposite if shut), €1.25 includes a helpful explanation by the knowledgeable and justly proud caretaker*, is its very lovely church in light honey-coloured stone. It was originally a massive five-naved space, but was partitioned after a fire destroyed half of it in the 19th century. The exterior highlight is an excellent 13th-century Gothic portal featuring Christ and the Apostles, while the museum has some well-displayed Roman finds as well as a couple of top-notch pieces; a couple of Flemish tapestries featuring the life of Alexander the Great, and a Diego de Siloe polychrome of San Miguel, the pretty-boy bully. It's fairly plain, a reflection of the Inquisition passing into irrelevance. In the church itself, two works of the German school stand out; the ornate pulpit, from around 1500, and a large baptismal font. A 16th-century Plateresque *retablo* of Santiago is one of many that adorn the building, so monumental for such a small town.

A statue of **Octavian** stands in a square nearby. The town of Segisama was used as a base in 26 BC for his campaigns against the Cantabrians and Asturians. The inscription reads *Ipse venit Segisamam, castro posuit* (then he came to Segisama and set up camp).

Don't leave town without checking out the **Ermita de San Isidro**, dominated by a massive 6-m carved crucifix that once would have stood at a crossroads to comfort weary travelling souls. Under Christ is the Tree of Knowledge, Adam, Eve, Cain and Abel. It dates from the 16th century and is a lovely work. Atop it is a nesting pelican; it was formerly believed that a pelican short of fish to feed the kids would wound itself in the breast to let them feed on its own blood. This became a metaphor for Christ's sacrifice, and pelicans are a common motif in Castilian religious sculpture.

but a late 19th-century restoration brought mixed benefits. While the building owes its good condition to this, it also has lost some of the weathered charm that makes the Romanesque dear. That said, the purity of its lines make it well worth a visit. Inside, it's the capitals of the pillars that attract the attention. While some were sculpted during the restoration (they are marked with an R, with creditable honesty), the others are excellent examples of Romanesque sculpture. There are no Biblical scenes – many of the motifs are vegetal, and some are curious juxtapositions of people and animals, particularly lions and birds. The church is crowned by an octagonal tower as well as two distinctive turrets.

Nearby, **San Pedro** is an attractive Gothic building with a small museum. There's a small **tourist information centre** on the main crossroads in town.

Villalcázar de Sirga

The Camino continues through an awesomely empty landscape before arriving at the village of Villalcázar de Sirga, which is built around a memorable church, **Santa María la Blanca** ⓘ *May to mid-Oct daily 1030-1400, 1700-1930, mid-Oct to Apr Sat 1200-1345, 1630-1800, Sun 1200-1345, €1, pilgrims €0.20*. It's a majestic sight, a massive Gothic affair quite out of proportion to everything else around it. The exterior highlights include a carved rose window and a portal topped by a frieze depicting the Pantocrator with evangelists and apostles, and, below, Mary in the Annunciation and the Adoration. Inside, particularly noteworthy are the painted tombs of the Infante don Felipe, prince and brother of King Alfonso X, and his wife. Both date from the late 13th century.

Carrión de los Condes and beyond → *For listings, see pages 85-86.*

Carrión de los Condes provides some relief after the hard slog across the Castilian plain, with a greener feel around the Carrión, the river on which the town lies. A couple of shabby churches can be found north of the main road, but the nicest part of town is around the plaza to the south of it. The **Iglesia de Santiago** is the town's showpiece, with an excellent late 12th-century façade, an unusual affair with zigzag columns and an actor doing a backflip among the figures on the archivolt. The Christ in Majesty has been described as the most impressive in Spain. There's also a small **museum** ① *Jun-Sep 1100-1400, 1700-2000, Oct-May Sat and Sun only, €1,* inside. Another church, **Santa María**, is a clean-lined affair with a large porch and some chessboard patterning. It's relatively unadorned inside apart from a massive gilt *retablo*. A statue of St Michael is camp even by his lofty standards; the archangel looks as if he's just stepped off the set of *Starlight Express*. On Thursday mornings, a market stretches between the two churches. There's a nice park by the river too. Just west of town, the monastery of **San Zoilo** has been converted into a beautiful hotel (see Where to stay, page 85).

La Olmeda and Quintanilla
Near Carrión are two of the little-known highlights of Palencia province, the Roman villas of La Olmeda and Quintanilla. **La Olmeda** ① *T979 119 997, www.villaromanalaolmeda.com, Tue-Sun 1030-1830, €5,* 18 km north of Carrión, near the town of Saldaña and just outside Pedrosa de la Vega, is the more impressive. Dating from the late first century AD, it was a sizeable building with defensive turrets, many rooms, and an attached bathhouse. Around the large central courtyard, rooms are decorated with geometrical and vegetal mosaic flooring, but in a larger room is a superb mosaic with Achilles and Ulysses as well as a hunting scene, with all manner of beasts in a flurry of complex activity. There are regular free guided tours (with English audio available), and multilingual information panels. There's also a café here.

A couple of kilometres away, **Saldaña** itself, an attractive if hard-bitten *meseta* town, has some of the finds from the two villas assembled in a **museum** set in an old church. There are some excellent pieces, particularly those found at a funerary complex by the Olmeda villa. Your entry ticket for Olmeda is valid here. Buses run to Saldaña via the turn-off for La Olmeda from Carrión de los Condes.

Quintanilla, just off the N120 west of Carrión, and 4 km south of the Camino, taking a left turn at Calzadilla de la Cueza, has a large **villa** ① *Apr-Sep Tue-Sun 1000-1400, 1700-2000; Oct and Mar 1030-1330, 1600-1800; closed Nov-Feb; €3,* featuring some excellent mosaics as well as a hypocaust underfloor heating system for the cold Castilian winters. The entry fee is €6 if you're going to visit both villas.

Carrión to Sahagún
It's 38 km from Carrión to Sahagún, so many pilgrims choose to spend the night short of here, but wherever you choose, allow some time in this, the first town in León province.

It's a flat but tough stage through typical *meseta* scenery. Some 12 km from Carrión, the Camino crosses the Cañada Real Leonesa, one of the historic transhumance routes used by herders to take livestock from the higher summer pasturelands to the winter grazing zones some 600 to 700 km south.

The Camino passes through **Calzadilla de la Cueza**, a deep-Spain farming village (from here you can detour to the Roman villa at Quintanilla), and then **Terradillos de los Templarios**, named for the Knights Templar who once maintained a pilgrim shelter here.

Beyond here, you pass through **San Nicolás** and then past the pretty Romanesque chapel of the **Virgen del Puente** before reaching Sahagún.

Sahagún and beyond → *For listings, see pages 85-86.*

Sahagún is one of those rare towns whose population is only a quarter of that it housed in the Middle Ages. These days it's a likeably out-of-the-way place; wandering its dusty streets it's hard to imagine that Sahagún was ever anything more than what it is today – an insignificant agricultural town of the thirsty *meseta*. Sahagún's main attraction is its collection of *mudéjar* buildings. These differ from Aragonese *mudéjar* and are to some extent Romanesque buildings made of brick.

The area around Sahagún was settled by Romans and the town is named for an early Christian basilica dedicated to a local saint, Facundo (the Latin name was *Sanctum Facundum*). The town began to thrive once Santiago-fever got going, and it gained real power and prestige when King Alfonso VI invited a community of Cluny monks to establish the Roman rite in the area. They built their monastery, San Benito, on the site of the old Visigothic church; once Alfonso had granted it massive privileges and lands, it became one of the most powerful religious centres of Spain's north.

Sahagún's most famous son was a 16th-century Franciscan missionary to the Americas, Friar Bernardino, a remarkable character. His respect for Aztec culture made him a controversial figure at the time; he mastered the *náhuatl* language and wrote texts in it. He is commemorated in his hometown by a small bust near the Plaza Mayor.

The **Iglesia de San Lorenzo** is the most emblematic of Sahagún's *mudéjar* buildings; a church dating from the early 13th century and characterized by a pretty belltower punctured with three rows of arches. The interior is less impressive, remodelled in later periods. It's worth climbing the tower if restoration work permits.

The **Iglesia de San Tirso** dates from the 12th century and is similar, with a smaller but pretty tower. The interior has suffered through neglect, but it's worth popping in to see the floats from Sahagún's well-known **Semana Santa** celebrations, as well as a well-carved 13th-century tomb, later reused. A spectacular church on the hill, **Santuario de la Virgen Peregrina**, formerly a Franciscan monastery, is finally undergoing much-needed restoration; when it reopens it should be the crowning *mudéjar* glory of the town. Especially notable is the little chapel at the back of the church, where fragments of superb Mozarabic stucco work were found when the plaster that covered them began to flake off in the mid-20th century. The chapel was commissioned by a local noble in the 15th century to house his own bones.

By the church is what's left of the **Monasterio de San Benito**; a clocktower and a Gothic chapel. The portal also survived and has been placed across the road behind the building; it's an ornate baroque work from the 17th century with impressive lions. Nearby, in the still-functioning Benedictine **Monasterio de Santa Cruz** ⓘ *guided tours Tue-Sat 1000,*

1100, 1200, 1600, 1700, 1800, Sun during mornings only, €2, is a small museum of religious art that also has architectural and sculptural fragments from the burned monastery.

Around Sahagún
If your legs aren't weary from peregrination, or if you've got a car, there's a good excursion from Sahagún. It's an hour's walk south to the **Convento de San Pedro de las Dueñas**, which preserves some excellent Romanesque capitals and attractive *mudéjar* brickwork. The keyholder is a curious old man named Pablo; if he doesn't appear, seek him out in the house below the castle by the main road.

Head east from the convent for around half an hour to **Grajal de Campos**, with an excellent castle of Moorish origin but beefed up in the 15th and 16th centuries. It's a very imposing structure indeed. There's not a great deal to see inside, but it's fun to climb the crumbling stairs and walls. While you're in town, have a look at the nearby *palacio*, which has seen better days but preserves an attractively down-at-heel patio. From here, it's about an hour back to Sahagún.

Sahagún to León
It's about 55 km from Sahagún to the capital of the province, a two-day walk that can be broken in any number of the Leonese villages along the trail. Bercianos del Real Camino, El Burgo Ranero, Reliegos, and **Mansilla de las Mulas** all have decent places to stay and typical adobe houses. There are few mules around in Mansilla de las Mulas these days, and what remains of its once proud heritage are the ruins of its fortifications. Some 8 km north, however, is the lovely Mozarabic **Iglesia de San Miguel de Escalada** ⓘ *Oct-Mar Tue-Sun 1040-1400, 1500-1750; Apr-Sep Tue-Sun 1015-1400, 1630-2000*. Dating from the 10th century, it was built by a group of Christian refugees from Córdoba. There's a pretty horseshoe-arched porch; the interior is attractively bare of ornament; the arches are set on columns reused from an earlier structure, and are beautifully subtle. A triple arch divides the altar area from the rest of the church. It's a lovely place and well worth the detour.

West from Burgos listings

For hotel and restaurant price codes and other relevant information, see pages 12-19.

Where to stay

Burgos to Carrión de los Condes *p80*
€ Albergue Restaurante El Puntido, C Iglesia 6, Hontanas, T947 378 597, www.puntido.com. Warmly welcoming and well-equipped pilgrim hostel, with a cheap and filling set menu served in the restaurant.

Castrojeriz and beyond *p80*
€€ Hotel Cachava, C Real 93, T947 378 547, www.lacachava.com. On the paved main street that winds through town, this is a welcoming choice for pilgrims to put their deserving feet up for a night. Rooms are simply decorated and comfortable, and meals and bikes are available for guests. There's a patio/garden to relax in on sunny days.
€ Camping Camino de Santiago, C Virgen del Manzano s/n, T947 377 255, www.campingcamino.com. This friendly campsite has a pilgrim hostel as well as bungalow accommodation.

Frómista *p80*
€ Albergue Canal de Castilla, C Estación, T979 810 193, www.alberguepelegrinos fromista.com. By the railway as you enter Frómista, this offers decent bunk accommodation in a barn-like dormitory. Evening meals available at a decent price. Open Apr-Oct.
€ Hostal San Telmo, C Martin Veña 8, T979 811 028, www.turismofromista.com. A great place to stay; a large, light and tranquil *casa rural* with large garden/courtyard and charming but cheap rooms.

Sasamón *p81*
There are various *casas rurales* for complete let; check www.toprural.com for details.
€ Casa Gloria, C Arco 1, T947 370 059. The village's main accommodation option, this is right opposite the church. It's cordial, clean and well presented; the simple heated rooms have spick and span white-sheeted beds and small bathrooms. The owner will lend you a bike, and you can eat downstairs.

Villalcázar de Sirga *p81*
€ Hostal Las Cántigas, C Condes de Toreno 1, T979 880 015, www.hostallascantigas.es. This excellent modern *hostal* is right by the church of Santa María la Blanca in this tiny and tranquil village. It makes a great rural base and is well priced. Rooms have bathroom, heating and there's a bar and restaurant.

Carrión de los Condes and beyond *p82*
€€ Real Monasterio San Zoilo, T979 880 050, www.sanzoilo.com. The best of several options. A characterful setting in an old monastery with a peaceful grassed garden. There's also a good restaurant with atmospheric beamed ceiling, offering quality local produce at fair prices.
€ Albergue Espíritu Santo, Plaza San Juan 4, T979 880 052. An excellent nun-run pilgrim hostel, with spacious, comfortable sleeping quarters (beds not bunks) and a welcoming attitude.
€ Hospedería Albe, C Collantes 21, T979 880 913, www.hostalalbe.es. Hospitable, pleasant and cool, with charming rustic decoration. A couple of rooms have their own kitchenette and cost a few euros more. Prices are very fair.

Sahagún and beyond *p83*
€€-€ Hostal El Ruedo, Plaza Mayor 1, T987 780 075, www.restauranteelruedo.com. This is a good choice, on the main plaza with clean modern rooms, recently renovated and equipped to hotel standard, above an *asador*. There are only 4 rooms so you might want to book ahead during peak pilgrim season.
€ Domus Viatoris, C Arco Travesía 25, T987 780 975, www.domusviatoris.com.

Helpful and cordial private pilgrim hostel with a good atmosphere and adequate if noisy dorm beds. There are also hostal-grade private rooms which are a good deal, and a restaurant.

Sahagún to León *p84*
€ Albergue La Parada, C Escuela 7, Reliegos, T987 317 880, www.alberguelaparada.com. New pilgrim hostel that's the best bet for a night's stop between Sahagún and León, as well as being about halfway. Friendly and comfortable, with good-value private rooms also available, and a restaurant.

Restaurants

Castrojeriz *p80*
€ La Taberna, C General Mola 43, T947 377 120. One of a handful of cheap restaurants catering to locals and pilgrims. It's decent and also has internet access and simple rooms.

Villalcázar de Sirga *p81*
€€ El Mesón de Villasirga, Plaza Mayor s/n, T979 888 022, www.mesondevillasirga.com. Great Castilian cooking at this hearty local.

Carrión de los Condes *p82*
€€ Bodegón El Resbalón, C Fernán Gómez 17, T979 880 799. This dark and inviting spot is in an attractively refurbished traditional building. Stone and wood give a typical bodega feel, and the typical local cuisine matches it. The €10 *menú* is worth waiting for.

Sahagún *p83*
€€€ Restaurante Luis, Plaza Mayor 4, T987 781 085. Sahagún is famous for its *puerros* (leeks), and the best place to try them is here; it's a great restaurant with a log fire, courtyard and a large fresco depicting market day. There's a *menú* for €12 at lunchtimes but it's much more interesting to go à la carte.

Transport

Castrojeriz *p80*
Bus Buses run from from **Burgos** to Castrojeriz twice a day (none on Sun).

Sasamón *p81*
Bus There are 2 buses a day to Sasamón from **Burgos** (none on Sun).

Frómista *p80*
Bus and train There are regular services to **Palencia**.

Carrión de los Condes *p82*
Bus Regular buses to **Palencia**, and services to **Burgos** and **León**.

Sahagún *p83*
Bus A few buses stop in Sahagún but they are significantly slower than the train.

Train There are a dozen or so feasible daily trains linking **León** and Sahagún, a journey of 30 mins. Some of the trains continue to **Grajal**, 5 mins away, before heading onto **Palencia**.

Sahagún to León *p84*
Bus There are buses at least hourly from **León** to **Mansilla** (20 mins). 2 buses continue Mon-Fri, and 1 Sat to **San Miguel de la Escalada** (40 mins).

León

León is one of the loveliest of Northern Spain's cities, with a proud architectural legacy, an elegant new town and an excellent tapas bar scene. Once capital of Christian Spain, it preserves an outstanding reminder of its glory days in its Gothic cathedral, one of the nation's finest buildings. After crossing the dusty *meseta* from Burgos, pilgrims arriving here should put their feet up for a couple of days and enjoy what León has to offer.

Arriving in León → *Phone code: 987. Population: 135,119. Altitude: 870 m.*
Getting there and around   León's bus and RENFE train stations are close to each other just across the river from the new town, a 10-minute walk from the old town. ▶▶ *See Transport, page 96.*

Best time to visit   Like Burgos, León's high-altitude results in freezing winters and roasting summers; spring and autumn are good times to visit, as there's little rain.

Tourist information   León's helpful main **tourist office** ⓘ *T987 237 082, Plaza de la Regla s/n, oficinadeturismodeleon@jcyl.es, Oct-Apr Mon-Sat 0930-1400, 1600-1900, Sun 0930-1700, May-Sep daily 0900-2000*, is opposite the cathedral.

Background

León was founded as a Roman fortress in AD 68 to protect the road that transported the gold from the mines in El Bierzo to the west. It became the base of the *Legio Septima*, the seventh legion of Imperial Rome; this is where the name originates (although León means 'lion' in Spanish). The city was Christianized in the third century and is one of the oldest bishoprics in western Europe. After being reconquered in the mid-eighth century, León became the official residence of the Asturian royal line in the early 10th century; the royals were thereafter known as kings of León. The city was recaptured and sacked several times by the Moors until it was retaken for the final time by Alfonso V in 1002. León then enjoyed a period of power and glory as the centre of Reconquista pride and prestige; the city flourished on protection paid from the fragmented *taifa* states.

As the Reconquista moved further south, however, León found itself increasingly put in the shade by the young whippersnapper Castilla, which had seceded from it in the 10th century. In 1230 the crowns were united, and León is still bound to Castilla to this day, a fact bemoaned by many – spraycans are often taken to the castles on the coat of arms of the region, leaving only the Leonese lion. When the Flemish Habsburg Carlos V took the throne of Spain, León feared further isolation and became one of the prime movers in the *comunero* rebellion. One of the most extreme of the *comuneros* was a Leonese named Gonzalo de Guzmán, who declared a "war of fire, sack and blood" on the aristocracy. The rebellion was heavily put down, and León languished for centuries.

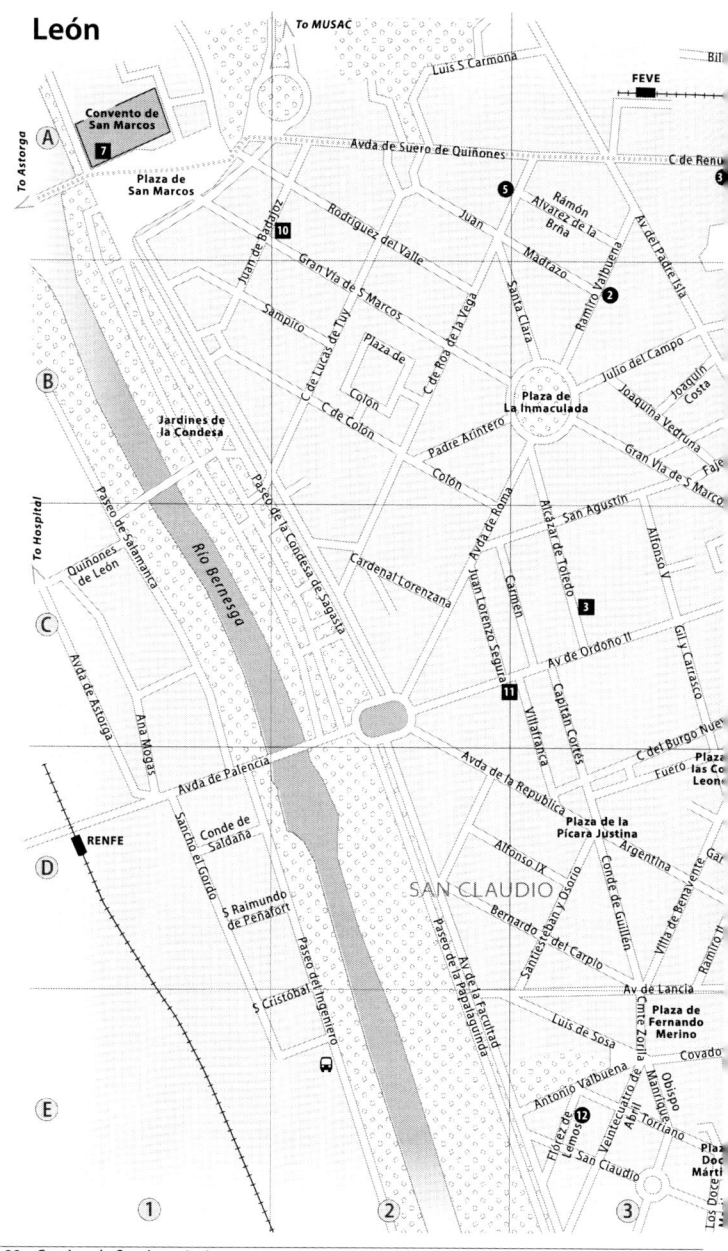

León

To MUSAC

To Astorga

Convento de San Marcos

Plaza de San Marcos

Luis S. Carmona

FEVE

Avda de Suero de Quiñones

C. de Renu

Juan de Badajoz

Rodríguez del Valle

Gran Vía de S Marcos

Sampiro

C de Lucas de Tuy

Plaza de Colón

C de Roa de la Vega

C de Colón

Juan Madrazo

Santa Clara

Ramiro Valbuena

Ramón Álvarez de la Brña

Av del Padre Isla

Jardines de la Condesa

To Hospital

Paseo de Salamanca

Quiñones de León

Río Bernesga

Paseo de la Condesa de Sagasta

Padre Arintero

Colón

Plaza de La Inmaculada

Julio del Campo

Joaquín Costa

Joaquina Vedruna

Gran Vía de S Marco

Faje

Avda de Astorga

Ana Mogas

Cardenal Lorenzana

Avda de Roma

Juan Lorenzo Segura

San Agustín

Alcázar de Toledo

Carmen

Alfonso V

Gil y Carrasco

Av de Ordoño II

Capitán Cortés

Villafranca

C del Burgo Nue

Plaza las Co Leon

Avda de Palencia

Avda de la República

RENFE

Sancho el Gordo

Conde de Saldaña

S Raimundo de Peñafort

Plaza de la Pícara Justina

Alfonso IX

SAN CLAUDIO

Bernardo del Carpio

Santiesteban y Osorio

Conde de Guillén

Argentina

Villa de Benavente Gal

Ramiro II

S Cristóbal del Ingeniero

Paseo de la Papalaguinda

Av de la Facultad

Luis de Sosa

Av de Lancia

Plaza de Fernando Merino

Covado

Antonio Valbuena

Flórez de Lemos

Veinticuatro de Abril

San Claudio

Obispo Manrique

Torriano

Plaza Doc Martí

Los Doce

(1) (2) (3)

88 • Camino de Santiago León

Where to stay

Albergue de las Benedictinas **12**
Hostal Albany **2** *C5*
Hostal Bayón **3** *C3*
Hostal Casco Antiguo **1** *B5*
Hostal Guzmán el Bueno **5** *B4*
La Posada Regia **6** *C4*
Parador de San Marcos **7** *A1*
París **8** *C5*
Pensión Blanca **11** *C2*
QH **4** *B5*
Quindós **10** *A2*
Reina **9** *D4*

Restaurants

Alfonso Valderas **1** *C4*
Casa Condeso **11** *B5*
El Besugo **27** *C5*
El Gran Café **6** *B5*
El Palomo **7** *C5*
Ezequiel **5** *A2*
Fornos **3** *B4*
La Competencia **10** *C5*
La Esponja **8** *B4*
La Poveda **2** *B3*
La Ribera **30** *B4*
La Trébede **14** *B4*
Las Termas **9** *C5*
L'Union **12** *E3*
Sabor de Grecia **32** *A3*

Bars & clubs

Cervecería Céltica **17** *B5*
León Antiguo **21** *B4*
Planet Móngogo **31** *A4*
Taxman **16** *A5*

···· Camino de Santiago

Camino de Santiago León • 89

The region's coal provided some prosperity in the 19th century, but it has really only been relatively recently that the city has lifted itself from stagnating regional market town to what it is today; a relatively modern and dynamic Spanish city.

Places in León → *For listings, see pages 93-96.*

León's **old town** is to the east of the River Bernesga and surrounded by the boulevards of the newer city. Walk up the pedestrianized Calle Ancha and prepare to be stunned by the appearance of the white Gothic cathedral, a jewel in Spain's architectural crown.

Cathedral

ⓘ *www.catedraldeleon.org, May-Sep Mon-Fri 0930-1330, 1600-2000, Sat 0930-1200, 1400-1800, Sun 0930-1100, 1400-2000, Oct-Apr Mon-Sat 0930-1330, 1600-1900, Sun 0930-1400, €5.*
Effectively begun in the early 13th century, León's cathedral is constructed over the old Roman baths; this, combined with the poor quality of the stone used and the huge quantity of stained glass, historically made the building fairly unstable. A late 19th-century restoration replaced many of the more decayed stones, an impressive engineering feat that required removing and replacing whole sections of the building.

Approaching the cathedral up Calle Ancha, its spectacular bulk is suddenly revealed. The main western façade is flanked by two bright towers, mostly original Gothic but capped with later crowns, the northern (left hand) one by one of the Churriguera brothers. Walking around the outside, there's some superb buttressing as well as numerous quirky gargoyles and pinnacles. Back at the main door, investigate the triple-arched façade, expressively carved. The central portal features a jovial Christ above a graphic Hell, with demons cheerfully stuffing sinners into cooking pots. To the right are scenes from the life of the Virgin; a brief biography of her son is on the left side.

The beautifully untouched Gothic interior of the cathedral is illuminated by a riot of stained glass, a patchwork of colour that completely changes the building's character depending on the time of day and amount of sun outside. The sheer quantity of glass is impressive; some 1700 sq m. The oldest glass is to be found in the apse and in the large rose window above the main entrance; some of it dates to the 13th century, while other panels span later centuries. There's a general theme to it all; the natural world is depicted at low levels, along with the sciences and arts; normal folk, including nobles, are in the middle, while saints, prophets, kings and angels occupy the top positions. Between midnight and 0100, the floodlights are turned off and the building illuminated from the inside, a spectacular sight. From April to September, at weekends there are very worthwhile visits at 2330 to a platform that allows a close-up appreciation of the stained glass under floodlights; book ahead.

Ongoing restoration work means that you can visit a platform in the cathedral's interior (accessed outside, down the side of the building) which lets you get up close to some of the magnificent stained glass. It's an excellent experience, especially the visits at 2330 at weekends, which allow you to appreciate the glass under floodlights.

Another of the cathedral's appealing attributes is that, although there's a Renaissance *trascoro* illustrating the Adoration and Nativity, there's a transparent panel allowing a perspective of the whole church, a rarity in Spanish cathedrals. The *coro* itself is beautifully and humourously carved of walnut, although you'll have to join one of the frequent guided tours to inspect it at close quarters. The *retablo* is an excellent painted work by Nicolás Francés, although not complete. Scenes from the lives of the Virgin and the city's patron, San Froilán, are depicted.

Much venerated is the 13th-century statue of the Virgen Blanca, in one of the apsidal chapels; there's also a replica of the elegant sculpture in the portal. Inside the north door of the cathedral is another Virgin, also with child; she's known as the Virgin of the Die, after an unlucky gambler lobbed his six-sider at the statue, causing the Christ-child's nose to bleed.

Also worth a peek are two excellent 13th-century tombs in the transepts. Holding the remains of two bishops involved in the cathedral's construction, they are carved with scenes from the prelates' lives; although heavily damaged, the representations are superb.

The **cathedral museum** ⓘ *Oct-Apr Tue-Fri 1000-1330, 1600-1900, Sat 1000-1330; May-Sep Mon-Fri 1000-1330, 1600-2000, Sat 1000-1200, 1400-1900, Sun 1000-1100, 1400-2000, €5, €2 cloister only, last museum visit 1 hr before closing*, is housed in the cloisters and sacristy. Most of the cloister is Renaissance in style, with several tombs of wealthy nobles and frescoes; note too the star vaulting. The museum, part of which is accessed up a beautiful Plateresque stair, has a good collection, with many notable pieces. Outstanding items include a Mozarabic bible dating from the 10th century, fragments of stained glasswork, and a superb crucifixion by Juan de Juni, portraying a twisted, anguished Christ.

Basílica de San Isidoro

ⓘ *Sep-Jun Mon-Sat 1000-1330, 1600-1830, Sun 1000-1330, Jul-Aug Mon-Sat 0900-2000, Sun 0900-1400, church free, Panteón €5, free Thu afternoon.*

As well as the Gothic cathedral, León also has a cracker of a Romanesque ensemble in the Basílica de San Isidoro. Consecrated in the 11th century over an earlier church, it was renamed in 1063 when Fernando I managed to get that learned saint's remains repatriated from Sevilla.

The complex is built into the medieval city walls, much of which is preserved. The façade is beautiful, particularly in the morning or evening light; it's pure Romanesque in essence, although the balustrade and pedimental shield were added, harmoniously, during the Renaissance, and there are Gothic additions in other parts of the building. Facing the building, the right-hand doorway is named the **Puerta del Perdón** (door of forgiveness); pilgrims could gain absolution by passing through here if they were too infirm to continue their journey to Santiago. The door is topped by a good relief of the Descent from the Cross and Ascension.

To the left is the **Puerta del Cordero** (door of the lamb), with an even more impressive tympanum depicting Abraham's sacrifice. Atop this door is the Renaissance pediment, decorated with a large shield surmounted by San Isidoro in Reconquista mode (like Santiago, this bookish scholar made surprise horseback appearances to fight Moors several centuries after his death). The interior of the church is dark and attractive, with later Gothic elements in accord with the Romanesque; large multifoil arches add a Moorish element. The *retablo* dates from the 16th century and surrounds a monstrance in which the Host is permanently on display (the basilica is one of only two churches in Northern Spain to have been granted this right). Below is a casket containing the remains of Isidore himself – or whoever it was whose bones were found in Sevilla long after the saint's burial place had been forgotten.

The real treasure of San Isidoro lies through another exterior door which gives access to the **museum**. On entering, the first chamber you are given access to is the Panteón Real, an astonishing crypt that is the resting place of 11 kings of León and their families. The arches, the ceiling and some of the tombs are covered with Romanesque wallpainting in a superb state of preservation (it's barely needed any restoration). There are scenes from the New Testament as well as agricultural life; if you're at all jaded with religious art and architecture, this sublime space will fix it. The short columns are crowned with well-carved capitals, mostly vegetal, but some with Biblical scenes or motifs derived from Visigothic traditions.

The next stop on the visit is the first of the two cloisters, above which rises the emblematic **Torre del Gallo** (tower of the cock), topped by a curious gold-plated weathercock that wouldn't look out of place at White Hart Lane. The original is now in the museum; recent studies have revealed that it was made in sixth-century Sasanian Persia.

The treasury and library is the other highlight of the visit to the museum. Although the complex was sacked and badly damaged by French troops in the Napoleonic Wars, most of the priceless collection of artefacts and books survived. More remains of San Isidoro reside in an 11th-century reliquary beautifully decorated in Mozarabic style; another reliquary is equally finely carved from ivory. The ornate chalice of Doña Urraca is made from two Roman cups and studded with gems. The library contains some beautiful works, of which the highlight is a 10th-century Mozarabic bible.

Convento de San Marcos

León's other great monument is the San Marcos convent by the river, which doubles as a sumptuous parador. Not a bad place to stay, you might think; so, no doubt, did generations of pilgrims who laid their road-dusted heads down here when it was administered as a monastery and hostel by the Knights of Santiago.

The massive façade is the highlight. It postdates the pilgrim era and is 100 m long, pure Plateresque overlaid by a baroque pediment, and sensitively dignified by a well-designed modern plaza. The church itself is attractive if rather unremarkable; more inspiring is the adjoining cloister with its figure-adorned arches. You can also access it from the parador. There are daily tours of the hotel, but it's easy enough to take a stroll around the ground floor areas; the bar lounge, and cloister are attractive and open to the public.

Next to the parador on the riverbank a crowd gather at weekends and on some weekday evenings to watch the curious game of *bolos*, in which old men toss a wooden ball at skittles aiming, not to knock them over, but to roll it in an arc between them.

Beyond the parador, cheerful coloured panels greet the visitor to **MUSAC** ① *T987 090 000, www.musac.es, Tue-Fri 1100-1400, 1700-2000, Sat-Sun 1100-1500, 1700-2100, €5, free Sun afternoon*, an upbeat contemporary art museum with rotating temporary exhibitions of varying quality. There's a cute gift shop and good café-restaurant here.

Old town

On the edge of León's old town, the **Museo de León** ① *Plaza Santo Domingo 8, T987 236 405, Tue-Sat 1000-1400, 1600-1900 (1700-2000 summer), Sun 1000-1400, €1.20*, opened its doors in early 2007 to some acclaim. It's a very impressive modern display that comprehensively covers the city's significant Roman, royal, and Jewish past, with good information in English too. Among the pieces on display is the famous Cristo de Carraza, an exquisite 11th century ivory crucifix.

Other sights in the old town include the nearby **Casa Botines**, a *palacio* built by Gaudí in subdued (for him) fairytale style. It now functions as an exhibition centre, but the top floors are a bank. The building's façade features St George sticking it to a dragon; a bronze sculpture of Gaudí observes his creation narrowly from a park bench outside. Next door is the elegant **Palacio de los Guzmanes**, a 16th-century Renaissance palace with a fine façade and beautiful patio. Across the square, the old Ayuntamiento is from the same period; next to it is the fine tower of **San Marcelo**.

Wandering around León's old quarter will reveal many time-worn architectural treasures and hidden nooks. The area north of Calle Ancha contains several, but the area south is the most interesting. This is the **Húmedo**, the 'wet' barrio, named after its massive collection of tapas bars, the most popular of which are around Plaza de San Martín, which hums with life most evenings and explodes at weekends. Near here is the beautiful **Plaza Mayor**, an extremely elegant porticoed 18th-century design that holds a fascinating and extremely traditional Wednesday and Saturday morning fruit and veg market. Delve a little further into the area and you'll come to the **Plaza de Santa María del Camino**, popularly known as Plaza del Grano (grain square) for its one-time wheat exchange. It's a lovely time-worn space with rough cobbles, wooden arcades and a pretty Romanesque church.

León listings

For hotel and restaurant price codes and other relevant information, see pages 12-19.

Where to stay

León *p87, map p88*

€€€€ Parador de San Marcos, Plaza San Marcos 7, T987 237 300, www.parador. es. One of Spain's most attractive hotels, housed in the former monastery and pilgrim hostel of San Marcos. The furnishings are elegant but not over the top, and the building itself is a treasure. The rooms are comfortable and attractive, even if they don't quite live up to the rest of the building. The restaurant is excellent.

€€€-€€ Q!H Hotel, Av de los Cubos 6, T987 875 580, www.qhehoteles.es. This brand-new boutique hotel has an excellent location on a wide pedestrian street just a few paces from the cathedral (some of the rooms have great close-up views of it) but in a quiet zone. The rooms are decorated with comfortable modern style, and the staff are most helpful. There's a spa complex and café too.

€€ Hostal Albany, C Paloma 13, T987 264 600, www.albanyleon.com. Right by the cathedral, this excellent modern hostal offers compact, comfortable rooms, friendly staff, and a worthwhile restaurant and pastry shop on site. There's no parking particularly close by though.

€€ Hostal Guzmán el Bueno, C López Castrillón 6, T987 236 412, www.hostal guzman.es. This is a good choice in the old town, with attractive woody rooms in a spruce old building in the barrio of the Cid. They're a little dark because it's on a narrow street, but they are well equipped, and the management is friendly.

€€ Hotel París, C Ancha 18, T987 238 600, www.hotelparisleon.com. This is something of a León hub; a bright family-run hotel on the main pedestrian street near the cathedral. The rooms are well-equipped and very comfortable for the price – with minibar, good bathroom and pillow menu. There's also a good café, and atmospheric downstairs restaurant and tapas bar.

€€ Hotel Quindós, Gran Vía de San Marcos 38, T987 236 200, www.hotelquindos.com. This is a very pleasant modern hotel near San Marcos, with inventively chic decor, modern art on the walls, rooms all decorated differently from each other and with plenty of colour, as well as an excellent restaurant. Good value.

€€ La Posada Regia, C Regidores 9, T987 218 820, www.regialeon.com. This is a superb, characterful place to stay in León's old quarter. Just off busy pedestrian C Ancha, this 14th-century building has enticing rooms with floorboards, pastel shades and many thoughtful touches; get one away from the street though, as there's a motorcycle shop next door. There's an equally charming new annexe opposite. The restaurant is good, but overpriced. Underground parking is very close by. Recommended.

€ Albergue de las Benedictinas, Plaza Santa María del Camino s/n, T987 252 866. In a convent on León's prettiest square, this pilgrim hostel has an appealing location and decent facilities, though the dorms are pretty tightly packed.

€ Hostal Bayón, C Alcázar de Toledo 6, T987 231 446. This is a fine and homely choice, with comfy rooms with en suite or shared bath in a friendly *pensión*. It's got character and it's quiet and leafy with house plants.

€ Hostal Casco Antiguo, C Cardenal Landázuri 11, T987 074 000, www.h-cascoantiguo.com. This newish spot is attractively modern and enjoys a fabulous location in the heart of old León, very close to the cathedral but on a quiet street. The rooms aren't huge but have good bathrooms; an added plus are the ruins of a Roman camp in the basement.

€ Hotel Reina, C Puerta de la Reina 2, T987 205 200. This hotel was a faded beauty until enterprising new management took it over; now it is charmingly Spanish retro and offers excellent value. Rooms are bright and cheery, and come with or without old-fashioned bathroom (only 2 rooms use each shared one). There's a lift and roof terrace, and always a genuine welcome. Recommended.

€ Pensión Blanca, C Villafranca 2, T987 251 991/678 660 244. This is an exceptional budget option; the rooms are light and colourful, tastefully decorated with brand new furnishings. Rooms have private or shared bathroom; guests have use of a kitchen and there's free internet access and a friendly owner. Breakfast is included in the price, and you can have your laundry done. Highly recommended.

Restaurants

León *p87, map p88*
Eating in León is a pleasure. Nearly all the tapas bars give a free snack with every drink; it's standard practice to order a *corto* (short beer) to take full advantage. The most concentrated tapas zone is around Plaza San Martín in the Barrio Húmedo; for a more sophisticated scene, head across C Ancha into the Barrio Romántico around Plaza Torres de Omaña.

€€€ Casa Condeso, Plaza Torres de Omaña 5, T987 170 613. The gold paint and turquoise frills around the lampshades mark this place as out of the ordinary, and the great *menú del día* (€15 weekdays) is equally memorable, with great modern cuisine in old-fashioned portions; it's worth phoning ahead for a spot in the attractive dining room. Recommended.

€€ Alfonso Valderas, Arco de Animas 1, T987 200 505. Famous for its *bacalao* (cod), this elegant but down-to-earth upstairs restaurant does it in myriad tasty ways. But don't be dissuaded if salt cod isn't your thing: the grilled meats are truly excellent, as are all the starters. Excellent service. Recommended.

€€ El Palomo, C Escalerilla 8, T987 254 225. A good little restaurant in the Húmedo area, with well-priced, high-quality fare and a friendly attitude. The cuisine is typically Leonese, with plenty of dishes to share as well as steaks and fine fish dishes. Order à la carte. Recommended.

€€ Ezequiel, C Roa de la Vega 4, T987 172 177, www.embutidosezequiel.es. Make a beeline for this combined chorizo shop and bar to try traditional Leonese cured meats. The tapas are incredibly generous and filling, but if you're still hungry, grab a table and try regional specialities like *botillo* or *cocido*. Good salads and warm-hearted service round out the experience. Recommended.

€€ La Esponja, Pl del Cid 18, T987 237 504. In the heart of the best barrio for tapas, this restaurant has warm rustic decor and attentive service. There's a simple, cheap, and good *menú del día* and excellent traditional à la carte options at reasonable prices.

€€ La Poveda, C Ramiro Valbuena 9, T987 227 155. This traditional restaurant fills up fast, for the quality is very high. Dishes are mostly *raciones*, and are absolutely delicious – the *sesos* (brains) have incredible flavour and texture, and the octopus is as good as you'll get outside Galicia.

€€ Las Termas, C Paloma 13, T987 264 600, www.restaurantelastermas.es. An excellent lunch *menú* is the main reason to come to this spot near the cathedral. For €16, you get a wide choice of generously sized dishes. Keep your eyes peeled for rice dishes for 2, normally on Thu; they're prepared fresh to order, and are enormous and delicious. The desserts are always tasty too, as they own the pastry shop round the corner.

€ El Besugo, C Azabachería 10, T987 256 995. This is an old-style León tapas bar; a big spacious place that doesn't deal in frills but rather simple free *morcilla* and *jamón*. There are tables to devour reliable and good-value *raciones* of the same sort of fare, and an upstairs restaurant.

€ Fornos, C El Cid 8, T680 857 544. This longstanding León favourite in new premises specializes in traditional Leonese fare, accompanied by a range of wines. Grab a table and try the delicious *ensaladilla rusa*, calamari, the *mollejas*, or any of the other tasty *raciones*. Good tapas at the bar too.

€ La Competencia, C Conde Rebolledo 17/C Mulhacín 8, T987 212 312, www.pizzerialacompetencia.com. A León classic, this deservedly popular place serves very good cheap pizzas in 2 locations in the heart of the Barrio Húmedo. They serve until late at weekends; the 2-level bar at C Mulhacín is also much visited as a tapas bar.

€ La Ribera, C Fernando González Regueral 8, T987 270 408. The locals crowded into this place will show you that it's one of León's best tapas options. Once you squeeze your way to the bar, you'll find out why; as well as the home-made fried potatoes, you can enjoy some of the tastiest innards around: tripe, kidneys and *asadurilla* to remember. If that's not your thing, try the delicious mussels or calamari. Recommended.

€ La Trébede, Pl Torres de Omaña 1. Decorated with everything from old farming implements to stuffed reptiles, this cosy neighbourhood bar is consistently busy. There's always an interesting tapa to go with your wine, and the chatty buzz makes this one of the town's best.

€ L'Unión, C Flórez de Lemos 3, T987 261 710, www.vegetarianoleon.com. Quality vegetarian places are thin on the ground in Spain, but this place certainly fits the bill. Simple decor, but excellent and innovative plates are served in generous quantity and can be washed down with organic wine. The *menú* is great value for €10.50.

€ Sabor de Grecia, C Renueva 11, T987 224 628. A welcoming family-run restaurant not far from San Isidoro, this is much visited for its short but very delicious menu of Greek cuisine. Dishes such as meatballs or broad beans ooze with flavour, and can be accompanied by a number of Greek wines. Recommended.

Cafés

El Gran Café, C Cervantes 9, T987 272 301, www.elgrancafeleon.com. This classic-looking café is a popular and atmospheric spot for an afternoon coffee, but it really hits its straps in the evenings, when there's regular live music. Tue jam sessions are lots of fun and pack the place out.

Bars and clubs

León *p87, map p88*
León's nightlife is busy; the **Barrio Húmedo** is the best place for concentrated action – wander around these streets and you'll find any number of bars that will suit you.

Cervecería Céltica, C Cervantes 10, T987 072 438. This large and bright bar has an excellent range of Belgian beers, and several draught options, all expertly poured. Always buzzy and cheerful.

León Antiguo, Plaza Ordoño IV s/n, T987 226 956. A good bar with a friendly upmarket vibe and a nice outdoor terrace in the quieter part of the old town. Always busy and cheerful.

Planet Móngogo, Plaza Puerta Castillo 5. Open Tue-Sun from 1800. People come from all over Northern Spain to visit this unique bar/restaurant, which blends trash horror, psychobilly, and high-quality, low-priced 'Hell-Mex' food among a riot of voodoo, zebra stripes and leopard spots. It's a spot you won't forget in a hurry. Highly recommended.

Taxman, C Babia 6. By the car park behind the cathedral, this bar has a loyal following thanks to its excellent service, good coffee, and beautifully poured drinks. The theme is The Beatles, whose mugshots are everywhere, but they happily play other music on request.

Festivals

León *p87, map p88*
Mar/Apr León's Semana Santa (Easter Week) is a very traditional, serious affair, with many mournful processions conducted by striking hooded *cofradías* (religious brotherhoods and sisterhoods). Carrying the *pasos* (floats bearing sculptures of Jesus and Mary) is thirsty work; relief comes in the form of *limonada*, a *sangría*-like punch; a throwback to Christian Spain's dark past is that going out to drink a few is traditionally known as *matar judíos* ('kill Jews').
Late Jun The feasts of San Juan (24 Jun) and San Pedro (28 Jun) are León's major fiestas of the year. There's a good range of activities over 10 days, including bullfights, concerts and high alcohol consumption.
Early Oct Fiesta de San Froilán, the city's patron, is the first weekend of Oct. There's a Moorish/medieval market, processions and dances; there's also a good Celtic music festival.

Shopping

León *p87, map p88*
The main shopping street is Av Ordoño II in the new town; more quirky shops can be found in the old town.

Books
Galatea, C Sierra Pambley 1, T987 272 652, near the cathedral, has a surprising and high-quality selection of English-language fiction and non-fiction.
Iguazú, C Plegarias 7, T987 208 066. A good place to go for maps and travel literature.

Transport

León *p87, map p88*
Bus Within the province, **Astorga** (30-45 mins) is served hourly, **Sahagún** 2-3 times daily (1 hr), **Ponferrada** hourly (1-2 hrs), and Villafranca del Bierzo 3 times daily (2½ hrs).

There are regular departures to **Madrid** and other major cities in the area, including **Burgos** and **Valladolid** (via its airport).

Train From the RENFE station, trains run to **Madrid** 9 times a day (2¾-4½ hrs, €35-45), north to **Oviedo** (2 hrs, €9-20) and **Gijón** 7 times, east to Barcelona 3 times daily (10-11 hrs) via **Palencia**, **Burgos**, **Logroño**, **Vitoria**, **Pamplona** and **Zaragoza**, and 2 daily westwards to **A Coruña** and **Santiago**.

A dozen trains run east to **Sahagún**, and several daily go west to **Astorga** and **Ponferrada**.

Directory

León *p87, map p88*
Medical services Hospital Virgen Blanca, C Altos de Nava, T987 237 400. Call 112 in an emergency. **Police** Paseo del Parque s/n, T987 255 500.

West of León

Although joined in semi-autonomous harmony with Castilla, the province of León is fairly distinct, and offers a different experience to the vast Castilian plain. In fact, it's got a bit of everything; a look at the map confirms that it's part *meseta*, part mountain and part fertile valley.

León was an important early kingdom of the Christian Reconquest, but soon lost ground and importance as the battlegrounds moved further south and power became focused around Valladolid and then Madrid. Mining has been a constant part of the area's history: the Romans extracted gold in major operations in the west of the province, while coal, cobalt and copper are all still extracted, although with limited future.

The west of the province is a region of hills and valleys known as El Bierzo. It's a busy, rural zone of grapevines, vegetables, mines and more; further exploration reveals superb natural enclaves and vibrant local fiestas.

The pilgrim route heads west from León, stopping in the towns of Astorga, Ponferrada and Villafranca del Bierzo; they are all good places to regain lost strength for the climb into Galicia and the last haul of the journey.

The Maragatos

The matter of origin of the Maragatos has provoked much scholarly and unscholarly debate. They have been variously touted as descendants of Moorish prisoners, Sueves, Visigoths and Phoenicians, but no one is really sure. Until fairly recently they kept pretty much to themselves; it is still common to see them in their characteristic national dress. The men wear a red waistcoat, bowler-style hat and a black tunic, while the women have a shawl and a headscarf.

The Maragatos are famous for their *cocido*, which is served in reverse to the standard Spanish custom; the meal starts with the stewed meats: usually a bit of everything, chicken, lamb, sausage and chunks of pork from various parts of the pig. The chickpea and cabbage part of the stew follows on a separate plate, and is washed down by the broth after. There are many restaurants in Astorga serving it up, but some of the best are in the small villages of the *maragatería*, the surrounding district.

León to Astorga

The road (and the Camino de Santiago) west from León starts out through urban sprawl to the village of **Virgen del Camino**, where a modern church houses a respected Virgin. Beyond here, the village of **Hospital de Orbigo**, reached via a long medieval bridge, is a reasonably attractive little place famous for its trout soup, and the best option for pilgrims to stop over between León and Astorga, with several decent *albergues* to choose from. The bridge was the scene of a curious event in 1434. A local noble, iron chain around his neck and doubtless suffering some form of insecurity, decided to take up residence on the bridge for the fortnight leading up to the feast day of Santiago. Passing pilgrims were forced to either declare his chosen lady the most beautiful in Christendom or have a joust with the knight or one of his heavies: just what a penniless peregrine needed after another hard day's slog across the plains. The event became known as the *Paso Honroso*; how fair the fights were is not known, but the knights unhorsed over 700 pilgrims, killing one and wounding several more. Ah, for the days of chivalry. In early June, the event is commemorated in a fiesta, with everyone dressed in medieval costume, and jousts held on the *vega* below the bridge.

Astorga and around → *For listings, see pages 102-104.*

While Astorga has an interesting history, nothing much goes on here now. However, it's a very pleasant, relaxed place with some attractive buildings and a peaceful small-town atmosphere. Astorga and its surrounding villages are particularly famous for being the home of the Maragatos (see box, above), a distinct ethnic group that for centuries were considered the bravest and most trustworthy of muleteers and guides.

As a major Roman centre for administering the gold-mining region further to the west, Astorga was known as Asturica Augusta, having been founded by Augustus during his campaigns against the never-say-die tribes of the northwest of the peninsula. Astorga was one of the earliest of Christian communities in Spain; the archbishop of Carthage, San Cipriano, wrote a letter to the presbyter and faithful of the town as early as AD 254. After the disintegration of the Empire, the area was settled by the Sueves who made the journey from Swabia, now in southwest Germany. They made Astorga their capital and fought constantly with the Visigothic rulers until Astorga finally fell for good in the sixth century.

Astorga's most important sight is its **cathedral** ⓘ *Oct-Apr Mon 0900-1030, Tue-Sat 0900-1400, 1600-1800, Sun 1100-1400, May-Sep Mon 0900-1030, Tue-Sat 0900-1400, 1600-2000, Sun 1000-1400, cathedral free, but entry after 1100 includes the Museo Diocesano, €2.50*, on which construction began in the 15th century. The best view of the cathedral is to be had from below it, outside the city walls. Most of it is in late Gothic style, but the façade and towers are later baroque constructions and seem overlarge and ornate for the comparatively small town. The sculptural reliefs depict events from Christ's life, and are flanked by numerous cherubs and flights of Churrigueresque fancy. Inside, the marble *retablo* is impressive, while the highlight of the are the paintings of the temptations and trials of St Anthony, who is bothered during his hermitage by some memorable demons.

Next to the cathedral, the **Palacio Episcopal** ⓘ *Tue-Sat 1100-1400, 1600-1800, Sun 1100-1400; summer Tue-Sat 1000-1400, 1600-2000, Sun 1000-1400, €3 (€5 including Museo Diocesano)*, is something of a contrast. In 1887 a Catalan bishop was appointed to Astorga. Not prepared to settle for a modest prefab bungalow on the edge of town, he decided that his residence was to be built by his mate, a man called Gaudí. The townsfolk were horrified, but the result is a fairytale-style castle with pointy turrets. Little of the interior was designed by the man, as he was kept away by the hostility of the locals, but there are a couple of nice touches, notably in the bishop's throne room and chapel. Much of the (chilly) interior is taken up by the **Museo de los Caminos**, a collection of art and artefacts relating to the pilgrimage to Santiago. The garden is guarded by some scary angels. The **tourist office** ⓘ *Tue-Sat 1000-1400, 1600-1900, Sun 1000-1400*, is opposite the Palacio Episcopal.

Astorga's **Plaza Mayor** is attractive, and notable for the figures of a Maragato man and woman that strike the hour on the town hall clock. Some of the city's Roman heritage can be seen at the **Museo Romano** ⓘ *Tue-Sat 1000-1400, 1600-1800 (1700-1930 summer), Sun 1100-1400, €3*, constructed over some of the old forum by the Ayuntamiento. Finds from many of the archaeological excavations around the town are on display. There are many **Roman remains** of interest around the town; the tourist office will provide a map of the *Ruta Romana*; there are guided tours in the summer.

Another museum is the **Museo de Chocolate** ⓘ *Tue-Sat 1030-1400, 1600-1800 (1630-1900 summer), Sun 1100-1400, €2.50*, where you can learn how chocolate was, and is, made.

Around Astorga

Some 5 km from Astorga, and an easy detour off the Camino, **Castrillo de los Polvazares** is somewhat touristy, but it's the most attractive of the **Maragato villages** (see box, opposite). Built of muddy red stone, it's been attractively restored, and you still expect the rattle of mulecarts down its cobbled streets. There are many other less-developed Maragato villages around that are worth checking out if you've got transport. There are around 40 or 50 of them in all; some of the nicest are **Murias de Rechivaldo**, **Luyego** and **Santiago Millas**. All have at least one hearty restaurant dishing up the famed *cocido*.

Astorga to Ponferrada

It's a tough first day out from Astorga, a slow but unremitting climb of some 600 m until you reach the semi-abandoned mountain village of **Foncebadón**, which sits at 1430 m. There's a clutch of pilgrim hostels here, and a convivial atmosphere. Even in summer, nights can be freezing and visibility low, so be prepared.

Just beyond Foncebadón, the Cruz de Ferro marks the high point between the Maragatería and the Bierzo region. There's an iron cross here atop a tall mast; it's a pilgrim tradition to add a stone to the cairn by tossing it over your shoulder with your back to the cross.

From here, it's a tiring and often steep descent down a stony path to the fertile Bierzo valleys.

El Bierzo → *For listings, see pages 102-104.*

The Bierzo is crisscrossed by middling mountain ranges and pretty valleys. The Romans mined gold and other metals here, and some coal mines are still creaking on towards their inevitable closure. It's now mainly famous for red wine and vegetables; its peppers have DO (*denominación de origen*) status and are famous throughout Spain. There are many hidden corners of the region to investigate; it's one of Northern Spain's least known and most interesting corners that could merit a sizeable guidebook on its own.

Molinaseca

Some 5 km southeast of Ponferrada, on the Camino de Santiago, this excellent stone village, famous for its *embutidos* – chorizo, *salchichón* and the like – sits by a babbling river, scene of a frenetic water-fight during the village fiestas. It's full of bodegas that have been converted into bars, where the typical order is a cheap local wine that comes with a hunk of bread and slice of *chorizo*. It's particularly popular on Sundays with folk from Ponferrada. There's a pilgrim hostel here, and plenty of accommodation and eating options. For pilgrims it may make a more relaxing stay than Ponferrada itself.

Ponferrada

Although afflicted by rampant urban sprawl, industrial Ponferrada has a small, attractive old centre above the river Sil. It's a fast-growing and vibrant young city and capital of the Bierzo region, whose fruity red wines are growing in fame outside Spain. The main feature of the centre is a superb **Templar castle** ⓘ *Tue-Sat 1030-1400, 1600-1800, Sun 1100-1400, open until 2030 Jul-Aug, €6, free Wed*, low but formidable, with a series of defensive walls and a steep underground passage descending to the river.

Some lovely buildings are preserved in the old town; check out the small lanes around the **Plaza de Ayuntamiento**, an attractive space in itself; nearby a pretty clocktower arches across the street. The **Basílica de la Virgen de Encina** sits in another square and is an attractive building. The **Museo del Bierzo** ⓘ *Tue-Sat 1100-1400, 1600-1900 (1700-2030 May-Sep), Sun 1100-1400, €2.70*, set in an old *palacio* in the centre, is a good display, with items of interest from the region's Celtic cultures as well as the Templar period. There's a nice patio and cobbled courtyard. There's also a small **railway museum** ⓘ *Tue-Sat 1100-1400, 1600-1900 (May-Sep 1700-2030), Sun 1100-1400, €2.70*, on the edge of the new town, with several lovable old locomotives. The **tourist office** is by the castle walls.

Valle del Silencio

One of the most charming spots in Northern Spain is this hidden valley south of Ponferrada. The treeless plains of Castilla seem light years away as you wind through grape vines into the narrow valley carved by the River Oza. Chestnuts and oaks, as well as abundant animal and bird life accompany the cheerful stream through villages that are utterly tranquil and rural. A circular walk around the valley, waymarked PR L-E 14, is an excellent way to spend a day; it takes about six hours.

The village of **Villafrancos** is one of the prettiest in the valley, with a delightfully picturesque stone bridge, and villagers going about their business as if the passing of centuries is a curious but inconsequential matter.

Perched below the hamlet of **San Pedro de Monte**, signposted down a side road, is a monastery, mostly in ruins but of a venerable age. You can visit its baroque church, which has a Romanesque tower. The Valle del Silencio road ends at **Peñalba de Santiago**, and you feel it's done well to get this far. Peñalba, a village of slate where three mountain ranges meet, has eked out an existence on chestnuts for centuries. The village, though, is in good modern repair (restored a few years ago to beautiful effect); it's a grey beauty, with wooden balconies and an ends-of-the-earth feel. Enjoy a glass of home-made wine and a tapa of *cecina* at Cantina opposite the church, a bar steeped in tradition and the focus of village life.

The centrepiece of the village is a 10th-century **Mozarabic church** ⓘ *Oct-Mar Wed-Sat 1040-1400, 1600-1750, Sun 1040-1400, Apr-Sep Wed-Sat 1015-1400, 1630-2000, Sun 1015-1400*, which belies its solid exterior with elegant horseshoe arches inside, as well as many fragments of wall painting.

It's about a four- to five-hour stroll from Ponferrada to Peñalba, through beautiful surroundings; much of the distance is a marked trail that follows the river. ▶▶ *See Transport, page 104.*

Through the Bierzo

It's an easy day's walk from Ponferrada to **Villafranca del Bierzo**, for many pilgrims the last overnight stop before entering Galicia itself. En-route you'll see several typical Bierzo settlements. By adding a worthwhile extra 3 km to your route (turn off at Camponaraya and rejoin in Cacabelos), you can take in the noble semi-ruined monastery of **Santa María de Carracedo** ⓘ *Oct-Mar Tue-Sun 1000-1400, 1600-1800, Apr-Sep Tue-Sun 0930-1430, 1700-2000, €1.80.*

Villafranca del Bierzo

The next stop after Ponferrada for most Santiago-bound walkers is Villafranca del Bierzo. An attractive town, it's a nice spot to gather strength and spirit before the long ascent into Galicia. In medieval times, many pilgrims were by this stage not physically capable of continuing into the harsher terrain and weather conditions. That being the case, if they reached the church here, they were granted the same absolutions and indulgences as if they had completed the whole journey to Santiago. The **Iglesia de Santiago** is where they had to go, at least from when it was built in the late 12th century. Although Romanesque, it's unusual in form, with a cavernous, barn-like interior with a calming feel. There's a crucifixion above the simple altar, with Christ looking very old and careworn; the side chapel is a more recent affair with an 18th-century *retablo*. The side door, the Puerta del Perdón, is what the pilgrims had to touch to receive all the spiritual benefits of their journey. It has some nice capitals around it, including one of the three wise men cosily bunked up in a single bed.

Nearby, the foursquare **castle** has big crumbly walls as well as a restored section. It's still lived in and therefore cannot be visited. There's a late **Gothic Colegiata** with some local architectural influences; near here make a point of walking down Calle del Agua, a superbly atmospheric street lined with old buildings. Villafranca's **tourist office** ⓘ *daily 1000-1400, 1600-1900 (2000 summer)*, is very helpful.

West of León listings

For hotel and restaurant price codes and other relevant information, see pages 12-19.

Where to stay

León to Astorga *p98*
€ Albergue San Miguel, C Alvarez Vega 35, Hospital de Orbigo, T987 388 285, www.alberguesanmiguel.com. Excellent pilgrim stop with a welcoming attitude and good atmosphere. No dinners but there's a kitchen and plenty of options in the village.

Astorga *p98*
€€ Hotel La Peseta, Plaza San Bartolomé 3, T987 617 275, www.restaurantelapeseta.com. Good rooms above what is widely considered one of Astorga's best restaurants. The rooms are excellent for this price, and the staff incredibly welcoming.
€ Albergue Siervas de María, Pl San Francisco 3, T987 616 034, www.caminodesantiagoastorga.com. Deservedly popular hostel run by the local Friends of the Camino association. There's a big capacity, but the dorms are spacious and uncrowded. Facilities, which include free Internet terminals, are excellent.
€ Pensión García, Bajada Postigo 3, T987 616 046. One of the cheaper choices in town, this is clean and decent, if fairly unremarkable.

Around Astorga *p99*
€€ Cuca la Vaina, C Jardín s/n, Castrillo de los Polvazares, T987 691 078, www.cucalavaina.es. If you're exploring the area, this is a top base in the village of Castrillo de los Polvazares, with a lively bar and excellent restaurant. The rooms are rustic and beautiful, with elaborately carved headboards, and much-needed heating in winter.

Astorga to Ponferrada *p99*
€ Albergue Domus Dei, C Real s/n, Foncebadón. Actually set in the back of the village church, this isn't perhaps the most luxurious of Foncebadón's various pilgrim hostels, but it gets close to the heart of the pilgrimage with its genuine welcome, communal prayer/meditation time and convivial shared meals. Open Apr-Oct.

Molinaseca *p100*
€ Albergue de Peregrinos de Molinaseca, Av Fraga Iribarne s/n, T987 453 077. There are 2 *albergues* in Molinaseca, 1 municipal and 1 private, both run by the same person and both good. This, the municipal one, is simple but comfortable.

Ponferrada *p100*
Few of Ponferrada's accommodations are in the old town; most are in the new zone across the river.
€€ Hostal La Encina, C Comendador 4, T987 409 632, www.hostallaencina.com. Parked right beside the castle, this is pricier than some of the many cheaper *hostales* around Ponfe, but worth it for the warm rustic decor and the amiable owner.
€€ Hotel Bierzo Plaza, Plaza del Ayuntamiento 4, T987 409 001, www.aroihoteles.com. This appealing modern hotel has an excellent location in central Ponferrada, on the town hall square and warm, professional service. The rooms are decorated with a light touch, and are good value for the price. There's a popular café downstairs. Recommended.
€ Albergue San Nicolás de Flüe, C la Loma s/n, T987 413 381. Named after the patron saint of Switzerland, this is a very comfortable and well-equipped place, with just 4 berths in most of the rooms.

Villafranca del Bierzo *p101*
There are several good places to stay in Villafranca.
€€€ Parador Villafranca del Bierzo, Av Calvo Sotelo-Constitución s/n, T987 540 175, www.parador.es. Recently renovated in neo-rustic style, this

comfortable modern parador offers good views, a garden, outdoor pools, and a high level of service and food.

€€ Hotel San Francisco, Plaza Mayor/ Generalísimo 6, T987 540 465, www. hotelsanfrancisco.org. Closed Dec-Feb. This is a solid option on the attractive main plaza. As it's right in the centre, you pay a little for location, but it's an enjoyable place to stay.

€ Albergue de la Piedra, C Espíritu Santo 14, T987 540 260, www.alberguedelapiedra. com. Spotless and super-comfortable private hostel with a spacious dorm with comfortable mattresses, and inexpensive private rooms as well as a locked bike shed and a great kitchen.

Restaurants

Astorga *p98*
€€ Hostal La Peseta, Plaza San Bartolomé 3, T987 617 275. See Where to stay, above. The best *cocido* in town.

€€ Parrillada Serrano, C Portería 2, T987 617 866, www.restauranteserrano.es. This is spacious and cosily stylish; there's a big range of dishes (including an excellent fish soup) and a good-value *menú*.

€ Cubasol, C Ovalle 10, T987 616 489. Traditional and no-frills place for cheap *raciones* of octopus, calamari, or sweetbreads. There's a cheap *menú del día* too.

€ Pizzería Venecia, C Matías Rodríguez 2, T987 618 463. Popular with all types of Astorgan, this is an inexpensive option with poor service and excellent pizza.

Cafés
Café Kavafis, C Mártires de Somiedo 5, T987 615 363. This cosy little place has internet access and books, including by the Alexandrine poet after whom it is named. The peaceful atmosphere changes at weekends, when it becomes a small disco, with good DJs.

Around Astorga *p99*
€€ Casa Juan Andrés, C Real 24, Castrillo de los Polvazares, T987 691 065, www.casajuan andres.es. Not the cheapest of the village's places, but this cosy place up the far end offers the best *cocido* in town in a beautifully decorated traditional courtyard house.

Ponferrada *p100*
There are many good tapas bars in Ponferrada, some in the old centre, and some around Plaza Fernando Miranda.

€€ Las Cuadras, Trasero de la Cava 2, T987 419 373. A good dark Spanish restaurant down the side of the castle with gutsy fishes and meats and a good set lunch. The tables are characterfully set around a central atrium.

€ El Bodegón, Travesía Pelayo 2, T987 411 019. Atmospheric central tapas bar in a spacious old stone wine cellar. A hearty dish of potatoes with sauce comes free with your drink.

€ Fragata, Av Montearenas s/n, Santo Tomás de las Olas, T987 401 231. It's worth tracking down this no-frills place on the edge of Ponferrada to gorge on some of Northern Spain's finest octopus, served in the traditional manner. Great value, but book ahead.

€ La Bodeguilla, Plaza Fernando Miranda 5, T987 411 119. One of the city's best tapas bars, this has wine-inspired decor, with wooden cases, hanging 'vines', and a soft padded bar. It's a popular meeting point for its delicious ham *pinchos*.

€ La Fonda, Plaza del Ayuntamiento 10, T987 425 794, with a nice covered terrace and excellent *alubias* (stewed beans) and generous meat dishes. *Menú del día* for €12.

Villafranca del Bierzo *p279*
€ Mesón Don Nacho, C Truqueles 2, T987 540 076, tucked off the main road just short of the square, is a cellar-type place offering an excellent *menú* for €10 full of hearty things like stews, tripe, and *caldo gallego*, a fortifying Galician soup.

€ Sevilla, Plaza Mayor s/n. Serves a good-value lunch *menú* with plenty of choice and lots of seating outside on the square. There's also internet access and friendly people running it.

Bars and clubs

Ponferrada *p100*
Ponferrada has a famously boisterous nightlife; in the streets behind the **Temple** hotel there are any number of *discobares* with all types of music. Later on, the action moves out to the large bars in the purpose-built complex known as La Gran Manzana.

A rather unique venue in the heart of the old town is **Sala Tararí**, C del Reloj 17, www.salatarari.com, an excellent bar with an inclusive feel, friendly folk, regular high-quality concerts, and a rocking Thu night jam session that's worth timing your visit to experience.

Festivals

Astorga *p98*
Aug A Roman festival, togas and all.

Transport

Astorga *p98*
Bus There are 15 daily buses from **León** to Astorga. There are a few trains too, but the station is inconveniently situated 20 mins' walk from the centre.

Ponferrada *p100*
Bus Ponferrada's bus station is across the river from the old town; it's a bit of a trudge, but there are frequent city buses crossing the river. Many buses go to **León**, several a day go on west to **Villafranca**, and several continue into **Galicia**, mostly to **Lugo** and **Santiago**.

Train Trains run east to **León** via **Astorga** 6 times a day, and some go west to **A Coruña**, **Ourense** and **Vigo**. The train station is also across the river from the old town.

Valle del Silencio *p100*
Bus There are only 2 buses monthly from **Ponferrada** up the valley to Peñalba de Santiago.

Villafranca del Bierzo *p101*
Bus Villafranca is served by ALSA buses from **León** and **Ponferrada**. Many buses continue into **Galicia**.

Route through Galicia

Thrust out into the Atlantic like Spain's storm shield, and dotted with hill villages and dolmens, remote Galicia reverberates with Celtic history. The *gaita*, or bagpipe, is a strong element of Galicia's musical heritage. Another point it shares with other Celtic nations is its rainfall, which is high; in the northwest, it rains 150 days of the year.

The course of Galicia's history was changed forever when the tomb of the apostle St James was allegedly discovered here. Pilgrims flocked to Galicia, progressing from across Europe, as they have as they now do again. The twin towers of the marvellous baroque cathedral in the noble granite city of Santiago de Compostela, which grew up around the tomb, is a fitting welcome for them.

The climb from western León province into Galicia is one of the most gruelling parts of the Camino de Santiago, particularly if the local weather is on form. The first stop, O Cebreiro, is a pretty village that offers a well-deserved welcome; from here, the route to Santiago takes you through rolling green hills and a number of interesting Galician towns.

Galicians have a reputation for being superstitious and introspective, not hard to understand when you've seen the Atlantic storms in full force. A Celtic melancholy known as *morriña* is also a feature, expressed in the poems of Galicia's favourite writer, Rosalía de Castro. To visitors, though, Gallegos are generous and friendly; the region's cities are as open and convivial as anywhere in Northern Spain. You'll also notice that Galicia's a little lighter on your finances than other parts of the country: both accommodation and restaurants offer significant value here.

Piedrafita and O Cebreiro

The most spectacular approach into Galicia is via the pass of **Piedrafita**, a wind- and rain-swept mountain location that can be hostile in the extreme. Sir John Moore and his ragtag British forces were pursued up here by the French army, and many died of cold. Not much further on, they found themselves without explosive to blow up a bridge behind them, and were forced to ditch all their gold over the edge so that they could travel faster and avoid being set upon from behind.

From Villafranca, the first 20 km as you follow the Valcarce valley slope only gently uphill, but you are then confronted with a long, wearisome ascent of some 600 m over 7 km into Galicia and the pilgrim's rest stop of **O Cebreiro**. There will be few days on the Camino when you'll be gladder to put your feet up. In many ways, this tiny village of attractive stone buildings is where the modern Camino de Santiago was reborn. The church and former pilgrim hostel were rebuilt in the 1960s and the energetic parish priest, Elías Valiña, found suitable people to run hostels in other waystations and began to popularize the notion of the pilgrim way once again.

Although O Cebreiro can be indescribably bleak as the winds, rains and snows roll in and the power fails, it's atmospheric and friendly and has all the services a weary pilgrim could desire. Here you'll see reconstructed *pallozas*, a circular dwelling of stone walls and straw roofs originating in Celtic pre-Roman Galicia. The church has a reliquary donated by Fernando and Isabel to accompany the chalice, which is known as the 'Grail of Galicia', after the host and communion wine became real flesh and blood one day as a skeptical priest went through the motions at Mass. In high summer, pilgrims can outnumber locals (of whom there are 31) by 30 or 40 times.

Samos

Your first full day in Galicia is a significantly easier one. About 20 km after leaving O Cebreiro, in the village of **Triacastela** (where some choose to spend the night), pilgrims have a choice of routes, which meet up again further down the track. The more interesting, but slightly longer, goes via the village of **Samos** (31 km from O Cebreiro, and a great place to spend the night). Significantly wetter than the Greek island where Pythagoras was born, this Samos is wholly dominated by the large monastery of **San Julián** ⓘ *www.abadiadesamos.com, Mon-Sat 1000-1230, 1630-1830, Sun 1245-1330, 1630-1830, €3; admission by interesting tour only, leaving on the ½ hr*. The Benedictines first came here in the sixth century, and a tiny slate chapel by the river dates back to the ninth and 10th; it's shaded by a large cypress tree. The main monastery is a huge structure entered via its elegant western façade. If you think it looks a bit too square, you're right; towers were planned but the coffers ran dry before they could be erected. Ask at the monastery for a guide to visit the little chapel by the river it it's not already open.

Much of the interior of the monastery has been rebuilt: in 1951 a monk took a candle too close to a fermenting barrel in the distillery and burned most of the complex down. Although a Romanesque doorway is still in place where it used to give access to the old church, most of the architecture is baroque, but a far more elegant and restrained baroque than is usual in these parts. There are two cloisters; a pretty fountain depicting water nymphs from Greek mythology is the highlight of the smaller one, its pagan overtones appear not to trouble the monks, whose cells and eating quarters are here. Sixteen Benedictines still live here and run a small farm on the edge of the village.

The larger cloister abuts the raised church and is centred around a statue of Feijóo, the notable and enlightened writer who was a monk here early in his career. He donated much money derived from his writings to enable the dome of the church to be completed. The upper level sleeps guests (males can apply in writing or by phone, T982 546 046, to join the community for a contemplative break) and was decorated in the 1960s with a series of murals to replace those paintings lost in the fire. They're pretty bad – the artist painted cinema posters for a living – but give the monks credit for courage; it would have been all too easy to whack in a series of insipid replicas.

The church itself is large, elegant, and fairly bare. An Asturian cross above the altar is a reference to the kings that generously donated money to the early monastery; statues of them flank the nave. The dome, as with the one in the sacristy, has a touch of the Italian about it.

Sarria

The two separate branches of the Camino converge before Sarria, the major town on this stretch of the Camino, and a starting point for many, as from here to Santiago is the minimum distance to achieve the *compostela* certificate. Sarria is a bit dull: a busy service and transport centre for the region, without a great deal to see. In the old town, on the side of the hill, there's a simple Romanesque church with a charming cloister and above it, a privately owned castle that needs a couple of ravens as a finishing touch to its creeper-swathed tower. The attractive pedestrianized main street that these are on is full of pilgrim hostels and peregrine-friendly eateries; it also houses a tourist information office. Sarria is famous for antiques, and there are many such shops in the town, and also several places peddling convincing replicas. The riverbank makes a relaxing spot to sit outside on a summer terrace.

Portomarín

It's an up and down day through frequent bad weather from Sarria to Portomarín, and you'll notice the Camino more crowded than before. At first glance you wouldn't know it, but this village is only about 40 years old. The original lies underwater, submerged when the river Miño was dammed. Hearteningly, the villagers were helped to move the historic buildings to the new site, and Portomarín escaped becoming the sad and soulless concrete shambles that many such relocated villages in Spain are. The main street is attractive, with an arcade and whitewashed buildings, and the Romanesque parish church is well worth a look for its rose window and beautifully carved tall portals.

Portomarín to Santiago

It's just 93 km from Portomarín to the long-awaited spires of Santiago, and there are numerous ways of breaking up the journey. To be truthful, the towns and villages along this stretch aren't the most characterful you'll have encountered along the Camino, but that matters little with the delights of Santiago just over the horizon.

Many walkers pass the next night in **Palas de Rei**; if you've got time en route, it's worth the detour north from Portos to see the impressive Romanesque, later Templar church at Vilar de Donas. Palas de Rei ("palace of the king") according to tradition, is named for having been the seat of a Visigothic monarch in the eighth century.

The next day, shadowing the main road, takes you through **Melide**, the geographical centre of Galicia, with a very attractive plaza and a moderately interesting church with Romanesque origins. Options to spend this night include the cheese-producing capital of **Arzúa**, from where it's 39 km to the Galician capital.

A flattish but largely uninteresting day from here takes you to **Lavacolla**, where pilgrims used to bathe in the river so as to be clean when arriving at the apostle's tomb (the name may derive from the Latin for 'wash arse'). Ascending the hill of **Monte del Gozo**, now cluttered with tasteless *hostales* and roadside brothels, the first pilgrim to spot the cathedral would be dubbed the 'king' of the group. A large metal pilgrim figure marks the beginnings of the long outskirts of Santiago itself. It's a good idea, especially in busy periods, to overnight shortly before Santiago, thus arriving first the next morning to grab a cheap bed before everyone else.

Route through Galicia listings

For hotel and restaurant price codes and other relevant information, see pages 12-19.

Where to stay

O Cebreiro *p106*
There are several options in O Cebreiro, all offering similar comforts: cosy rooms in refurbished stone buildings, a convivial pilgrim bar, and warming home-cooked food.
€€ Hotel O Cebreiro, O Cebreiro, T982 367 125, www.hotelcebreiro.com. Just down from the church, this offers small but comfortable rooms, a range of traditional Galician cuisine, and outdoor tables in the heart of the village.
€ Albergue de O Cebreiro, T660 396 809. With marvellous mountain vistas, this crowded pilgrim hostel is reasonably equipped and fills pretty fast.

Samos *p106*
€ Albergue Monasterio de Samos, T982 546 046, www.abadiadesamos.com. While it's not the best-equipped pilgrim hostel on the *camino*, this is in the monastery itself and makes a very atmospheric and welcoming place to stay.

Sarria *p107*
€€ Alfonso IX, Rúa do Peregrino 29, T982 530 005, www.nh-hoteles.com. The town's most luxurious option, this chain hotel is modern and pleasant; the rooms have all the facilities (some are equipped for disabled visitors), and it also boasts a gym, sauna, and swimming pool as well as a restaurant. Better value than most of this chain's hotels. Extras are overpriced though.
€ Albergue San Lázaro, C San Lázaro 7, T982 530 626, www.alberguesanlazaro.com. The most welcoming of Sarria's several pilgrim hostels, this is an attractive and most appealing place to overnight.

Portomarín *p107*
€€ Pousada de Portomarín, Av Sarria s/n, T982 545 200, www.pousadadeportomarin.com. Not the most attractive of the buildings along the Camino de Santiago, this nevertheless makes a good choice by the river a short stroll from the centre of Portomarín. Rooms are large and comfortable, if curiously furnished, and there's a pool among other facilities.
€ Albergue Manuel, C Rúa do Miño 1, T982 545 385, www.pensionmanuel.com. Efficient and helpful modern independent pilgrim hostel. With no curfew, and private pension rooms also available, it's a flexible option.

Portomarín to Santiago *p107*
€ Albergue del Monte do Gozo, Ctra Aeropuerto Km 2, Monte do Gozo, T660 396 827. This giant hostel is a favourite last-night stop, allowing a short day into Santiago the next morning. There are excellent facilities and a demob-happy atmosphere.
€ Albergue de Melide, Rúa San Antonio s/n, Melide, T660 396 822. Large and well-appointed official pilgrim hostel with partitioned dorm beds and plenty of places.

€ Albergue los Caminantes, C Santiago 14, Arzúa, T647 020 600, www.arzua.albergueloscaminantes.com. The best option in Arzúa, this private pilgrim hostel has a genuine welcome and bright, well-spaced dormitory beds.

€ Albergue Os Chacotes, C As Lagartas s/n, Palas de Rei, T607 481 536. New, comfortable and clean government-run pilgrim hostel that you pass about 15 mins before the centre of town. A good option with a decent restaurant alongside.

Restaurants

O Cebreiro *p106*
O Cebreiro has several places to eat, all serving inexpensive mountain food to hungry pilgrims.

Sarria *p107*
€ Anduriñas, Rúa Maior 29, T982 532 598. On the main pedestrian street, this place does filling plates of meat, eggs, and salad for hungry pilgrims, as well as traditional Galician favourites.

Portomarín *p107*
€ O Mesón do Rodríguez, T982 545 054. This bastion of peregrine comforts on the main street, is a good place for a meal; the food is generously proportioned and compassionately priced.

Santiago de Compostela

"The true capital of Spain." *Roads to Santiago*, Cees Nooteboom.

Archaeologists in the ninth century weren't known for their academic rigour, so when a tomb was discovered here at that time it was rather staggeringly concluded to be that of the apostle Santiago, or Saint James. Christianity was in bullish mode, and the spot grew into the major pilgrimage destination in Europe as people walked thousands of miles to pay their respects, reduce their time in purgatory, or atone for their crimes.

The pilgrimage had an enormous cultural, social, and architectural effect across Northern Spain, and Santiago soon transcended its dubious beginnings to become one of the most magical cities in Spain, its cathedral the undisputed highlight of a superb ensemble of mossy granite buildings and narrow pedestrian lanes.

The late 20th century saw a massive revival of the pilgrimage tradition which has continued to grow in the new millennium. More than a 100,000 pilgrims arrive annually and Santiago is today a flourishing, happy place, seat of the Galician parliament and lively with students. Don't come for a suntan, though; HV Morton accurately if unkindly described the city as a "medieval aquarium", but the regular rain can add to the character of the place, at least for the first three days or so. Simply walking the streets here is a pleasure (even in the rain), particularly Rúa Vilar and Rúa Nova and the streets around the old university buildings.

Arriving in Santiago de Compostela → *Phone code: 981. Population: 95,092.*

Getting there
The traditional way to get to Santiago is the five-week walk from the French Pyrenees, or from some closer point, but there are ways to cheat. **Ryanair** runs from London Stansted, Frankfurt Hahn and Milan Bergamo, as well as several Spanish airports, to Santiago's airport (SCQ) 11 km east of town in Lavacolla. There are also daily flights from London run by **BA/Iberia**, as well as frequent internal connections and flights to other European destinations. Buses run from the airport to the the bus station via the centre. Another bus runs from Praza de Galicia to coincide with Ryanair flights. Santiago is well served by interurban buses. The bus station is a 20-minute walk northeast of the centre. Bus Nos 5 and C5 run there from Praza de Galicia via Rúa da Virxe da Cerca. If arriving by bus, head up the hill directly opposite the bus station café and turn left at the big intersection. The train station is south of the centre, about a 15-minute walk down Rúa de Hórreo (off Praza Galicia). There are trains to the rest of Galicia and Spain. ▸▸ *See Transport, page 124.*

Getting around
The interesting bits of town are mostly very close together. The main places you'll need public transport to access are the airport and the bus station.

Tourist information
Santiago has several tourist information offices. The three most useful are the **municipal office** ⓘ *Rúa do Vilar 63, T981 555 129, www.santiagoturismo.com, daily 0900-1400, 1600-1900*; the nearby **Galician regional office** ⓘ *Rúa do Vilar 30, T981 584 081, ot.santiago@xunta.es, Mon-Fri 1000-2000, Sat 1100-1400, 1700-1900, Sun 1100-1400*, and a **kiosk** ⓘ *Praza de Galicia, T981 584 400, Mon-Sat 1000-1400, 1600-1900*. There's also an information office at the airport. Galicia's tourist board, **Turgalicia**, publishes useful booklets and brochures. The website, www.turgalicia.es, is also worth a browse.

The **pilgrim office** ⓘ *Rúa do Vilar 1, T981 568 846, www.peregrinossantiago.es, Easter-Oct 0900-2100, Nov-Easter Mon-Sat 1000-2000, Sun 1000-1400, 1600-2000*, is around the corner from the cathedral. This is where you can get your pilgrim passports examined and pick up the *compostela* certificate. The process has been streamlined somewhat, but there are still long queues in summer. A pile of gleefully abandoned wooden sticks sits inside the door.

Background

Relics have been a big deal in Christendom since the early Middle Ages, and especially in Spain. Christ physically ascended into heaven, and the Virgin was bodily assumed there too. With the big two out of the question, the apostles were just about the best physical remains an ambitious church could hope for. But whether you believe that the bones of Saint James are, or were ever, under the altar of the cathedral (see box, page 112) is beside the point; the city has transcended its origins completely, as the number of atheist pilgrims trudging towards it attests.

After the discovery of the tomb in the early ninth century, pilgrims soon began flooding in, and the city had achieved such prosperity by AD 968 that it was sacked by none other than the Vikings, who were never averse to a long voyage for a bit of plunder. Some 29 years later Santiago had another bad day, when Al-Manzur came from the south and sacked it again. Legend says that an old monk was praying by the tomb of Saint James

Saint James and the Camino de Santiago

The patron saint of Spain is one of the most revered of figures in the country. St James, or Santiago, was the son of Zebedee, brother of the apostle John, and a fisherman who gave up his nets to follow Christ. In AD 44 he was martyred at swordpoint by King Herod Agrippa. Several centuries later, a small west European kingdom flexing its Christian muscles was in need of a holy warrior.

We move to Galicia, and a spot near the end of the world, Finisterre. In the early ninth century, 800 years after James was martyred and thousands of miles away, a shepherd was guided by an angel and stars to a tomb in the woods at a place now called Compostela. The local bishop, evidently not a man to reserve judgement, deemed it to be St James himself. The news spread fast, and gave the Christians new faith for their fight against the Moors. Even handier than faith on a muddy battlefield is a back-from-the-dead apostle on a white charger, and Santiago obliged. He brutally slew hundreds of hapless Muslims in battle, winning himself the nickname Matamoros, or slayer of Moors.

All very well, but how and why was his body in Spain in the first place? He had, after all, been killed in Caesarea. But tradition, however historically debatable, has it that he preached in Spain at some point, and the Virgin Mary is said to have appeared to him in Zaragoza (at the time called Caesarea too; a possible source of the confusion). James went back to the Holy Land with a few keen Spanish converts. After his death the followers rescued his body and set forth for home with it. Not experts in boat buying, they selected a stone yacht, but with the saint on board, they managed to navigate it to the Pillars of Hercules and around to Galicia. Along the way, the saint performed a miracle, saving a gentleman whose panicked horse had dashed headlong into the sea with him in the saddle. Man and horse rose from the seabed safe and sound; some traditions hold that they were covered in scallop shells; this became the apostle's symbol. His followers landed near Padrón and requested oxen from the local pagan queen so that they could transport the body inland. In mockery, she gave them a pair of ferocious bulls, but the apostle intervened and transformed them into docile beasts, thus converting the amazed queen. After the long

while chaos reigned around. The Moorish warlord himself burst in and was so impressed by the old man's courage that he swore on his honour to safeguard the tomb and the monk from all harm.

Although the city was razed to the ground, Santiago continued to flourish as Saint James became a sort of patron-cum-field marshal of the Reconquista. Pilgrims came from across Europe and the cathedral was constructed to receive them in appropriate style; they used to bed down for the night in its interior. Constant architectural modifications followed from Santiago's swelling coffers, which also paid for the 40-something churches in the small city. This restructuring reached its peak in the 17th and early 18th centuries, from which period most of the granite centre that exists today dates. A rapid decline followed as pilgrimage waned and A Coruña thrived at Santiago's expense. The French occupied Santiago during the Napoleonic Wars, and carried off a large amount of plunder.

The late 20th century brought a rapid revival as the age of tourism descended on Spain in force. Santiago is high on many visitors' lists and the comparatively recent surge journey, Santiago's loyal companions buried him and he was conveniently forgotten until the shepherd's discovery centuries later.

The pilgrims News that an apostle's tomb was in Christian Galicia travelled fast. A church was built and granted a perpetual *voto*, a tax payable by every inhabitant of Spain; this was levied until the 19th century. Pilgrims began to make the journey to Galicia to venerate the saint's remains. Most of the early pilgrims were from France, and the main route across Northern Spain came to be known as the Camino Francés. Waystations for pilgrims were set up, and French settlers and monks became a significant presence in the towns and villages along the route, and continued to be so; many of the churches and cathedrals are based on models from France. In the 12th century a French monk, Aimery Picaud, wrote the *Codex Calixtinus*, part of which was an entertaining guidebook for pilgrims making the journey to Santiago; the dangers mentioned include robbers, con-artists and wolves.

The pilgrimage became phenomenally popular, helped along by the Pope's declaration that all pilgrims to Santiago would have their time in Purgatory halved; if they went on a Holy Year (when the feast of St James, 25 July, falls on a Sunday) they would get a full remission (plenary indulgence). They came from all over Europe; some by boat (Chaucer's Wife of Bath made the journey), some walking for more than a year. At its peak, some half a million pilgrims arrived annually in Santiago, which rapidly became a flourishing city.

The pilgrimage declined in the 19th century, although there was a brief revival when the bones of Santiago, missing for a couple of centuries, were rediscovered (it was proved because a fragment of St James's skull from Pistoia in Italy fit exactly into a handy notch in the Compostela skull) and by the mid-20th century only a handful of people were following the route, whose pilgrim hostels had long since disappeared.

However, in the late 20th century there was a surprising revival in the pilgrimage, whose popularity has continued to grow. Well over 100,000 pilgrims arrive in Santiago on foot and bicycle every year, many more in Holy Years (the next is 2021).

in popularity of the Camino sees pilgrims of all creeds making the journey in whole or part on foot or bicycle. Although A Coruña remains the provincial capital, Santiago is the seat of the Xunta (semi-autonomous Galician government established in 1982), which has provided a further boost to the town's economy.

Cathedral and around

ⓘ *www.catedraldesantiago.es, Cathedral 0730-2100, except during Mass; entry at these times is via the Praza das Praterías only. There's a Mass for pilgrims daily at 1200, and evening Mass at 1930; both last for about 45 mins. Admission is free, apart from the museum (see below).*
Santiago's past, present and future is wrapped up in its cathedral and its emblematic grey towers. Pilgrims trudge for weeks to reach it, many tourists visit Galicia specifically to see it, and locals go to Mass and confession in it as part of their day-to-day lives.

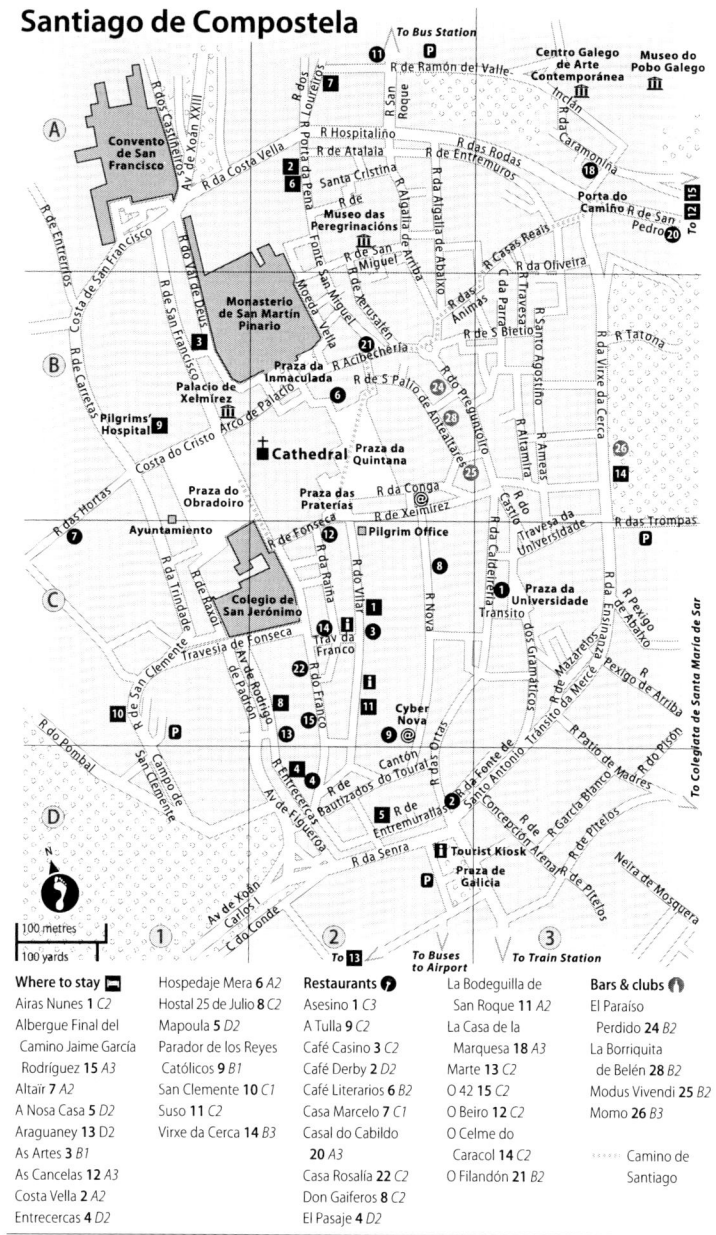

Santiago de Compostela

Where to stay	Hospedaje Mera **6** *A2*	Restaurants	La Bodeguilla de	Bars & clubs
Airas Nunes **1** *C2*	Hostal 25 de Julio **8** *C2*	Asesino **1** *C3*	San Roque **11** *A2*	El Paraíso
Albergue Final del	Mapoula **5** *D2*	A Tulla **9** *C2*	La Casa de la	Perdido **24** *B2*
Camino Jaime García	Parador de los Reyes	Café Casino **3** *C2*	Marquesa **18** *A3*	La Borriquita
Rodríguez **15** *A3*	Católicos **9** *B1*	Café Derby **2** *D2*	Marte **13** *C2*	de Belén **28** *B2*
Altaïr **7** *A2*	San Clemente **10** *C1*	Café Literarios **6** *B2*	O 42 **15** *C2*	Modus Vivendi **25** *B2*
A Nosa Casa **5** *D2*	Suso **11** *C2*	Casa Marcelo **7** *C1*	O Beiro **12** *C2*	Momo **26** *B3*
Araguaney **13** *D2*	Virxe da Cerca **14** *B3*	Casal do Cabildo	O Celme do	
As Artes **3** *B1*		**20** *A3*	Caracol **14** *C2*	····· Camino de
As Cancelas **12** *A3*		Casa Rosalía **22** *C2*	O Filandón **21** *B2*	Santiago
Costa Vella **2** *A2*		Don Gaiferos **8** *C2*		
Entrecercas **4** *D2*		El Pasaje **4** *D2*		

114 • Camino de Santiago Santiago de Compostela

While the original Romanesque interior is superbly preserved, what first greets most visitors is the western façade and its twin towers. Granite is the perfect stone to express a more sober face of Spanish baroque; its stern colour renders the style epic rather than whimsical, and it's hard enough to chisel that masons concentrated on broader, nobler lines rather than intricacy. The façade rises high above the square, the moss-stained stone towers (which incorporate the original Romanesque ones) seem to say 'Heaven this way'. The façade was added in the 18th century and is reached by a complex double staircase that predates it.

The plaza that it dominates, named **Obradoiro**, is the main gateway to the cathedral, but it's worth strolling around the building before you enter. Walking clockwise, you pass the façade of the Romanesque **Palacio de Xelmírez**, which adjoins it and forms part of the cathedral museum. Turning the corner, you emerge in the **Praza da Inmaculada**, where the north façade is a slightly underwhelming 18th-century baroque construction that replaced the earlier Romanesque portal, which, from fragments of stone and textual descriptions, was superb. It faces the **Monasterio de San Martín Pinario**, with a huge façade that's wasted next to this magnificent cathedral; this part of it is now a student residence. The plaza used to be known as the *Azabachería*; this is where craftsmen made and sold rosaries made of jet (*azabache*) to the arriving pilgrims.

Continuing around, the **Praza da Quintana** is a curious space, with an upper and lower half; these are known as the halves of the living (the top) and the dead (below); the area used to be a cemetery. A plaque here is dedicated to the Literary Batallion, a corps of student volunteers who fought the French in the Napoleonic wars. The portal on this side is known as the Puerta Santa, or holy door. It is only opened during Holy Years, when the feast day of Santiago (25 July) falls on a Sunday. The façade is 17th century, but contains figures salvaged from the Romanesque stone choir. The 18th-century clocktower soars over the square.

The last square on the circuit is **Praza das Praterías**, with an entrance to the cathedral through an original portal, the oldest that remains, with scenes from the life of Christ.

Come back to the western façade and ascend the complex staircase. Once through the baroque doorway, you're confronted with the original Romanesque façade, the **Pórtico de la Gloria**. Built 1168-1188 by a man named Master Mateo, it is one of the finest pieces of sculpture in Spain, and a fitting welcome for weary pilgrims. Three doorless arches are intricately carved with Biblical scenes; a superb Last Judgement on the right, and variously interpreted Old Testament scenes on the left. In the centre Santiago himself sits under Christ and the Evangelists, who are surrounded by elders of the Apocalypse playing medieval musical instruments.

Upon entering the church, pilgrims queue to touch the pillar by the feet of Santiago; over the centuries five clear finger marks have been worn in the stone. On the other side of the pillar, carved with the Tree of Jesse, many then bump heads with the figure of Master Mateo, hoping that some of his genius will rub off. Many mistakenly butt the head under Santiago's feet; this is in fact Samson; Master Mateo faces into the church.

The interior itself is still attractively Romanesque in the main. High barrel vaulting and the lack of a *coro* in the centre of the nave give an excellent perspective down the church, although it's a pity the original stone *coro* by Master Mateo was destroyed in the early 17th century to make way for a wooden one that is no longer there either (the stone one has been re-assembled in the cathedral museum, the wooden one in the Monasterio de San Martín Pinario).

The massive altar is over-ornate and features some rather out-of-place cherubs on the *baldacchino* (baldachin), which is topped by an image of Santiago in Moor-killing mode; the whole thing belongs on a circus caravan. Above in the cupola is the eye-in-triangle symbol of the all-seeing God. Behind the altar is the image of Santiago himself. Pilgrims ascend behind the statue and give it an *abrazo* (embrace); this, a kiss to the back of his head, and a confession below, was the symbolic end to the pilgrimage.

There are various masses daily, with a special pilgrim one at midday. On occasions during the celebration of Mass, a large silver *botafumeiro* (censer) is hung from the ceiling at the crossing and slowly swung by eight men until it covers the whole length of the transept and reaches frightening velocities, diffusing incense and sparks all the while. It's a fantastic and unnerving thing to see, and it's only flown off twice (once in a Mass celebrated for Catherine of Aragón to wish her luck on her journey to wed Henry VIII in England; it was considered a bad omen, as it proved to be). The *botafumeiro* is an expensive thing to light, and is swung only on religious holidays or when a group of pilgrims get €240 together to pay for it. It needs to be reserved at least two days in advance. Contact peregrinos@archicompostela.org.

Cathedral museum
ⓘ *Oct-May Mon-Sat 1000-1330, 1600-1830, Jun-Sep 1000-1400, 1600-2000, Sun 1000-1400, €5.*
Back in the Praza do Obradoiro, investigate the Romanesque **crypt** at the base of the main staircase. One of the three sections of the cathedral museum, it was built by Master Mateo to support the weight of his Romanesque façade above; it's an interesting space dominated by a sturdy load-bearing pillar. There are reproductions of some of the musical instruments that appear on the façade above, as well as some processional crosses and, interestingly, the 14th-century battle-horn of Alfonso XI, made from an elephant's tusk.

The main section of the museum is accessed from the cathedral or the Praza do Obradoiro. Entering from the square, the first rooms contain fragments of Romanesque sculpture, including one of the *Punishment of the Damned*, with two naked sinners having their sensitive bits eaten by beasts. The highlight of this section is the reconstruction of the stone **coro** by Master Mateo, which must have looked superb in the cathedral until it was destroyed in 1603 to make way for a wooden one. Some granite slabs elegantly painted in *mudéjar* style are also noteworthy. Upstairs, there's a range of religious sculpture in both polychrome wood and granite, including a sensitive San Sebastián in gold shorts and a fine *Last Judgement*, with an hirsute San Miguel presiding over the psychostasis (weighing of souls). There's also a wooden relief of the bells of the original church being carried back from Córdoba, whither they had been taken after Al-Manzur sacked the city. They were triumphantly reclaimed during the Reconquista, although, underwhelmingly, they were allegedly found in a pantry, being used to hold olive oil.

The **cloister** is absolutely massive in scale, and has a slightly neglected feel. The star vaulting is ornate Gothic and the arches heavily elegant. There are several tombs and fragments around, as well as some large, 18th-century bells. A small **library** contains one of the *botafumeiros* (see above), and there are some mediocre tapestries; but don't despair, there are some better ones upstairs, especially three depicting the life of Achilles by Rubens. Others are factory-made ones depicting rural life, some based on Goya cartoons.

Between the cloister and the cathedral is the **treasury**, a rather vulgar display of wealth donated by various bigwigs; the collection includes a goblet that belonged to Marshal Pétain. Next to this is the **Panteón**, which contains tombs of various kings of León and other nobles. There's also an immense *retablo* holding the cathedral's impressive collection of relics; these include the head of the other apostle James, the Lesser (Alpheus), encased in a gilt bust, and a spine from the crown of thorns.

The other section of the museum, on the other side of the cathedral façade, is the **Palacio de Xelmírez**, interesting for being a Romanesque civil building (it was built as an archbishop's residence), although it was heavily modified in the 16th century. Features include an attractive patio and large kitchen and two beautiful halls.

Praza de Obradoiro

The other buildings on the Praza do Obradoiro are also interesting. To the left as you face the cathedral is the massive **Pilgrims' Hospital**, built by Fernando and Isabel, the Catholic Monarchs. Now a parador, pilgrims still have the right a free meal here if they are one of the first 10 to queue for 0900, 1200 or 1900 sittings. The hotel has four pretty courtyards named after the evangelists and several elegant halls. Access is limited if you aren't a guest, but the bits you are allowed to wander around are worthwhile.

Opposite the cathedral, the **Ayuntamiento** is housed in an attractive neoclassical building, while the fourth side, opposite the parador, is partly taken up by the **Colegio de San Jerónimo**, a 15th-century structure now part of the university, with a nice little patio and a portal that looks distinctly Romanesque; perhaps the architects didn't want to clash with the Pórtico de la Gloria of the cathedral. Next to it, the **Colegio de Santiago Alfeo** is a Renaissance construction used by the local government.

Monasterio de San Martín Pinario and around

North of the cathedral, the **San Martín Pinario monastery** ⓘ *Tue-Sun 1100-1330, 1600-1830, €2*, is half restricted to students, but you can enter the church and museum from the back. The door is high and rather overbearing; it's reached via an attractive downward staircase. The interior is lofty and bare, with a massive dome. In contrast to the sober architectural lines is the huge altarpiece, described by the 19th-century traveller Richard Ford: "In the *retablo*, of vilest Churrigueresque, Santiago and San Martín ride together in a fricasee of gilt gingerbread."

Similarly decorative *retablos* adorn the side chapels. Of more interest is the *coro* behind the altar; see if you can find the hidden door that the monks used to enter through. The museum has some old printing presses, an interesting old pharmacy and the wooden choir from the cathedral. There's also a multimedia exhibition on Galicia.

Near to the monastery is the **Convento de San Francisco**, founded by Saint Francis when he made the pilgrimage here in the early 13th century, and the newish **Museo das Peregrinacións** ⓘ *www.mdperegrinacions.com, Tue-Fri 1000-2000, Sat 1030-1330, 1700-2000, Sun 1030-1330, pilgrims free, free on Sat afternoon*, a three-floor display about the pilgrimage to Santiago, images and iconography of the saint, the Pórtico de la Gloria, and the medieval life of the town. It's reasonably interesting, more so if you're a pilgrim, but ducks a few crucial Saint James issues.

Extension to Cape Finisterre

You've walked across Spain through the heat and the cold and the wet, your blisters have blisters of their own, and you've just reached Santiago. Time to pick up your *compostela* certificate, snap your staff, go to the pilgrim Mass, admire the cathedral, and then put your feet up and feast on seafood or scoff a rather large gin and tonic feeling deservedly rather proud of yourself. After all, unlike the medieval pilgrims, you don't have to turn around and walk all the way back home again; there are budget airlines to do that for you.

So it's all over. Or is it? Not for everyone, for a growing number of pilgrims are choosing to shoulder the pack for three more days and continue westwards to Cape Finisterre. There's a certain logic at work here. You've walked right across Spain, but actually, you haven't, for there are still 90 km to the west coast. So why not finish the job? Another reason is that, in the hurly-burly of arrival at Santiago you sometimes realize that you would have liked a day or two more's walking to gather your thoughts or continue a conversation with someone you've met along the way.

The third reason is the wild beauty of the cape that the Romans considered to be the end of the world. Sitting on the clifftop as the sun sets into the Atlantic in front of you is a fitting end-of-journey experience, both awe inspiring and peacefully contemplative.

Route

Though as always you can divide up the 90 km in whichever way you prefer, most walkers take a short first day, to be able to do things in Santiago in the morning, and a longer third day – you want to be at the cape in the late afternoon so no need to hurry. Remember to bring your *credencial* with you; even though you've reached Santiago, you'll still need it to be able to stay in the *albergues* along this stretch.

Thus, the first day is a fairly easy walk, with not-too-onerous up-and-down stretches through pleasant pastures and light woodland, some 20 km from Santiago to the small town of **Negreira**, dignified by the well-known Pazo de Cotón, a curious stone mansion with medieval origins, connected to its chapel by an arch. There are several *albergues* in Negreira.

The next day is a rigorous one that starts with a long, steady climb of some

Around Porta do Camino

At the eastern end of town, opposite the Porta do Camino where pilgrims enter the city, are two more museums. The **Museo do Pobo Galego** ⓘ *T981 583 620, www.museodopobo.es, Tue-Sat 1000-1400, 1600-2000, Sun 1100-1400, free*, was originally founded by Saint Dominic as a monastery. Inside is a monumental cloister and many ethnographic exhibits relating to Galician life. It's worth a look just for the architecture, including a stunning spiral staircase. There's also a chapel where the poet Rosalía de Castro is buried. Next to the museum, the **Centro Galego de Arte Contemporánea** ⓘ *www.cgac.org, Tue-Sun 1100-2000, free*, is a modern building whose attractive white spaces provide a break from the timeworn granite. Exhibitions are of a high international standard; check their website for what's on. There's also a bookshop and café.

250 vertical metres over the course of some 10 km, and then continues with rises and descents, passing through several typical Galician villages, and via viewpoints with some fine perspectives over the green countryside. Most walkers end up in **Olveiroa**, but there are several *albergue* options over the last stretch.

From Olveiroa, the last day – though there are several appealing places to break the walk – takes you 35 km to the end of your journey.

The first section is picturesque, following the Xallas river valley, and about halfway through the day you hit the coast at **Cee**. Follow on through the town of Fisterra to the cape and lighthouse at **Cabo Finisterre**, 2 km further along the road (a slow and often weather-beaten uphill trudge).

Now, just to sort a couple of things out: the most westerly point in mainland Europe is not Cabo Finisterre but a headland near Lisbon. In fact, the most westerly point in Spain is a little further up the coast, but Finisterre has won the audience vote. Part of its appeal comes from its name, derived from the Latin for 'end of the earth', part from its dramatic location: a small finger of land jutting into the mighty Atlantic. Gazing westwards from the rocks around its scruffy lighthouse (which houses a small pilgrimage exhibition) is a magical experience, particularly at sunset; imagine what it would have been like if you believed the world ended somewhere out there, dropping off into a void.

Fittingly, the clifftop is marked with a cross and a sculpture of a pair of worn-out boots. Many pilgrims leave their own boots here, or burn their hiking clothes, though this is discouraged.

When you've tired of the view, turn around and it's an easy downhill stroll back into Fisterra, where there are several good fish restaurants and several *albergues* and other accommodation options. Three buses a day head back to Santiago, but if you've stayed for the sunset, you'll have to overnight here.

If you still can't accept that the walk's over, you can continue a further day up the coast to the authentic Galician fishing town of **Muxía**. It's more dramatic to do this in reverse, adding an extra day from Olveiroa to Muxía, then down the coast to Fisterra from there. The trail between Muxía and Fisterra is well marked both ways.

Colegiata de Santa María de Sar

The Colegiata de Santa María de Sar is a Romanesque church a 15-minute walk south of the centre. Built in the 12th century, on insecure ground, it is remarkable chiefly for the alarming lean of its interior columns; after the Lisbon earthquake of 1755, massive buttresses had to be added. There's a small **museum** ⓘ *Mon-Sat 1000-1300, 1600-1900, €0.60*, with a tiny bit of Saint Peter in a reliquary, and a cloister, of which one side survives with carvings attributed to Master Mateo. To get there from the Rúa Fonte de San Antonio off Praza de Galicia, take the second right down Rúa Patio de Madres and follow it down the hill; the church is on your right after the railway bridge.

Santiago de Compostela listings

For hotel and restaurant price codes and other relevant information, see pages 12-19.

Where to stay

Santiago de Compostela *p110, map p114*
There are well over 100 places to stay in Santiago, with plenty in the budget range to cater for the pilgrim traffic. Many restaurants in the centre have a few cheap rooms too. Rooms can be hard to find in summer, but it's just a matter of persistence.

€€€€ Hotel Araguaney, C Alfredo Brañas 5, T981 559 600, www.araguaney.com. Not in the old town, but not far from Praza Galicia, this hotel has rather bland decor but makes up for it with good service, and plenty of space, comfort and facilities in the rooms. There's also a high-quality restaurant. You can often get much lower rates through travel agents or online discounters.

€€€€ Parador de los Reyes Católicos, Praza do Obradoiro 1, T981 582 200, www.parador.es. Although these days it's beyond the budgets of many 21st-century peregrines, the pilgrims' hostel built by the Catholic monarchs is a luxurious place to lie up and is by far the city's most atmospheric place to stay. Built around 4 beautiful courtyards, it's worth splashing out for the history and location alone. It's on the cathedral square, and the rooms lack nothing of the class of the building.

€€€ Hotel Altaïr, Rúa dos Loureiros 12, T981 554 712, www.altairhotel.net. Modern, effortlessly attractive and stylish, this boutique hotel blends warm minimalism in the superbly comfortable rooms with exposed stone reflecting the centre of historic Santiago. Attentive staff and tasty breakfasts set you up perfectly for getting to know Compostela. Recommended.

€€€ Virxe da Cerca, Rúa Virxe da Cerca 27, T981 569 350, www.pousadasdecompostela.com. This lovely old stone building on the road circling Santiago's old town has been converted into this stylish and characterful hotel. While the rooms are as well equipped as in any big hotel, there's a more enchanting feel here, particularly around the delightful central patio. Rooms in the historic section are slightly dearer. Recommended.

€€€-€€ Hotel As Artes, Travesía de dos Puertas 2, T981 555 254, www.asartes.com. A very short stroll away from the cathedral, this is a winning boutique choice with rooms named after artists of various media. If room size is a priority, look elsewhere, but if you don't mind a compact, cosy retreat in a fabulous location, you'll be charmed.

€€ Costa Vella, Porta da Peña 17, T981 569 530, www.costavella.com. This smart, comfortable hotel is one of the best in this price range. It's got a romantic feel, not least for its fantastic garden studded with apple and lemon trees and offering fantastic views. Some of the rooms overlook it (they are slightly more expensive); the interior decor is stylish and beautiful, and the welcome from the owners is genuine. Highly recommended.

€€ Hostal 25 de Julio, Av Rodrigo de Padrón 4, T981 582 295, www.25dejulio.com. This intimate little luxury *pensión* is a charming choice. It's run by *simpático* management with an aesthetic eye. The rooms abound in good taste and are soft on mind and body. There's disabled access and an alluring little café too. It's cheaper if you stay more than 1 night.

€€ Hotel Airas Nunes, Rúa do Vilar 17, T981 569 350, www.pousadasdecompostela.com. Right in the thick of things, this modern and stylish hotel has excellent facilities and plenty of attractive charm in a 17th-century building. Rooms are on the small side but comfortable and the location is hard to better. Bottom end of this price category.

€€ Hotel Entrecercas, Rúa Entrecercas 11, T981 571 151, www.entrecercas.es. A charming little hotel that's central but tucked away from the busier parts. It has charm as well as courteous and helpful management. Breakfast included. Underground parking close by. Recommended.

€€ Hotel San Clemente, Rúa San Clemente 28, T981 569 260, www.pousadasdecompostela.com. An excellent option located in the old town below and close to the cathedral. The charm of the old house still shines through, but the rooms are equipped to modern standards with good if small bathrooms and free Wi-Fi.

€ Albergue Final del Camino Jaime García Rodríguez, Rúa Moscova s/n, T981 587 324. Run by the archdiocese, this modern pilgrim hostel is a fitting place to end the Camino. It's comfortable and excellently equipped, although a bit of a walk from the centre. No limit as to how long you can stay.

€ A Nosa Casa, Rúa Entremurallas 9, T981 585 926, www.anosacasa.com. This friendly family-run spot is close to Praza Galicia, on an atmospheric old town street that can be loud at weekends. Handy for the Ryanair bus, but you won't get the hire car very close.

€ Hospedaje Mera, Porta da Pena 15, T981 583 867, www.hospedajemera.com. This quiet and cheap option is on a pedestrian street in the centre of town. Facilities are basic – there are rooms with and without bathroom available – but some rooms have balconies and views, and it's in a great location.

€ Mapoula, Rúa Entremurallas 10, T981 580 124, www.mapoula.com. Good value for money, this is set on a narrow little street in the old town not far from Praza de Galicia. Comfortable beds, modern en suite bathrooms, and Wi-Fi make it solid budget accommodation. Noisy at weekends.

€ Suso, Rúa Vilar 65, T981 586 611, www.hostalsuso.com. This central pilgrims' favourite is handy for everything in town. Its spacious (not the singles), en suite rooms are very good value year-round (it's worth getting here early to avoid disappointment) and there's a friendly vibe from management and the happy walkers at journey's end (unlike the pilgrims of yesteryear, they don't have to turn around and walk back home again). Highly recommended.

Camping

As Cancelas, T981 580 266, www.campingascancelas.com. Open year-round. A good campsite within 30 mins' walk of the heart of town, and frequently served by city bus No 9. There are various family-sized bungalows as well as a shop and a pool.

Restaurants

Santiago de Compostela *p110, map p114*

Seafood is the thing to eat in Santiago, as indeed in much of Galicia. One of the main streets, Rúa Franco, is something of a tourist trap (although locals eat here too); prices are high and quality variable. *Vieiras* (scallops) are an obvious choice, served in a bacon and onion sauce, but they're expensive at about €6 per scallop. *Percebes* are also popular, as are *cigalas* (a word to the wise: *cigalas* are expensive and menus often somewhat misleadingly list the price per 100 g; 6 chubby *cigalas* can weigh well over 500 g). *Tarta de Santiago* is an almond cake often engraved with a sword; patisseries along Rúa Franco give out free morsels to taste.

€€€ Casa Marcelo, Rúa das Hortas 3, T981 558 850, www.casamarcelo.net. Open Tue-Sat. This little gourmet's paradise is on one of Santiago's most picturesque streets just below the Praza do Obradoiro. You won't spend hours browsing the menu, for it's *table d'hôte* only. The feast on offer changes daily, but consists of 5-6 courses full of delicate flavours for €75. Recommended.

€€€ Don Gaiferos, Rúa Nova 23, T981 583 894, www.dongaiferos.com. A dark and moody but modernized place that offers plenty of choice of the finest Galician produce in a good location close to the cathedral. Excellent daily seafood specials, but you might also be tempted by the meat on offer; the *tournedos* are delicious, and the steak tartare just as it should be. Mains are €17-25, and there's a degustation menu.

€€€ El Pasaje, Rúa Franco 54, T981 557 081, www.restaurantepasaje.com. A class above the other fish restaurants on this street, this is at the open end near the Alameda and has room for 3 or 4 outdoor tables. The seafood is sublime, though expensive. The fish cooked *a la parrilla* is memorable, and there's a fine range of wine to accompany it. The *zamburiñas* (mini-scallops) make a fine appetizer. Be aware of the price/weight equation. Recommended.

€€ Asesino, Praza Universidad 16, T981 581 568, www.restaurantegonzabaasesino.com. Discreetly signposted, this restaurant opposite the university is a long-standing Santiago classic that opens when it chooses, and offers excellent home-style food accompanied by appropriately familiar bric-a-brac decor. Almost everything is worthwhile, but the *navajas* (razor shells) are particularly succulent.

€€ Casal do Cabildo, Rúa de San Pedro 18, T981 583 057, www.casaldocabildo.com. Off the beaten track, but still in an attractive part of Santiago close to the heart of things, this is one of several good mid-range restaurants on this street. There's great meat at good prices and huge platters of seafood on a bed of chips.

€€ La Casa de la Marquesa, Costa de San Domingos 2. T981 573 958, www.lacasadelamarquesa.es. Nicely positioned near the modern art gallery, and with an appealing terrace with outdoor tables, this place is frequented by smart young Santiago folk and offers upmarket meals and tapas, as well as creditable sushi twice a week.

€€ Marte, Av Rodrigo de Padrón 11, T981 584 905. Cops usually know where to eat well at sensible prices, so it's a good sign that this no-nonsense family-run place is much patronized by the police station opposite. The *menú del día* is superb value for €15 (there's an even cheaper one for €9) and doesn't hold back on the seafood; there's turbot, monkfish and plenty more. There's a terrace outside too. Top value. Recommended.

€€ O 42, Rúa Franco 42, T981 581 009, www.restauranteo42.com. This place on the main eat street certainly doesn't try to curry favour with pilgrims or tourists except through being authentic. The seafood is slightly pricier than at neighbouring places, but it's top quality, especially the octopus and *navajas* (razor clams). Sit at the rustic wooden tables to enjoy the traditional Santiago *raciones*.

€€ O Beiro, Rúa da Raíña 3, T981 581 370. Stocked with hundreds of wines from all over Spain, this is the place for an impromptu tasting session. The shop has an atmospheric back bar, with flagstones and a low wood-beamed ceiling, where you can try several of their wines by the glass or any of them (and there's over a 1000) by the bottle. There's a free tapa with every glass, and other local produce for sale. Recommended.

€€ O Celme do Caracol, C Raíña 22, T981 571 746, www.ocelmedocaracol.com. A buzz with upbeat Galician chat, this happy place a few paces from the cathedral turns out truly delicious bistro-style Galician fare in its intimate 2-level space. Downstairs, the bar pours good wines by the glass, and complements them with generous free tapas from the semi-open kitchen. Find a table, and enjoy a marvellous seafood soup, top salads, and, as the name suggests, snails in a spicy sauce. Prices are more than fair.

€ A Tulla, Ruela de Entreruas 1, T981 580 889. In a tiny square reached by the narrowest of passageways, this secluded, rustic, and enchanting spot looks like Grandma's house and does simple, delicious old-style Galician cooking from an open kitchen. There's a great vegetarian set menu as well. Recommended.

€ Casa Rosalía, Rúa Franco 10, T981 568 441. A tempting array of tapas is on view at the counter in this busy bar in Santiago central. There's prompt service, and it's a fine spot for a quiet bite with a glass of wine... try something like the octopus pâté.

€ La Bodeguilla de San Roque, Rúa San Roque 13, T981 564 379, www.bodeguilla desanroque.com. A good bar, popular with students for its cheap and filling *raciones*. These are best eaten in the pretty upstairs *comedor* which also serves up a value-packed *menú del día*.

€ O Filandón, C Azabachería 6, T981 572 378. This cosy wine bar is popular with arriving pilgrims, whose messages on paper serviettes adorn the walls. There's an excellent atmosphere and very good service from the personable boss.

Cafés

There's nowhere better in town for a relaxing outdoor drink than the garden of the **Costa Vella** hotel (see Where to stay, above).

Café Casino, Rúa do Vilar 35, T981 577 503, www.cafecasino.es. This historic café is awash with 19th-century plushness. It's a massive space, beautiful, elegant and popular with young and old for evening coffee.

Café Derby, C Huérfanas 29, T981 586 417, www.cafederby.com. Just turned 80 years old, this noble old café seems to have changed little, and it's much the better for it. Polite service, cosy worn seating, cut-glass chandeliers, and plenty of space make it a Santiago classic.

Café Literarios, Praza Quintana 1, T981 565 630. A great spot on this attractive and unusual square, named after the redoubtable student batallion of this granite city. It's still got an arty feel inside, while the terrace gazes over the architectural glories of the old centre.

Bars and clubs

Santiago de Compostela *p110, map p114*

The student nightlife kicks off around Rúa Nova de Abaixos near Praza Roxa. Get the free newspaper *Compostelán* or *7 Días Santiago* for bar, club events and other venue listings.

El Paraíso Perdido, Rúa San Paio de Antealtares 3. This basement bar has an intriguing 'hell gate' entrance. Inside it's decorated with mosaics, and there's a chilled-out, buzzy, hippy-trippy atmosphere.

La Borriquita de Belén, Rúa San Paio de Antealtares 22. A sociable and lively bar tucked away behind the cathedral and playing host to regular live jazz and traditionally influenced Galician bands.

Modus Vivendi, Praza Feijóo 1, T981 576 109, www.pubmodusvivendi.net. Once a stable, you can still use the old horse trough as a table. The stone arches lend a medieval ambience to what is one of Santiago's friendliest and most characterful drinking options. Recommended.

Momo, Rúa da Virxe da Cerca 23, www.pub momo.com. This massive, super-characterful bar on the edge of the old town comes equipped with its own old street and zebra crossing. In summer the terrace opens – it's a fantastic spot to be, with great views.

Entertainment

Santiago de Compostela *p110, map p114*

Check the website www.compostelacultura.org for upcoming concerts and events.

Auditorio de Galicia, T981 552 290, www.auditoriodegalicia.org. North of town. Classical concerts and opera.

Festivals

Santiago de Compostela *p110, map p114*

25 Jul Santiago's main fiesta is the day of St James himself. When this day falls on a Sun, it's known as a **Holy Year** (the next one is 2021). Apart from partying, there's a solemn Mass and a spectacular pyrotechnic display the night before.

Shopping

Santiago de Compostela *p110, map p114*

Bookshops
Librería Universitas, Rúa Fernando III el Santo 3, T981 592 438; Librería San Pablo, Rúa do Vilar 37, T981 552 180.

Food and drink
The Mercado de Abastos is a lively food market in the old town on Praza de Abastos. O Beiro, Rúa da Raíña 3, www.obeiro.com, is a good place to buy (as well as drink) Galician and other Spanish wines.

Gems
Santiago is a good place to purchase *azabache* (jet), but beware of vendors near the cathedral who make a living preying on tourists.

Transport

Santiago de Compostela *p110, map p114*
Buy a copy of the newspaper *El Correo Gallego* for a complete list of transport times.

Air
Buses connect the airport with the city centre and bus station, stopping at the corner of Av Xeneral Pardiñas and Rúa da República de El Salvador; they run approximately hourly. A **Ryanair** bus runs from Praza Galicia to coincide with their flights.

Bus
Local Within Galicia, buses run hourly to **A Coruña** (via motorway 45 mins, via road 1 hr 20 mins), 3 a day to **Fisterra** and **Camariñas**. 8 buses to **Lugo**, hourly ones to **Pontevedra** (45 mins) and **Vigo**, and 7 to **Ourense**.

Services connect with **Bilbao** (3 daily, 12 hrs), **Ponferrada** (5 daily, 3½-4 hrs), **Madrid** (5-6 daily, 8-9 hrs), **Oviedo** (5 a day, 5 hrs 30 mins) and **Gijón**, and **Salamanca** (2 daily, 6 hrs 15 mins) via **Zamora**, among other destinations.

Train
Trains run regularly to **A Coruña** (45 mins, €6.85), **Vigo** (1 hr 20 mins, from €8.70); there's also a sleeper and a day train to **Madrid** (9½ hrs and 5¾ hrs respectively, €51-55).

Directory

Santiago de Compostela *p110, map p114*

Laundry Lavandeira, Av Rosalía de Castro 116, T981 942 110. A self-service laundromat with plenty of machines. **Medical services** The Hospital Xeral is fairly central on Rúa das Galeras, T981 950 000. **Police and emergency** T112 for an emergency; T092 contacts the municipal police. The handiest police station is on Av Rodrigo de Padrón around the corner from the post office.

Contents

126 Index

Footnotes

Index

A
accommodation 12
Agroturismos 13
air travel 6
Arzúa 107
Astorga 98, 102
Astún 41
Atapuerca 75

B
banks 20
beer 18
Berceo 62
budgets 21
Burgos 68
　background 69
　bars and clubs 78
　Cartuja de Miraflores 75
　Cathedral 69
　eating 77
　entertainment 79
　festivals 79
　hotels 76
　Iglesia de San Nicolás 73
　Monasterio de las Huelgas 74
　transport 79
Burguete 27
buses 10

C
campsites 13
Candanchú 41
Canfranc 41
　listings 48
Canfranc-Estación 41
Canfranc Valley 41
car 7
Carrión de los Condes 82
　listings 85
Cartuja de Miraflores 75
casas rurales 13
Castrillo de los Polvazares 99
Castrojeriz 80
　listings 85

Charlemagne 29
Codex Calixtinus 113
compostela 10
Convento de San Pedro de las Dueñas 84
costs 21
credencial 10
cuisine 14
currency 20

D
drink 17

E
El Bierzo 100
El Cid 72
Ermita de Santa María de Arcos 61
Estella 51
　listings 53

F
ferry 8
Fiesta de San Fermín 31
fiestas 19
Foncebadón 99
food 14
　vegetarian 17
Frómista 80
　listings 85

G
Gares 51
Grajal de Campos 84

H
health 20
holidays 19
Holy Grail 42
Hospital de Orbigo 98
Hugonell 62

I
Iruña 28

J
Jaca 41
　listings 48

L
La Cueva de las Güixas 41
language 20
La Olmeda 82
Le Chanson de Roland 29
León 87
　bars and clubs 95
　Basílica de San Isidoro 91
　Cathedral 90
　Convento de San Marcos 92
　directory 96
　eating 94
　festivals 96
　history 87
　hotels 93
　Museo de León 92
　Old Town 92
　shopping 96
　transport 96
Lizarra 51
Logroño 57
　bars and clubs 67
　entertainment 67
　festivals 67
　history 57
　hotels 64
　transport 67
　wineries 58
Los Sanfermines 31
Luyego 99

M
Maragatos 98, 99
Marqués de Murrieta de Ygay 58
Melide 107
Molinaseca 100
Monasterio de Irache 52
Monasterio de San Juan de la Peña 44

126 • Footnotes Index

Monasterio de San Pedro
  de Cardeña 75
Monasterio de San Salvador
  de Leyre
    listings 49
Monasterio de Santa María
  la Real 60
Monasterio de Suso 61
Monasterio de Yuso 61
money 20
Monte del Gozo 108
Murias de Rechivaldo 99
Museo de Navarra,
  Pamplona 33

N
Nájera 60
  listings 64

O
O Cebreiro 106
  listings 108

P
Palacio de la Vega 52
Palas de Rei 107
Pamplona 28
  Cathedral 30
  history 29
  listings 35
  Plaza Consistorial 33
  Plaza del Castillo 30
  Primer Ensanche 33
Patxarán 37
Piedrafita 106
Ponferrada 100
  listings 102
Portomarín 107
  listings 108
Puente La Reina 51
  listings 53

Q
Quintanilla 82

R
restaurants 16
  price codes 13

Rioja 59
Roland 29
Roncesvalles 27
  listings 34
running bulls 31

S
safety 21
Sahagún 83
  listings 85
Saint James 112
Saldaña 82
Samos 106
San Fermín 31
Sangüesa 45
  listings 49
San Juan de la Peña 44
San Millán de Cogolla 61
  listings 65
San Pedro de Monte 101
San Salvador de Leyre 46
Santiago 112
Santiago de Compostela
  110
  See also Camino de
    Santiago 110
  bars and clubs 123
  Cathedral 113
  Cathedral museum 116
  Colegiata de Santa María
    de Sar 119
  directory 124
  eating 121
  entertainment 123
  festivals 123
  history 111
  hotels 120
  Monasterio de San
    Martín Pinario 117
  Porta do Camino 118
  Praza de Obradoiro 117
  shopping 124
  transport 124
Santiago Millas 99
Santo Domingo 62
Santo Domingo de la
  Calzada 62
  listings 65

Sarria 107
  listings 108
Sasamón 81
  listings 85
sleeping
  price codes 13
Somport tunnel 41
St James 112
St-Jean-Pied-de-Port 27
student travellers 9

T
tapas 16
taxes 21
taxis 12
tipping 22
tourist information 22
trains 7, 9
transport
  air 6
  bus 7, 10
  car 7
  ferry 8
  taxi 12
  train 7
Tricio 61

V
Valiña, Elías 106
Valle del Silencio 100
Viana 53
  listings 54
Villafranca del Bierzo 101
  listings 102
Villafrancos 101
Villalcázar de Sirga 81
  listings 85
Villanúa 41
Virgen del Camino 98

W
Western Navarra 51
wine 17
wineries 52, 58

Z
Zangoza 45

Titles available in the Footprint *Focus* range

Latin America	UK RRP	US RRP
Bahia & Salvador	£7.99	$11.95
Brazilian Amazon	£7.99	$11.95
Brazilian Pantanal	£6.99	$9.95
Buenos Aires & Pampas	£7.99	$11.95
Cartagena & Caribbean Coast	£7.99	$11.95
Costa Rica	£8.99	$12.95
Cuzco, La Paz & Lake Titicaca	£8.99	$12.95
El Salvador	£5.99	$8.95
Guadalajara & Pacific Coast	£6.99	$9.95
Guatemala	£8.99	$12.95
Guyana, Guyane & Suriname	£5.99	$8.95
Havana	£6.99	$9.95
Honduras	£7.99	$11.95
Nicaragua	£7.99	$11.95
Northeast Argentina & Uruguay	£8.99	$12.95
Paraguay	£5.99	$8.95
Quito & Galápagos Islands	£7.99	$11.95
Recife & Northeast Brazil	£7.99	$11.95
Rio de Janeiro	£8.99	$12.95
São Paulo	£5.99	$8.95
Uruguay	£6.99	$9.95
Venezuela	£8.99	$12.95
Yucatán Peninsula	£6.99	$9.95

Asia	UK RRP	US RRP
Angkor Wat	£5.99	$8.95
Bali & Lombok	£8.99	$12.95
Chennai & Tamil Nadu	£8.99	$12.95
Chiang Mai & Northern Thailand	£7.99	$11.95
Goa	£6.99	$9.95
Gulf of Thailand	£8.99	$12.95
Hanoi & Northern Vietnam	£8.99	$12.95
Ho Chi Minh City & Mekong Delta	£7.99	$11.95
Java	£7.99	$11.95
Kerala	£7.99	$11.95
Kolkata & West Bengal	£5.99	$8.95
Mumbai & Gujarat	£8.99	$12.95

Africa & Middle East	UK RRP	US RRP
Beirut	£6.99	$9.95
Cairo & Nile Delta	£8.99	$12.95
Damascus	£5.99	$8.95
Durban & KwaZulu Natal	£8.99	$12.95
Fès & Northern Morocco	£8.99	$12.95
Jerusalem	£8.99	$12.95
Johannesburg & Kruger National Park	£7.99	$11.95
Kenya's Beaches	£8.99	$12.95
Kilimanjaro & Northern Tanzania	£8.99	$12.95
Luxor to Aswan	£8.99	$12.95
Nairobi & Rift Valley	£7.99	$11.95
Red Sea & Sinai	£7.99	$11.95
Zanzibar & Pemba	£7.99	$11.95

Europe	UK RRP	US RRP
Bilbao & Basque Region	£6.99	$9.95
Brittany West Coast	£7.99	$11.95
Cádiz & Costa de la Luz	£6.99	$9.95
Granada & Sierra Nevada	£6.99	$9.95
Languedoc: Carcassonne to Montpellier	£7.99	$11.95
Málaga	£5.99	$8.95
Marseille & Western Provence	£7.99	$11.95
Orkney & Shetland Islands	£5.99	$8.95
Santander & Picos de Europa	£7.99	$11.95
Sardinia: Alghero & the North	£7.99	$11.95
Sardinia: Cagliari & the South	£7.99	$11.95
Seville	£5.99	$8.95
Sicily: Palermo & the Northwest	£7.99	$11.95
Sicily: Catania & the Southeast	£7.99	$11.95
Siena & Southern Tuscany	£7.99	$11.95
Sorrento, Capri & Amalfi Coast	£6.99	$9.95
Skye & Outer Hebrides	£6.99	$9.95
Verona & Lake Garda	£7.99	$11.95

North America	UK RRP	US RRP
Vancouver & Rockies	£8.99	$12.95

Australasia	UK RRP	US RRP
Brisbane & Queensland	£8.99	$12.95
Perth	£7.99	$11.95

For the latest books, e-books and a wealth of travel information, visit us at: www.footprinttravelguides.com.

footprinttravelguides.com

Join us on facebook for the latest travel news, product releases, offers and amazing competitions: www.facebook.com/footprintbooks.